Highway and Byways

Highway and Byways

Studies on Reform and Post-Communist Transition

János Kornai

The MIT Press
Cambridge, Massachusetts
London, England

This book originally appeared in Hungarian under the title *Útkeresés*,

Library of Congress Cataloging-in-Publication Data

Kornai, János.
[Útkeresés. English]
Highway and byways: studies on reform and post-communist transition/János Kornai.
p. cm
Includes bibliographical references and indexes.

ISBN 978-0-262-11198-0 (hc.: alk. paper) -- 978-0-262-52768-2 (pb.)

1. Mixed economy—Europe, Eastern. 2. Post-communism—Europe, Eastern. 3. Europe, Eastern—Economic policy—1989- 4. Europe, Eastern—Economic conditions—1989- I. Title.
HC244,K66913 1995
338.947—dc20 94-21566
CIP

The MIT Press is pleased to keep this title available in print by manufacturing single copies, on demand, via digital printing technology.

Contents

Preface

I have selected the eight studies in this volume from my writings in the last four years. Although each can be read and easily understood in isolation, there is a common theme linking them. The subject of each is the *search for a new road* by Hungary, and in addition by the whole Eastern European region that lived under the socialist system.[1]

The "first road" of capitalist development was abandoned first by the peoples of the former Tsarist empire, and later by the other peoples that came under communist-party rule, in favor of a new, "second road" that led to the development of the socialist system. Some decades later, it became increasingly plain that socialism in its classical form was a *blind alley*. The repression inflicted on friend and foe alike had reached an unbearable intensity, the frantic initial rate of growth had slowed down, and there was a steadily growing lag behind the developed capitalist countries in technical development, innovation, product quality, and human living conditions. Many, even of those who hitherto were devoted adherents of the socialist system, had lost their faith and begun to have doubts.

The first and second studies in the volume concern the *process of reform*, the initial stage in the search for a new road. Can a new, more comfortable, and attractive edifice be built on the old, unaltered foundations? The advocates of reform socialism hoped they could construct a new society that would differ from and improve on both capitalism and classical socialism. Reform socialism, in other words, was going to lead society off the first (capitalist) and second (Stalinist, classical socialist) roads onto a new kind of third road, which the advocates of reform socialism viewed not as an approach road leading back to the

1. This was alluded to in the title of the Hungarian edition of the book: *Útkeresés* (Search for a Road).

first, capitalist road, but as a third road *sui generis*, along which *permanent* progress might be made.

The first two studies examine why this venture—the biggest third-road experiment of the twentieth century—was bound to fail. For reform socialism proved to be a blind alley.[2]

That is not to say the reform process had no favorable results. The grip of repression was loosened and gaps appeared in the walls and barbed-wire fences dividing the socialist from the Western world. In the economy, managers gained greater autonomy and began to study the expectations and behavior patterns of the market economy, while an appearance was made by the formal and informal private sector, if only in a narrow field. But apart from such small changes for the better to be felt in daily life, the main favorable effect of the reform in world historical terms was the contribution it made, with elemental force, to eroding the socialist system. For the reform tried to combine elements that were mutually alien and incompatible with each other. There was to be "democratism," yet the sole rule of the Communist party was to remain; the market was to operate, yet state ownership was to remain dominant. So the thinking behind the reform constituted an attempt to mix fire and water. In place of the merciless, but coherent, classical system came an incoherent reform socialism replete with irreconcilable self-contradictions and tensions. An attempt to keep the power positions was made by a struggling leading stratum that had lost its faith and self-confidence and become steadily less able to lead and decide, and could no longer make tough, consistent use of repression, the great disciplinary method in the past. Once the two main political binding materials in the edifice of the socialist system, repression and

2. The debate on the economics of the reform, including the notions of market socialism, gains a special immediacy because certain ideas contained in them remain current and influential today. An example is the stubborn insistence by some politicians who otherwise consider themselves anti-communist on the need to maintain a broad state-owned sector. They fail to notice the inconsistency between advocating broad state ownership on the one hand and the solemnly avowed notions of market economy on the other. They want to maintain a broad state-owned sector for just the same reasons as the communist bureaucracy did: it provides a position of *power*.

Another example is the freeze on rents declared in Hungary in the summer of 1993—an act of crude interference in owners' rights to dispose over their assets and in the operation of the market. The highly predictable damaging effect of this measure will confirm the incompatibility between state micro regulation and true market coordination, which hardly needs further confirmation in any case, having emerged clearly from the experiments in market socialism.

the faith of the ruling stratum, had crumbled, the structure collapsed. Reform's place on the agenda was taken over by revolution.[3]

The second part of the volume deals with postsocialist development. The third study, as the starting material for this part, touches, albeit briefly, on the question of the difference between reform and revolution. As I see it, the distinguishing criterion in this context is not the speed of the change, or even whether it is peaceful or violent, but the depth and radicalism of the transformation. So long as the undivided power of the Communist party remains, along with the monopoly of the official party ideology, protected by administrative means, one can talk at most of a reform of the existing socialist system. A revolutionary change takes place when there is a profound transformation of the political structure in terms of these essential features. In several spheres, the changes in Hungary are seen to be of a *continual and gradual* nature: in the advance of private property and market mechanism based on free prices, in the macroeconomic situation, and in the introduction of legislation. But the continuity is associated at a certain point by a discontinuity: the one-party system comes to an end, and the period of parliamentary democracy based on a multiparty system commences. The termination of the sole rule of the Communist party removes the main road block, so that society can return to the first road, the road of capitalist development.[4]

It would be a mistake to envisage this road as some kind of motorway that plainly and necessarily links the point of departure with a sole conceivable future destination by the shortest possible route. Let us take the question of the *destination* first. Just as the socialist system is in fact a *family* of systems, whose members, while sharing the dominant characteristics, may differ from each other in many of their attributes, so capitalism is also a family of systems. A historian would certainly see in each country the unique and unrepeatable features of the construct that has come into being there, because of a certain constellation of unique and unrepeatable factors. Even if an attempt to generalize is made and a high degree of abstraction permitted, a vari-

3. A comprehensive, detailed analysis of the regularities in the operation of the socialist system and its reform and collapse is put forward in my 1992 book *The Socialist System*, some of whose ideas are summed up and augmented in the first two studies in this volume.

4. To continue the same metaphor, although the initiators of the reform intended the experiment to follow a separate, third road, it became in the end an approach road leading back to the first road. The reform was useful in preparing the ground for the postsocialist capitalist development.

ety of species of capitalism can still be distinguished. Here, for the sake of clarity, let us attach "geographical" labels to a few types: one can distinguish United States capitalism with its high degree of individualism and narrowly confined role for the state, Scandinavian welfare capitalism with its extensive redistribution, Japanese capitalism with its strong state intervention and interpenetration of bank capital and large-scale industrial capital, and so on. Which should be the pattern that we want to follow, or what combination of which patterns is it worth us aiming for, perhaps by developing features that have not emerged elsewhere before?

Let us assume that the destination is now clear, at least for the ruling parties and government in some particular country or other. Even then, there is still no map of any kind showing the route taken by the road that leads to it. Only from the height of a spaceship can the "first road" appear to be a single vast route. From the height of a helicopter it can clearly be seen that it consists of numerous greater or lesser main roads and side roads, zigzagging paths, ascents and precipitous slopes. This is also referred to in the English title of the volume, *Highway and Byways*.[5] Every highway and byway leads to capitalism eventually, of course, but precisely what kind do they lead to, how fast, at the cost of how many sacrifices, and with whom as the winners and whom as the losers? Each fork in the road poses a choice problem. So although most people accept and endorse the "main direction," there are innumerable dilemmas ahead.

The *crossroads* ahead of us in the postsocialist economy are considered in all the studies in the second part of the volume.[6] The third

5. There is a painting by the brilliant Swiss painter Paul Klee which shows a complicated road system. The title of the work is *Hauptweg und Nebenwege* (Highway and Byways). When I was shown a reproduction of the work by Albert O. Hirschman of the Princeton Institute for Advanced Study, in whose book *Journeys Toward Progress* it appears, I realized that this wonderful painting and its title precisely express what this volume sets out to convey. There is a web of highways, byways, and forks, but eventually they all lead in the same, upward direction. I am thankful to Albert O. Hirschman for the idea.

6. For a long time I took an exclusively positive approach to examining the socialist system and refrained from making proposals of a practical nature for the leadership. I departed radically from this practice in a book I wrote in 1989, *Indulatos röpirat a gazdasági átmenet ügyében* (Passionate Pamphlet in the Cause of Economic Transition; revised edition published in English as *The Road to a Free Economy. Shifting from a Socialist System: The Example of Hungary*, New York, W. W. Norton, 1990), where I summed up the proposals I recommended at the time to the parliament freely elected in 1990 and the legitimate government depending on the support of that parliament, tying them to certain

study presents the recommendations concerning the transformation, while the eighth and last study exclusively contains a positive description and prediction. The four intervening pieces of writing combine the positive and normative approaches. I have tried to make sure that it should always remain clear to the reader where the positive analysis of reality ends and the normative approach based on value judgments begins.

The "road" metaphor appeared in the title of my book *The Road to a Free Economy*, which to my knowledge was the first book on the subject of postsocialist transition. As I was writing it in the summer and autumn of 1989, I felt that some very grave difficulties were to be expected, but the matter of deciding what measures to recommend caused me less internal struggle than it does these days. I did not hesitate then to include the word "road" in the singular in the title of the book. Five years—full of joyful and bitter experiences—have passed since then. The plural in the title of this volume reflects my far clearer appreciation now than at that time of how socialist transition, while representing a clear choice of *the main road ahead* as the title of my earlier book implies, nonetheless leaves the decisions on numerous subsequent problems still open. Even at a distance of five years, I consider it was correct for me to state that Hungary and the other postsocialist countries should take the "First Road" to democracy and a market economy, not seek "Third Road" solutions. But I now have a better appreciation of how some important subquestions remained unanswered at that time.

I cannot agree with those who say that each such question has only one solution. In my view there is always a choice, even when the set of feasible alternatives has been narrowed by earlier historical development. There is never a single "compulsory course" in the strict sense, and politicians who claim the contrary simply want to reduce their responsibility in advance. This volume, like my previous writings, sets out to disseminate the opposite attitude: those who possess the right to decide, whether it be a parliamentary majority, a government or a minister, bear full responsibility for their decisions.

Even when some work of mine contains a proposal, it is usually a conditional proposal, in which the political and social conditions and consequences for implementing it are pointed out. I do not see myself

---

political conditions. The studies on the postsocialist transition in this volume develop further or, where I feel it is necessary, correct the normative ideas advanced in the book.

as a prophet whose inner prompting dictates what should be done at a particular time. I remain a researcher, even when I try to formulate practical economic-policy proposals. I place the primary emphasis on making plain what are the arguments for and against accepting the proposal, and what "price" and risk are attached to particular measures. I try to discover the traps, self-contradictions, pitfalls, and vicious circles concealed in the situation. I would like to shed light on the "trade-offs" between the choices made according to various values. Let complete self-confidence remain the privilege of politicians. The role in the social division of labor assigned to scientific researchers is to clarify the possible decision-making alternatives and the consequences of them, draw attention to the difficulties in good time, express the doubts and point out the uncertainties.

To that extent this volume and all eight studies in it are a direct sequel to two earlier collections of my studies: *Contradictions and Dilemmas* and *Vision and Reality, Market and State: Contradictions and Dilemmas Revisited*, whose titles convey the approach of a skeptical researcher weighing alternatives and opposing mutually conflicting values. The title of this book refers not only to the search by an actual society for a new road, but to my own personal research career as well. The first study, on market socialism, states clearly that wrestling with the dilemmas of reform socialism was the concern of a whole generation, and my concern as well. I too have struggled with the past and present conflicts of values with which these eight studies are concerned.

I think intellectual honesty requires me to publish each of the studies in its original form.[7] My view on a few questions has altered. This is either conveyed in one of the studies written later, with a critical reference to the earlier work, or brought to the reader's attention in foot-

7. This criterion also requires me in general to reprint the original studies without abbreviating them. Another argument for republication in full is the consideration mentioned earlier that each should be a rounded piece of reading matter understandable in itself, bearing in mind the needs of a reader, whether a researcher or a student, who happens to want to examine only part of the book, not the whole volume. I feel these two requisites outweigh the disadvantage that some study or other may contain a small amount of repetition of matter from an earlier study in the same volume. However, where such repetition could be avoided by making a slight cut without compromising the considerations stated before, I have done so, marking the cut with the sign [...].

Still consistent with the requirement that the *content* of the original text should appear is the fact that I have made some editorial changes to the texts from the *formal* point of view—for instance, in order to ensure typographical uniformity.

notes added subsequently (and clearly distinguishable from the original text), so that the changes in my ideas can be followed.[8]

I do not undertake in this volume to compare my earlier recommendations with the experience with implementing them or not implementing them. It would be impossible to keep the materials in a thoroughly up-to-date condition and augment them with the extra information that has come to light since they were written. Readers, and critics reviewing the book, will be able to try and compare the prediction, the recommendation and the actual events and assess the deviations between them. They will be able to see that the prediction on some matter or other has proved correct, and the forecast of some danger has been confirmed, while in other cases the situation turned out differently from the way predicted. Some proposals were adopted, while others remained as mere words. I would like to plan to return some day to these predictions and recommendations at a much later date, when I am separated by a sufficient distance from the events of 1990–1993 and can look on my earlier works almost as an outsider.

Only the third study is about the economy of a country other than my own one, namely the Soviet Union in its final days, although I tried there as well to express a more general message. A few studies deal with the whole postsocialist region, but the direct subject of most of them is Hungary. Not only in the studies in this volume, but throughout my whole career, I have always been first and foremost a Hungarian economist, directly experiencing the problems of his own country and seeking to help his own compatriots in the first place. The inspiration for my theoretical thinking has always come from Hungarian experience and the debates in the intellectual workshops of my own country. However, I have tried in these studies, most of which I delivered as lectures at international events, to see the aspects of the Hungarian situation from which generalizations can be made. It may be instructive for those outside the country to look at favorable experiences in Hungary, which can be presented as examples for other nations to follow, or at failures from which others can be warned, and so avoid the wrong turnings. I have feelings of solidarity with all countries struggling, like Hungary, with the difficulties of postsocialist transition.

---

8. I have also added subsequent footnotes in one or two places where, on rereading the text with present-day eyes, I felt that some supplementary explanation was needed in order to avoid any misunderstandings.

I have never felt any qualms about presenting the problems of this country to economists internationally. Openness, frankness, and unembellished presentation of our mistakes can only enhance the reputation and credibility of the country and the Hungarian intelligentsia in the eyes of the world. This can only help to ensure that others think along with us and assist us in overcoming the difficulties. I feel that Hungarian researchers can best serve their own nation's cause by not hiding themselves within the narrow bounds of provincialism and by remaining free of arrogance when encountering foreign scientific findings. Hungarian researchers, in my view, are doing the right thing when they present their own contributions and unanswered questions to the international profession and contribute to professional knowledge at home with accounts of findings and practical experiences known abroad. In this way they can make the thinking of their foreign colleagues more productive, and along with their fellow countrymen, receive new intellectual impulses. It was already worth attempting this in decades gone by, but the opportunities for international exchanges of views have been greater than ever before since the change of system.

This volume is open-ended: new experiences and new problems arise month by month. The jacket of the first, Hungarian volume of *Contradictions and Dilemmas* showed a laboratory test tube in which a map of Hungary could be seen. The great experiment *in vivo* on the body of the peoples of Hungary and the other postsocialist countries continues, and we could not avoid it even if we wanted to, as there is no historical precedent for the process that is now taking place. The studies have a dual purpose. I would like above all to ease matters for the subject of the experiment, helping to minimize the suffering and maximize the benefits of the experimentation that necessarily accompanies the transformation and change of system. In addition I have an intellectual, road-seeking, research objective before me. As the experiment is taking place anyway, let us make the fullest scientific use of it—for the sake of other peoples with similar problems and to enrich the historical knowledge and thinking of future generations.

Finally I would like to thank all those who have helped me in preparing this collection of studies. For each study separately I have mentioned the persons and institutions that played a part in its elaboration; here I would like to express once again my thanks to them collectively for their support. Cooperation in editing this volume came primarily from my closest associate, Mária Kovács, who worked as ever in a bright, conscientious, and dedicated way. I am grateful to Brian McLean and Julianna Parti for the excellent and faithful translation of the Hungarian text and to Zsuzsa Dániel and Ann Flack for the valuable editorial assistance, and to Ilona Lukács for compiling the index. I am pleased that The MIT Press was willing to bring out this collection of studies. I am especially grateful to Michael Sims and Ann Sochi for their editorial help.

1 Market Socialism Revisited[1]

The great transformation taking place in Eastern Europe, the Soviet Union, and China has revived the discussion about market socialism.[2] Since this study does not cover the whole issue, I would like to begin by delimiting the subject examined and briefly noting the methods of approach.

1. Initial conditions have a strong effect on any formation that actually occurs in history. Where did it start from before reaching its present state? Because of the differing circumstances in which the genesis occurred, it is worth distinguishing clearly between two subject areas. One is market socialism as a system to replace capitalism, and the other market socialism as a system to replace old-style, Stalinist, prereform socialism or, as I call it in my works, classical socialism.[3]

The subject of this study is the development and operation of market socialism during the process of reforming the socialist system.[4] I do

---

1. I owe thanks for valuable observations to Kenneth J. Arrow, Zsuzsa Dániel, Parta Dasgupta, Eric Maskin, Mária Kovács, Carla Krüger, and John M. Litwack. I am grateful to Brian McLean and Julianna Parti for their excellent translation.

2. The Soviet Union and Yugoslavia still existed when the lecture was delivered. This written text uses the terminology current at that time.

Almost every book and study discussing the reforms, particularly in the first stage of the changes, mentions the concept of market socialism. Market socialism is the main topic of some major pieces of writing; I pick out here the ones that had a thought-provoking effect on me while I was working on this study: P. Bardhan (1990), W. Brus and K. Laski (1989), A. de Jasay (1990), D. Lavoie (1985), J. Le Grand and S. Estrin, eds. (1989), A. Nove (1983), G. E. Schroeder (1988), and G. Temkin (1989).

3. The concept of "classical socialism" is clarified in more detail in my book *The Socialist System* (1992).

4. A terminological observation is needed. The term "socialism" in this study, as in my other works, denotes actual socioeconomic systems marked by the monopoly rule of the Communist party. While I am aware of the importance to adherents of socialist ideas of clarifying whether these systems merited the name "socialism," I use it in a value-free sense. It is what the countries concerned called or still call themselves, and I have abstained from renaming them.

not discuss at all the other issue of market-socialist-style reform of capitalism.

Of course the two sets of problems overlap, since both of them entail thoroughly weighing the same value choices and the same instruments. But when it comes to practical conclusions and normative proposals, they hold only in a specific context. What is true in the framework of reform socialism does not necessarily apply to the reforms of capitalism or vice versa. History does not move like a pendulum; having swung one way, it does not return to its original state. Explanations in which the unidirectional, "whence-and-whither" nature of history is ignored can easily lapse into serious fallacies.

2. Influential ideas tread a long path from their first formulation in theory to their realization in practice. For simplicity's sake, three stages in this path are distinguished here.

The vision: This may be a utopia presented in an outline form,[5] or a normative model of pure theory. The series of the latter was opened by E. Barone [1908] (1935); an outstanding work is the study by Oscar Lange (1936–37). Ideas related to Lange's can be found in the works of F. M. Taylor (1929) and A. P. Lerner (1946).[6] Because of its outstanding significance to the history of theory, the Lange Model will be returned to regularly in subsequent parts of this study.

The blueprint: This can appear in a variety of forms, for instance as the practical proposals of reform economists,[7] the political declarations of leaders, or resolutions on reform passed by a Communist party and government in power in a socialist country.

Realization: This covers what actually goes on in the economy, the de facto rules of the game, and the attitudes and behavioral regularities of the actors in the system.

Although the first stage is very important, it is not discussed here in all its details. The main subject of this study is political and economic

5. On the concept of vision, see J. A. Schumpeter (1954), R. Heilbroner (1990), and J. Kornai (1986*b*).

6. Formalization of the Lange-Taylor-Lerner models is dealt with in several works; I would stress the classic work of K. J. Arrow and L. Hurwicz (1960), E. Malinvaud's model (1967), and, of the most recent literature, the studies by I. Ortuno-Ortin, J. E. Roemer, and J. Silvestre (1990).

7. A few pioneering works are mentioned, grouped by countries. *Yugoslavia*: B. Kidric (for the works he wrote in the 1950s, see his 1985 volume); *Hungary*: Gy. Péter (1954*a*), (1954*b*), (1956), J. Kornai [1957] (1959); *Poland*: W. Brus [1961] (1972); *Czechoslovakia*: O. Sik (1966); *Soviet Union*: E. G. Liberman [1962] (1972); *China*: Y. Sun [1958–61] (1982).

history, not intellectual history, and so attention is centered on the blueprint and realization.[8] Although I admit the relevance of utopias and pure theoretical models, I would like to point out to Western readers that the practical experience of what took place in the socialist countries cannot be ignored even in the debate at the "visionary" level. The old ideas must be reconsidered in the light of the new evidence.

3. A whole range of countries went through a stage in which certain ingredients of market socialism were applied. Changes pointing in this direction occurred from 1949 onward in Yugoslavia and from 1953 in Hungary. Certain elements of market socialism appeared much later in Poland, the Soviet Union, China, and Vietnam. It is not possible here to discuss the matter country by country. Although there were appreciable differences between the specific formations that came into being in each country and its pace of historical development, an attempt will be made to formulate general statements. A common *prototype* will be outlined for each blueprint and for each practical realization. A prototype blueprint consists of a compression of thousands of political speeches, party programs, proposals submitted to the authorities, and resolutions passed by the state. A prototype realization is a generalized image of common practice, intended to describe what goes on in the offices of finance ministers or chief executives of state-owned firms and what are the characteristic tendencies in the economy.

The prototypes of both kinds result from a high degree of abstraction. They omit the less essential, ad hoc features and are intended to reflect the fundamental characteristics of market-socialist reforms. Neglecting the differences between countries, they focus on the properties in *common*.

This study sheds light on the problems posed by market socialism from various angles. The first part approaches the matter mainly from the point of view of *political economy*, and the second from the point of view of *philosophy*. The latter examines both the epistemological-methodological and the ethical-political aspects.

---

8. When Hayek (1935) took issue with the adherents of market socialism during the famous debate in the 1930s around the article by Oscar Lange, he stepped out of the realm of pure theoretical models by also bringing forward practical counterarguments that belong, according to the terminology of this study, to the blueprint stage.

I Blueprint and Historical Realization: The Viewpoint of Political Economy

The Blueprint

The main features of the prototype blueprint can be summed up as follows:

1. The political monopoly of the Communist party must be maintained. Some degree of political liberalization may occur: *glasnost'* may develop, that is, a higher degree of honesty in the provision of political information and greater tolerance for alternative views; there may be more openness in relations with the West. But no fundamental change in the political structure is permissible.

I propose to make a sharp distinction between two stages. In the first of these a *reform* of a market-socialist character takes place, while the Communist party's monopoly of power basically remains. The point of departure for the second stage is a *revolutionary* change in the political sphere, when the monopoly of the Communist party is broken and parliamentary democracy develops after free, multiparty elections. At that point the system commences the *transition* from socialism toward a capitalist market economy. The issues of this transition are extremely important, of course, but they are outside the scope of this study. Occasional references are made to the problems of the transition, but the subject here is the reform socialism associated with the names of Tito in Yugoslavia, Kádár in Hungary, Deng Xiaoping in China, Rakowski in Poland, and Gorbachev in the Soviet Union.

2. The predominance of public ownership must be maintained. Except in Yugoslavia's case, this means the predominance of state ownership. The specific characteristics of Yugoslav development cannot be dealt with here in detail, and the discussion that follows is concerned with state ownership. The observations, however, are applicable to Yugoslavia's case as well.

An important—perhaps the most important—component in the economic changes at the stage of historical realization is the evolution of the formal and informal private sector. Although it provides a relatively small proportion of production, it plays a big part in improving supply to the public and introducing property relations that conform with the market economy. But the idea of developing the private sector does not appear in the *blueprint* for market socialism before the actual transformation begins. The blueprint exclusively prescribes a renovation of the conditions under which state-owned firms operate. So in the rest of this study the remarks on market socialism refer exclusively to the state sector.

3. The relative share of decisions made at central level must diminish radically in favor of decentralized decisions made at local government or more frequently enterprise level.

A similar idea is expressed by another formula. A state-owned firm is linked vertically with its superior authorities and horizontally with its sellers and buyers. In the blueprint, the vertical links remain but the horizontal links are radically reinforced.

4. The main indicator of success for a firm is profit. The incentives for managers are to be tied to profits, and profit-sharing is to be introduced for the firm's workers.

5. The range of instruments available to the center must alter. Direct commands, the main instrument so far, should give way to indirect instruments or "economic levers." The blueprint's drafters assume that if firms are profit-maximizing, their actions can be influenced by changes in interest and exchange rates, taxes, subsidies, and specific prices. Centrally set prices and other financial parameters are to be strings pulled by the center to which firms will react like puppets.

6. The prototype blueprint does not clarify the kind of prices it seeks to introduce. Prices set by a decentralized process will reflect the market situation. But on what principles will centrally decided prices be set, including wages, interest rates, and exchange rates? The blueprint fails to say these must be market-clearing prices.

7. The economy must be opened up to relations with the capitalist world. The international credit market must also be entered, and it is worth raising loans from capitalist governments, banks, and firms in order to advance socialist development.

Let us look briefly at the best known vision, the Lange Model. The prototype blueprint is akin to it in aiming to operate profit-maximizing state-owned firms with a high degree of autonomy. It shares its aim of using central prices and financial levers to influence firms' decisions, but clearly departs from Lange theory in not stating firmly that market-clearing prices will be introduced.

The most important difference is that the blueprint contains a far richer set of rules. Pure theory can abstract away many important factors. Not so practice, which *must* settle all problems of choice one way or another. The prototype blueprint outlines many features of the system ignored in Lange's work and the theoretical controversy on market socialism in general.

That is not a shortcoming of the Lange Model or the debate on it. Richness of detail cannot be expected in an intellectual construct belonging to the realm of pure normative theory. But it is not a mere shortcoming, but a fatal fallacy to take the theoretical model too seriously, so to speak, and treat it as a blueprint.[9]

In fact even the blueprint falls far short of the complexity of reality, disregarding several considerations that prove highly important in practice. These will be returned to later.

The leitmotiv running through the seven attributes listed is that a new *Third System* must be created. This is to differ from the prereform, Stalinist classical socialism, but also from capitalism.[10] It is considered not as a transitory stage that leads from socialism to capitalism, but as a separate social formation, a lasting and robust new system.

The Economic Performance

In many features, if not in its entirety, the blueprint was applied for varying periods in the countries listed in the introduction. But it must be added that the historical realization differed from the blueprint in several respects, developing many characteristics that the drafters of the blueprint had not foreseen. Before turning to these departures, let us take a quick look at the economic performance produced by the blueprint's application. There is an ample body of empirical literature on the subject, and works discussing the issues of the transition to a market economy usually summarize the earlier period's economic successes and failures as well.[11] Rather than going into detail or presenting statistics, just a few of the main characteristics will be emphasized here.

9. This Oscar Lange himself never did.

10. This Third Road idea is well reflected in the following quotation from Gorbachev: "What alternatives are before us? . . . One is to maintain the command-administrative system, the strict planning, and the commands in culture as well as the economy. The other . . . suggests reverting to capitalism. Can we take either of these roads? No, we reject them . . ." (*Pravda*, November 26, 1989).

11. See, for instance, the articles of D. Lipton and J. Sachs (1990*a*), (1990*b*) and G. W. Kolodko (1991) on Poland, the article by J. Kornai (1986*b*) and the OECD report (1991) on Hungary, and the joint IMF, IBRD, OECD, and EBRD report (1990) on the Soviet Union.

• Signs of slowdown had appeared before the reform began and were among the motives for breaking with the old command economy. The market-socialist reforms at most bring a measure of temporary revival; they do not halt the downturn permanently. The economy arrives at a point of stagnation, and later, in fact, an absolute contraction of production sets in. If appreciable growth does appear in any sectors, as it did, for instance, in Chinese farming for a good many years, it is due not to the realization of the market-socialist blueprint at all, but to de facto privatization, which falls outside the original market-socialist blueprint, as mentioned earlier.[12]

• The stagnation or decline in GDP is accompanied by stagnation or decline in real consumption. Once again, the only countervailing force is the evolution of the private sector, which helps to improve supply and living conditions.

• Severe disequilibria are caused. Classical socialism is a chronic shortage economy, with distorted relative prices, but quite a stable general price level. Market-socialist reform is accompanied in most countries by a new, more complex problem: the "shortage-cum-inflation" syndrome. A grave and growing budget deficit develops, becoming one of the main factors fueling the growing inflation, which develops into open hyperinflation in some countries. In others the inflation is artificially repressed and a huge monetary overhang is created.

• There is no significant improvement in efficiency and factor productivity. Nor is there any tangible evidence in goods' quality, innovation, or technical advance.

• The share of foreign trade conducted with capitalist countries increases, but the performance in this field is again poor. There is a deficit in trade with the capitalist market. Foreign debt rises and certain countries reach the brink of insolvency.

If the blueprint was meant to create a Third System, it certainly did not prove its economic superiority over the First, modern capitalism. Nor can clear conclusions be drawn from a comparison with the Second System, classical socialism. On the one hand there are benefits. Although state-owned firms do not turn into real profit-maximizing economic units, some impression on the mentality of managers is made by the market-economic rhetoric, coupled with a few actual

12. [The problems of the Chinese reform are dealt with in footnote 20. *A new footnote added in the course of editing this volume*. Referred to as *New footnote* hereafter.]

measures. They learn to pay more heed to financial indicators and buyer requirements. (This eases the later, real transition toward a market economy after the great political changes have taken place.) The main factor tending to improve the economic situation is the development of the formal and informal private sector. Perhaps most importantly of all, life becomes more tolerable, mainly because there is a measure of political liberalization and human rights are asserted more easily. On the other hand there are serious negative consequences, primarily for the macroeconomic equilibrium. Take, for example, East Germany, Czechoslovakia, and Romania, three countries whose political leaders stubbornly resisted all market-socialist reforms, and compare them with Yugoslavia, Hungary, Poland, and the Soviet Union, which took the market-socialist road for varying periods. The macrosituation on the eve of the postsocialist transition is clearly worse in the second group than in the first: the budget deficit is greater, inflation faster (or the combination of shortage and inflation more acute), and foreign debt higher. The market-socialist experiments led to a situation in which the leadership lost control.

The economic leadership fails to understand what is happening. Repeated promises of an improvement cannot be kept, and this leads to frustration and protests from the general public. Since the reform has been coupled with political liberalization, the discontent takes open forms: demonstrations and protest meetings take place, and new parties opposed to the Communist party are organized. The old political system disintegrates.

So what has gone wrong with the market-oriented reform?

One view is that the original blueprint is basically a good one, but it has one or two shortcomings that need rectifying. "Reform the reform."

Another view is that the blueprint was wrongly implemented. The blueprint is in order, but it has not been applied in a consistent way because the bureaucrats and other conservative forces have sabotaged it.

In my view these factors are only a small part of the explanation. The main proposition in this study is that *the blueprint of market socialism is doomed to failure.* Although classical socialism causes great suffering and operates inefficiently, it is at least coherent. Combined with the "requisite" degree of brutal repression, it is viable and robust. The market-socialist reform, on the other hand, is not capable of becoming a robust system. In fact it is only its predecessor, classical socialism, in the process of falling apart.

The subsequent sections of this study advance arguments in favor of this proposition, grouped under the following themes: the role of the state and politics; property rights and the soft budget constraint; social discipline; and exit, entry, and natural selection.

The causal explanation for the failure is far from exhaustive. Several important issues are missing: for instance, the problem of prices and the related problem of information, mainly because they have been adequately covered in other works. In my view, however, the phenomena to be examined are among the main factors explaining the failure.

The Role of the State and Politics

The authors of the Lange Model and the purely theoretical ideas related to it do not refer specifically to a particular theory of the state. But some underlying tacit assumptions can be discerned, and these are not merely naive, but ultimately quite false. The theory assumes that the state will be content to perform three modest functions: (1) to determine the market-clearing prices, (2) to enforce the profit-maximization rule for state-owned firms, and (3) to perform some redistribution of personal incomes. The theory disregards the real nature of any modern state, let alone such an exceptionally powerful state as the one that operates under the socialist system.

The prototype blueprint is not so naive as the utopian pure theory. On the contrary, its axiomatic point of departure is a special form of state, the party-state. It postulates that on the one hand the Communist party's political monopoly is to remain, and on the other the market will coordinate a substantial proportion of the economic processes. Yet these two postulates cannot be satisfied together, because each precludes the realization of the other. That is the biggest flaw in the blueprint.

Let us look at the modern reformulation of market socialism in the light of contract theory and the so-called principal-agent model.[13] This suggests there is a specific kind of *contract* between the state-center and the manager of a state-owned firm, with the center as principal and the manager as agent acting on its behalf. Western theoretical economists today are often found to draw the following conclusion: the experiments in market socialism so far have failed because the

13. An overall view of this promising new line of research is provided by O. Hart and B. R. Holmström (1987) and J. E. Stiglitz (1987).

terms of the contract were wrong. With a better contract, the market-socialist system will work.

To counter this view, the main thesis put forward in the previous section can be rephrased like this: It is *impossible* to devise and enforce any contract between the state-center (as it actually exists in these countries) and the managers of firms (those actually operating in these countries) that would ensure an efficient allocation of resources. Let me draw attention to the qualifiers in parentheses. A contract between an imaginary principal and an imaginary agent is quite irrelevant to the subject of this study. Let me repeat for the sake of emphasis: our concern is with actual organizations and actual persons whose actions are dictated by their real natures and circumstances.

I hope that further research will produce an exact formulation of this assertion. In terms of strict logical proof, this assertion can only be rated as a conjecture for further research to prove or disprove. It can, if you like, be classed as a bold conjecture, as can the other assertions in this study. But the intuition rests on clear observation of a plain fact: thousands of highly intelligent, well-intentioned people in all the countries that experimented with market socialism were unable to hammer out and consistently implement a contract that was guaranteed to operate efficiently.

Here are a few arguments to support the conjecture:

1. It is a false assumption to expect any government (let alone an individual dictator or a politburo as a collective dictator under a Communist party–dominated political system) to maximize the social-welfare function. It is even doubtful whether any other well-defined utility function can be assumed. If there is an ultimate objective at all, it is to maintain the power of the political rulers, not further the welfare of society. The real motives are described more precisely, in fact, by saying that Communist leaders have multiple objectives. To mention just a few, these include fulfilling their deeply entrenched ideological obligations; in the case of smaller countries, faithfully serving the master-country, the Soviet Union; increasing their military might; accelerating growth in the shortest time possible; and, alongside all these, improving the population's standard of living, of course. It is an elementary truth to empirical political scientists that no politician ever has a consistent order of preferences. Unless stupid or stubborn, he or she will improvise, always adjusting to the contingencies, putting one thing first today and another tomorrow.

Since state ownership places the machinery of the whole economy in the hands of politicians, it is naive to expect that production can ever be "depoliticized." On the contrary, it will invariably be subject to the ever changing political winds. Important though efficiency, growth, technical advance, and so on remain as tasks, they can be easily pushed into second place if the day-to-day considerations of politics so require: for instance, if politicians give popularity priority over other tasks or need to extract more revenue for military purposes.

No politician wants to "sign a contract." They do not like to state their goals plainly, because it ties their hands and limits their room for maneuver. They do not want to be absolutely faithful to any kind of commitment or contract. They prefer flexible action adjusted ad hoc to the changing circumstances.

Even under modern capitalism, the business sphere primarily governed by criteria of profit and efficiency is never separated perfectly from the political sphere moved by considerations of power, but the separation goes quite a long way. The Communist monopoly of political power and predominant state ownership preclude that separation altogether.

2. Another approach is to look at *roles* instead of *objectives*. Capitalist owners basically fulfill one role: they behave as owners. In this role they primarily seek to enhance their income and the value of their property. The state, however, particularly the socialist state, has several concurrent roles. Apart from drawing income from its property, it performs the following other functions:

- legislator, setting the rules for the economy;
- police officer, enforcing the law;
- judge, arbitrating in cases of conflict;
- allocator, redistributing wealth and income;
- insurer, providing a cushion against risks, a dispenser of social security, and a paternalistic benefactor;
- union official, defending workers from managerial abuse.

Conflict between these roles is inevitable. In a democratic constitutional state they are separated, but market socialism, arising under the conditions of Communist power, conserves a political and governmental structure that combines these functions in a totalitarian party-state, instead of separating them.

The role of judge needs special mention. A contract between the state-center and a firm's manager is inevitably incomplete. If it covered every possible detail, it would be hopelessly complex and opaque, and its observance extremely expensive to check. But if the contract between the state-center and the manager fails to cover every detail, legal disputes may arise. Who adjudicates? There is no judicial independence in a totalitarian state. "Plaintiff," "defendant," and "judge" are all dependent on the party and all subordinate to the upper levels of the party-state bureaucracy.

3. Mention was made under point 1 of an individual fictional politician, but, in fact, every political leadership in existence is a coalition, and that applies under a one-party system as well. Within the coalition there are factions and power struggles. Any coalition is temporary and fragile. So whatever contract is drawn up between the state-center and the management of a firm, its enforcement and the conditions under which it can be renegotiated are subject to the power struggle. There is no stability and persistency, only capricious volatility. Even if the members of the coalition agree with the firm's management on the terms of their relations (the "contract") at a given time, its enforcement remains subject to momentary future configurations of power in the coalition.

4. Market socialism assumes that the bureaucracy exercises self-restraint. (Party apparatchiks are to be understood as included in the bureaucracy as an aggregate term; the members of the party apparatus are not just members of the bureaucracy, they are its core.) However great the bureaucracy's power, it is expected to refrain from using it and leave the decisions to the management of the firm and the market agreements between buyers and sellers.

This assumption rests on a vain hope. In fact the temptation is almost irresistible. If power gets into the hands of power-hungry people, they will use it. Moreover, it has become the tradition and routine for them to do so in the period of classical socialism. Both the bureaucrats and the citizens are used to that, and it is sometimes actually demanded even by those over whom the power is exercised. If there is a shortage of a product or service, for instance, the authorities are expected to intervene and organize an administrative distribution.

Oscar Lange's model sought to confine itself to two simple rules. The prototype blueprint intended the bureaucracy to have much greater power, but it set limits, saying where the role of the bureaucracy was to end and the role of the market to begin. But in reality the bureaucracy constantly oversteps the bounds with millions of interventions. Microregulation prevails.

The leadership under reform socialism appeals time and again to the bureaucracy to assist instead of obstructing the process of reform. This proves to be absurd, since the situation contains an innate contradiction. The bureaucracy cannot "assist," because its very existence is a basic obstacle to market-socialist reform.

The growth of the bureaucratic apparatus is not easy to halt, and a reduction is more hopeless still. Once a position in the bureaucracy has come into being, it is extremely difficult to abolish it. Far from falling, the number employed by the party-state and total spending can sometimes even rise during the experiments with market socialism.

There is a struggle going on around the reform, a struggle for power, prestige, influence, and privilege. The more autonomy individuals gain and the more scope there is for voluntary contracts between individuals, the less power bureaucrats are left with. So it is in their own interest to resist.

Property Rights and the Soft Budget Constraint

A return can be made here to an issue mentioned earlier, the "contract" between the principal and the agent. The following argument is often used to defend the concept of market socialism.

Ownership has been separated from control under modern capitalism. The owners of a large joint-stock company are a large number of shareholders, while control is concentrated in the hands of the senior executives. The former constitute the principal and the latter the agent. If this works well under capitalism, why should it not work well under market socialism, even though the owner is the state (or the government representing it)? After all, the output of General Motors is presumably no smaller than Albania's or Mongolia's.

This argument rests in my view on a false analogy, the criticism following from the ideas introduced in the previous section.

The *objectives* of the owners are radically different. Shareholders in General Motors seek financial gain in the first place in the short and long term, whereas the government under market socialism has complex motives that are ultimately subordinate to political goals.

The *instruments* in the hands of the owners are also different. The shareholders of General Motors can dispense financial rewards and penalties, with dismissal as the ultimate sanction; they do not have a KGB. A totalitarian party-state has countless administrative and ideological instruments available to it, though they have weakened since the classical socialist period.

So *the situation of the agent* differs fundamentally under the two sets of contractual circumstances. A General Motors manager has an exit: he or she can quit. (To stick with the U.S. car industry, Lee Iacocca left Ford after conflicts with Henry Ford, the main shareholder, and went to the rival firm of Chrysler as chief executive.) There is no real exit for a company manager under market socialism, since ultimately there is just one employer, the state. (Staying with the same analogy, it is like being able to move from Buick to Pontiac, but not escape from General Motors altogether.) Wherever managers go they are accompanied throughout life by a personnel file. Instead of jobs being allocated by a competitive labor market, top executives are assigned to them by a strongly centralized, ubiquitous network of personnel departments controlled by the party and secret police. A quarrel with the centralized bureaucracy can badly damage or even ruin a manager's career prospects, while good connections in the party and other branches of the bureaucratic apparatus open up a wide range of other careers, as a party functionary, for instance, a high-ranking official, or a diplomat.

This situation decides the motivation of the subordinate agent in the principal-agent relationship. The key trait is loyalty to superiors, not business success or concern for customers. A manager is a bureaucrat, a member of the *nomenklatura*.

A simple conclusion can be drawn: *there is no real decentralization without private ownership*. This well-known proposition was first emphasized strongly in the works of Mises and later expounded in more detail by the "property-rights school."[14] The practical experience of the socialist countries supplies new and convincing evidence to support the old truth. The experiments in applying market socialism confirm that the survival of state ownership inevitably conserves a high degree of centralization.

Let us look at the various property rights more closely.

(a) *Income*. The residual income of a capitalist joint-stock company, after deduction of expenses and taxes, clearly belongs to the share-

14. See L. von Mises [1920] (1935), and also A. A. Alchian (1965), (1974) and A. A. Alchian and H. Demsetz (1972). The position is summarized concisely in the title of W. G. Nutter's study (1968): "Markets without Property: A Grand Illusion."

holders. Though there are institutional owners as well, a high proportion of the shares are held by individuals with direct *personal interests.* With a firm under market socialism this income flows into the state treasury, which is quite *impersonal.* Even if part of the residual income is passed to the managers under various incentive schemes, the proportion is uncertain and the subject of constant negotiation.

(b) *Alienation.* Property rights in a capitalist joint-stock company are transferable, whereas the ownership of a market-socialist firm is inalienable: its sale is precluded by legal constraints.

(c) *Control.* A substantial part of this shifts from the center to the management of the firm, but the rights are not clearly separated, since the center continues to exercise control in a variety of ways. The line dividing the provinces of the superior state organizations and the firm's managers at any time depends on negotiation.

A clear, plain assignment of property rights is lacking. The key to grasping the situation is to see how every decision is based on ad hoc negotiations between the upper levels of the bureaucracy and the managers of the firm. The relative bargaining positions are uncertain. The superior bureaucratic authorities combine strength and weakness: strength in possessing the instruments of state power and weakness in being unable to resort to extreme instruments of terror. But the firm's managers are strong and weak too: strong in that they can resort to blackmail—"our output is vital in the shortage economy"; "we cannot dismiss our workers"—but weak because their careers depend on their superiors' grace and favor.

This is the context in which the syndrome of *soft budget constraint* emerges.[15] As mentioned before, the blueprint states profit to be the main indicator of a firm's success, but this is not taken seriously. With the prevailing political structure and predominance of state ownership there must be softness of the budget constraint. The state cannot let down an insolvent firm; it must bail it out. This conclusion can be drawn directly from what has been said about relations between the party-state and a state-owned firm.

Private ownership is an essential requirement for a hard budget constraint. Private owners can be left to their fate; it is their problem, not the state's. Softening of the budget constraint is the result of deep

15. This concept was introduced in my work *Economics of Shortage* (1980); for a more detailed explanation, see my (1986*a*) article and chapters 8 and 21 of the 1992 book.

state involvement, since the state bears ultimate responsibility for the fate of the firm.

Social Discipline

The bargaining that permeates society ties in with another noteworthy problem: social discipline.

Any complex process of coordination demands a measure of discipline. There must be a combination of positive and negative incentives, the carrot and the stick.

Discipline is needed at work to ensure full use of working hours, obedience to technological imperatives, and cooperation between the various phases of work.

Discipline is needed if pay or wages can become divorced from performance, which has harmful micro- and macroeconomic effects.

Discipline is needed in finance. Among the many facets of this multiple requirement is that persistently loss-making firms must be wound up, since their survival merely contributes to social costs.

Classical socialism rested on commands, mandatory planning instructions, and a brutal enforcement of obedience. There were rewards for discipline and loyalty to the party and the state, but harsh penalties for violations for discipline.

Capitalism applies market discipline mainly by economic means. Work discipline is reinforced by refined pay schemes, and most of all by the threat of dismissal and unemployment. Wage discipline is ensured by the self-interest of the owners, since extra pay unjustified by performance ultimately comes out of their pockets. Financial discipline in the business sphere is enforced primarily by the hard budget constraint: a firm that gets into difficulties will not be rescued by the state with tax breaks or subsidies, or with soft loans from the banking system.[16]

Under the reform pointing toward market socialism, the discipline of the command economy is lifted without true market discipline being applied. Softness is not confined to the budget constraint; all the other forms of discipline slacken too. Superiors and subordinates con-

---

16. Certain symptoms of the soft budget constraint syndrome appear in modern capitalism due to various factors: there are rescues of insolvent firms and even whole sectors. How inevitable this is and to what extent it brings an erosion of financial discipline, along with all the detrimental consequences known from the experience of the socialist countries, is a matter of debate.

nive to flout the law. Inspectors turn a blind eye to laxity and indiscipline. Laws and rules lose their prestige.

The breakdown of discipline is also to blame for the low efficiency at microlevel, and on a macrolevel it is the main contributor to the macrotensions—the wage spiral, excess state spending, and the practice of wantonly distributing credit and never demanding its repayment. All these phenomena ultimately bring about inflation, monetary overhang, and indebtedness.

Entry, Exit, and Natural Selection

In the discussion of market socialism to this point, the composition of the firms sector was taken for granted. In fact the multitude of firms is not constant, and the regularities governing entry and exit, birth and death, are extremely important.

One of capitalism's great virtues is the freedom of entry into all areas where it is unimpeded by monopolies. Opportunity is the mother of enterprise. The entrepreneur in Schumpeter's sense pools his or her talents with the financial resources of the lender.[17] Loan capital may come from various sources. The financial backing for the enterprise is provided by a competitive banking sector and a decentralized capital and money market.

Market socialism differs little from classical socialism in this respect. Entry is governed by bureaucratic decisions. The foundation of firms is the bureaucracy's task and privilege. There are strong monopolistic tendencies: why create rivals for oneself? Competition and the right of free entry are inseparable, and they are just what market socialism lacks.

The situation is similar on the exit side. With a hard budget constraint, a loss-making firm cannot survive. This applies invariably to the normally small and medium-sized firms in the noncorporate sector. Here the exit rate is very high, amounting to 20–30% of firms a year in many countries. The proportion is far lower in the corporate sector, but a similar selection effect operates there through the mechanism of corporate takeovers. If the earlier management was incapable of drawing the maximum profit from the firm, the potential new owners hope for new profitmaking opportunities by taking over control of

17. "Capitalism is that form of private property economy in which innovations are carried out by means of borrowed money," writes Schumpeter (1939, vol. 1, p. 223).

the shares, and this is usually accompanied by aggressive dismissal of the previous management.

These strict principles of selection fail to apply in an economy with a soft budget constraint. There is a bureaucratic redistribution of profits, which are taken from strong firms and given as assistance to weak ones. The state has sunk investments in an existing firm, and so it has a vested interest in its survival.[18] Exit is relatively rare, and when it does occur it is by an arbitrary bureaucratic decision.

The overall effect of the entry-exit rules set is that no rivalry occurs. A brief return must be made to an issue mentioned several times before: Can an effective "contract" be made between the state-center and a firm's manager? To the counterarguments advanced so far another can be added. For the "principal" (in this case the state-center) to gauge performance by the "agents" (in this context the managers of firms), it must be able to compare firms. But that requires free entry and competition, which makes a real comparison with winners and losers, not just paper assessments.[19]

Without free entry and without exit by the losers in the competition, the "creative destruction" that Schumpeter deemed so important cannot occur. Once the production structure has formed, it is frozen. That is one more reason for the low efficiency and weak performance.

To sum up, there are various arguments to support this study's main proposition that the failure of market socialism is not due to weaknesses in the blueprint or in the way it is implemented. Given certain fundamental features of the sociopolitical system—namely, the survival of the Communist party's political monopoly and the predominance of state ownership—the quest for a truly efficient economy is hopeless. There is a built-in instability, and the experiment sooner or later breaks down.[20]

---

18. This mechanism is formalized and its negative results graphically shown by M. Dewatripont and E. Maskin (1990). The effect of the phenomenon on innovation is analyzed by Y. Qian and C. Xu (1991).

19. Although this study does not deal with the issue of prices, it must be mentioned here that the comparative reports on paper of firms' performances are useless in any case because distorted and irrational prices are used to compile them.

20. [By the summer of 1994, as this volume is edited, the collapse of the reform-socialist experiment in the Soviet Union and Eastern Europe can already be described in the past tense. But the same does not apply in two other reform-socialist countries, Vietnam and China, where it survives and progresses successfully in many respects.

Some experts consider that the experience in China and Vietnam refutes the arguments just advanced for saying that the collapse of the market-socialist experiment is inevitable. I do not agree, and maintain my earlier position.

II Learning by Disappointment: The Epistemological and Ethical Viewpoint

Understanding the Process of Understanding

Some of the arguments against market socialism put forward in this study were known a good while before the present collapse of the Eastern European system. Reference was made earlier to Mises, Hayek, and the exponents of the "property-rights school," whose writings advance numerous objections still valid today. Why did the

---

I never claimed, either in my comprehensive book on the socialist system (1992) or in the studies in this volume, that reform socialism and the market-socialist changes made under it could have no success. Nor did I state that the reformed version of socialism could not survive in some country or other, for a considerable time, if conditions were favorable for it. I gave three examples in the book just mentioned (pp. 449–452) of countries in which a specific kind of "reform equilibrium" developed between the advocates and opponents of reform, amid advances and retreats and occasional dramatic conflicts. That was the case in Tito's Yugoslavia, Kádár's Hungary, and the China of Deng Xiaoping. The ruling Communist party managed to find the level of repression that would suffice to maintain its monopoly of power, while giving scope for a partial change in the property relations and coordination mechanisms. So it was possible for a specific kind of reform socialism to survive in Yugoslavia for more than 40 years and Hungary for 20. Reform socialism, having been prevalent in China for only 16 years and in Vietnam for even less time, may well survive there for a good deal longer.

All that can be said for certain about China and Vietnam, for the time being, is this: Although capitalist ownership is spreading in both countries, it is still subject to administrative constraints. Neither country has yet declared as an official government program the open privatization of firms hitherto in state ownership, or any intention of confining the state sector within narrow bounds. I would like to add my own forecast here. As the capitalist sector of the economy grows, it will sooner or later seek to articulate its interests politically, which will conflict with the monopoly of power held by the Communist party. Full capitalist development cannot unfold completely before parties supporting such a line wholeheartedly have formed and taken power. There is no telling yet whether the conflict between the situation in the political sphere and the forces of capitalist development will take a relatively peaceful form, as it did in Hungary, where the Communist party broke up and its successor organizations reconciled themselves to the loss of autocratic power, or whether there will be acts of violence.

On the basis of all this, I take the view that Chinese and Vietnamese reforms have certainly not refuted so far the hypothesis advanced on the grounds of the experience in Eastern Europe: that undivided communist political power and a capitalist economy cannot coexist within a single robust, stable system in a permanent way, over a long historical period. The historical test of this hypothesis is far from over. I would accept as refuting it a conjunction of the following three conditions: (1) if comprehensive privatization of the state sector in these two countries should begin as a declared government program and make steady progress; (2) if all political power should remain undivided in the hands of one legal party, a Communist party declaring itself to be a Marxist-Leninist party; and (3) if this situation should prove stable and capable of sustaining itself for a long time. *New footnote.*]

warnings fall on deaf ears in Eastern Europe? Why did reform politicians and reform economists not take the critics' words to heart? A broader problem lies behind these questions. What are the constraints on enlightenment and rational argument?

Some autobiographical elements appear in this part of the study; introspection contributes to the analysis. I envy those who never change their *Weltanschauung* from the moment they start to ponder the great issues of life to the day they die. No doubt this is not rare in relatively stable societies, but it is hardly possible in the troubled region of Eastern Europe. Many people, even those who tried to serve the same set of fundamental ethical principles throughout their lives, have come to change their philosophy, perhaps more than once, under the influence of disturbing experiences and dramatic changes in their social environment.

One side of people's lives is the history of their opinions. What doctrines did they subscribe to and when? In what period (if ever) were they faithful Marxists? When did they become adherents of reform, perhaps of market socialism itself, and when did they abandon hope of reforming the socialist system (assuming they went through that stage as well)? The discussion here does not cover the way *individuals* differ in the pace at which they go through the process of faith, disappointment, and enlightenment. The question I am interested in is what induced *large groups* of reform politicians and reform economists to devote themselves to the cause of market socialism. What drew them to it and what repelled them from it? The concern in this part of the study, as in the first, is not with individual cases, but with a *prototype* history of ideas: an intellectual movement and the general formulae of moral and political conviction that inspired it.

The question remains topical, because the idea has not been dispelled. It still influences many people despite the historical failure; the greater the difficulties encountered in the transition from socialism to capitalism, the greater the influence of market-socialist ideas tends to become.

The Struggle with Marxism

The reform politicians and reform economists of Eastern Europe were brought up in the Marxist intellectual tradition, with *Das Kapital* as their bible. Acceptance of market socialism is quite alien to the spirit of Marxism. Marx recognized the high degree of organization and efficiency *inside* the factory in a capitalist economy, but he emphasized that complete anarchy reigned on the market connecting the factories.[21] According to this concept, the market is a poorly operating, blind coordination mechanism based on *ex post* reactions to signals. So it must be replaced in the superior socialist society by conscious planning tuned to *ex ante* signals.

Nor was the market attacked merely by the spread of rational arguments. There was indoctrination that delved deep into the metarational, emotional realm, inducing prejudices against the market. A true Marxist views the market with suspicion and contempt. The need to free humanity from its market fetters is one reason why private property must be eliminated.

Overcoming these prejudices requires a great effort of will. Many formerly dogmatic Marxists never manage to overcome them entirely, an example being the frequent fulminations against "speculators," "profiteers," and "black-marketeers" even during the reform.

Despite this antipathy, market socialism seemed to many Communist politicians inclined toward reform to be a necessary concession. They wanted to retain the earlier structure of power, the political monopoly of the Communist party, because that for a Leninist was the prime consideration.[22] And they also wanted to retain the predominance of state ownership. These two attributes of socialism had more than an instrumental value in the Communist system of values, more than a purpose in terms of some other, ultimate aim like the welfare of the people or human happiness. They themselves possessed an intrinsic value, being absolutely indispensable characteristics for a system worthy of the name "socialist." So market socialism seemed to be a promising combination of socialism and capitalism: a dominant role is assigned to the fundamental socialist attributes in the power structure and property relations, and a little injection of capitalism is administered: some influence of the market on coordination. The new combination will improve efficiency without abandoning socialism.[23] As

21. ". . . the most complete anarchy reigns among . . . the capitalist themselves," Marx writes in *Capital* [1867–94]) (1978, chapter 51, p. 1021).

22. Stalin quotes Lenin's statement that "the question of power is the fundamental question of the revolution," adding himself: "The seizure of power is only the beginning. . . . The whole point is to retain power, to consolidate it, and make it invincible" (1947, p. 39).

23. As an illustration, a quotation from Gorbachev: "In short: the advantages of planning will be increasingly combined with the stimulating factors of the socialist market. But all of this will take place within the mainstream of socialist goals and principles of

long as politicians and economists retain their belief in this combination, they can be classed as *naive reformers.*

The reform camp broke up into conflicting groups as it became increasingly clear that *the alternatives were mutually exclusive.* There could *either* be socialism with Communist party rule and predominant state ownership *or* a genuine market economy.

Compatibility with Walrasian Thinking

Let us turn to another intellectual current: Walrasian economics.[24] Several groups must be considered here: (1) economists in Eastern Europe who were converts from Marxism to contemporary Western economic ideas; (2) again in Eastern Europe, a small number of economists, mainly of the older generation, who never went through a Marxist phase; and (3) Western economists who had an interest in market socialism.

The great attraction of Lange-type normative theories is the neat way they fit into the Walrasian tradition and combine nicely (on an intellectual plane, not in reality) with certain socialistic ideas such as a more equitable distribution of income through redistribution by the state. Even the ownership question can be ignored. What really matters is not ownership, but correctly setting the rules and drawing up the contracts with managers, which in turn assures the right motivation and rational prices.

The shortcomings of this view have been outlined in the first part of this study. The Walrasian Model, along with most of its later variants including the Lange-type Model, is a marvelous piece of intellectual machinery placed in a sociopolitical vacuum. It is a construction that lacks *a positive theory of politico-socioeconomic order* as a foundation. Walrasian economics and its more recent theoretical, mathematical-cum-economic kin like game theory, contract theory, and organization theory are very powerful tools for analysis. Analysts using them can arrive at sharp and relevant results, so long as the work is based on the

management" (1987, p. 91). A later statement: "The superiority of the market has been demonstrated on a world scale . . . it is really the regulated market economy which allows us to increase national wealth. . . . And, of course, state power is in our hands" (*Izvestia*, July 11, 1990).

24. The term "neoclassical" is intentionally avoided here in order to leave open the question of whether the Austrian school (including von Mises and Hayek, who have an outstanding role in connection with the subject of this study) belong inside or outside the neoclassical school.

right social theory. But they can reach misleading conclusions if their work is grounded on a false social theory, irrespective of whether their points of departure in social theory are spelled out or just implicit in the construction of the model.

The word "vacuum" has been used because the Lange Model lacks, among others, the following attributes required by a more complete theory:

- understanding of the sociopolitical environment of the actors and the institutions that influence their behavior;
- incorporation of the state, as an endogenous constituent of the system, in the overall theory of the economy;
- an explanation of how the preferences of decision makers and the changes in these preferences, the decision-making routines, and the political and social constraints on human actions are determined by the social circumstances and of the extent to which the social situation explains the goals of individuals and groups.

The Austrian school certainly offers a richer explanation of these attributes of the socioeconomic order than sterile application of Walrasian theory, but it is still not rich enough. Much can be learned from Marx if the explanatory theory of the economic order is being examined (although Marx and Hayek are admittedly strange bedfellows). Economists should make far greater use of the accumulated knowledge offered by modern sociology, political science, social psychology, and history. All this knowledge is required in order to reach the right normative conclusions.

There is nothing wrong with the tools of the Walrasian school, or, more widely, with the analytical methods of the neoclassical school, so long as they are treated with care and circumspection. But there are dangers in using them in an easygoing way because they tempt people to employ the wrong *research strategy*. Research should never *start* with formal analysis. The right questions must be put to start with; sound assumptions and sound conjectures must be devised. An erroneous strategy holds fewer dangers when the research is into "small" questions, especially if they can be compared with observable, repeatedly occurring facts. In that case it is simple to confront theory with praxis, which acts as a safeguard against serious error. An erroneous strategy becomes more dangerous in the case of "big" and rarely repeated issues, and more dangerous still, in fact positively fatal, with never-repeated future events of vast import like the transformation of whole societies. Starting the analysis "in the middle," with precise formalization but without very carefully weighing all the relevant political, sociological, and psychological assumptions and implications, can be very harmful indeed.

To add a personal note here, these ideas inspired me to write the book *Anti-Equilibrium* (1971). In retrospect I can see I was too harsh in my rejection of some analytical instruments that can actually do good service if they are used with sufficient precaution. I was not sufficiently confident in the Walrasian school's powers of rejuvenation, whereas prominent members of it have made great progress in expanding its range of tools and improving the realism of its models since then. Yet I still feel there was an element of justice in my bitter reproaches at that time. When I wrote the book, very widespread use was made of the narrow-minded, technique-oriented research strategy just outlined—starting research "in the middle" of the cognitive process by devising a formal model. Paucity of knowledge about the real workings of society often led to false positions. I might add that this approach is none too rare today. The artificial barrier and mutual mistrust between "institutionalists" and "analytical" economists still persists, damaging the usefulness of both approaches.

So far as I can see, the intellectual convenience of combining Walrasian thinking with socialistic principles of distribution still has an effect on the thinking of many economists. My request to my colleagues is to face up to Eastern European experience, especially the political, social, and psychological aspects of it; this may induce them to reexamine their adherence to the concept of market socialism.

Three Fallacies

Closely related to the issue discussed in the previous section are three fallacies with which I would like to take issue:

1. Schumpeter's pioneer theory on the role of the entrepreneur is highly relevant to the subject of this study: market socialism.[25] (See the section above on the role of entry, exit, and natural selection.) When the Walrasian normative theory was devised, the question was evaded of how "creative destruction" would occur in a Lange economy: elimination of obsolete technology and organization and introduction of revolutionary new products, technologies, and forms of organization.

25. See J. A. Schumpeter [1911] (1968).

Schumpeter later drew some far-reaching conclusions from his earlier theory and other observations on the future of capitalism and socialism.[26] Let me try, with a little simplification, to sum up his line of thinking. The main role in modern capitalism is played by large corporations, including monopoly firms. These have become bureaucratized to a great extent. The role of the entrepreneur has weakened. The bureaucratic monopoly firm is capable of taking over the entrepreneur's function, primarily in innovation. If it is the case that capitalism itself has become bureaucratic, and if Lange has proved anyway that market socialism is viable and efficient, it is best to acknowledge that socialism will replace capitalism. This is foreseeable, and even if it is not glad tidings, there is no need to oppose it.

This prophecy of Schumpeter's has been a subject of controversy ever since.[27] I am convinced that Schumpeter's reasoning here is erroneous.

First, the analysis of modern capitalism given by Schumpeter is biased and exaggerated. Luckily, the "entrepreneur" of Schumpeter's earlier works has not disappeared from the world of contemporary capitalism at all. On the contrary, it is often the entrepreneurs as battering rams for innovation who induce large corporations to innovate after all in spite of their indolent tendencies. Think, for example, of the role played in revolutionizing the computer industry by the founders of Microsoft or Apple, or other initially small ventures, in relation to the near-monopoly IBM. Strong bureaucratic tendencies have certainly arisen, and the role of the state has grown to a large extent. But those like myself, who know from personal experience what *real* bureaucratization of a system means, may be better placed to appreciate that the process of bureaucratization has not gone very far. Modern developed capitalism has basically remained a decentralized, competitive, private market economy.

Second, market socialism in real life did not fulfill the expectations of Lange or the later Schumpeter, as the first part of this study set out to show. Fifty years after the appearance of Schumpeter's book, its prophecy has been refuted by history. Instead of socialism replacing capitalism, capitalism is regaining lost territory that classical socialism ruled for a long time and the market-socialist experiments could only occupy temporarily.

26. J. A. Schumpeter [1942] (1976).

27. See, for instance, the volume published for the fortieth anniversary of the appearance of *Capitalism, Socialism and Democracy*, A. Heertje, ed. (1981).

2. Some reform economists familiar with contemporary Western theory favor the idea of market socialism for the following reason: They realize the various shortcomings in the operation of an unrestrained private market economy. The list is well known: the problems of externalities, public goods and monopolies, the income distributional troubles, and so forth. They are also aware of the many drawbacks of planning and overcentralized state control. The former they like to call market failures and the latter planning failures.

Now market socialism offers the prospect of a nice *complementarity*, with planning and the market coexisting peaceably side by side, each curbing the other's excesses. While the central authorities make corrective interventions when the market errs, the market and the partial degree of decentralization prevent the state from becoming excessively bureaucratic.[28]

No such nice complementarity materialized under the market-socialist reforms in Eastern Europe. The market failures persisted: the harmful externalities (air and water pollution, environmental damage, congestion), the monopoly position of vast state-owned firms, and the unjust distribution of income. At the same time, the market failed to gain vigor because it was throttled by the bureaucracy, which intervened even where the market had not failed.

3. There are a great many illusions about the potentials of "system design" and "system engineering." Some think they can be applied on a national scale, not just in a particular firm or smaller sector. The optimal schemes of organization and rules of operation must be thought out methodically. Once a wise and benevolent government possesses them, it will see they are implemented successfully.

That is not what happens in practice. Rules are only effective if they are compatible with the nature of the government and society concerned. Otherwise the implant will be rejected. The necessity for compatibility and coherence among the elements in a system is clearly recognized, but a detailed explanation is still lacking. Promising though the mathematical and economic researches into the compatibility of incentives are, they are still only in the initial stages of exploring the problem. They remain for the time being insufficiently associated with the non-formalized empirical studies of society's functioning and human behavior.

A high proportion of social institutions come into being by *evolution*. Again there is a process of natural selection. A large number of muta-

28. This idea also appeared in my book *Anti-Equilibrium* (1971, pp. 334–343).

tions occur, with some of the new institutions and rules that arise proving viable, while others disappear. One of the innate weaknesses of market socialism is that it is an artificial construct, a constructivist creature, to use Hayek's term.[29] Nor is it merely that the theoretical model and later the blueprint were artificial, for it also imposed a great many governmental interventions on people.

As an illustration, let me refer to one of the problems discussed in the first part of the study. Market socialism rests on the assumption that firms will behave *as if* they were profit maximizers. If that is so, they can be stimulated to do what the center wants by well-calibrated subsidies, tax concessions, administrative prices that ensure a high profit margin, and credit at concessionary interest rates. At the same time, firms can be dissuaded in a similar way from actions the center opposes by well-calibrated taxes, the setting of prices unfavorable to the firm, and deterrent interest rates. True, but to exert this influence, each bureaucratic agency builds up its own system of incentives and deterrents. Toward the end of the Hungarian experiment with market socialism, state-owned firms were subject to restraint or inducement from some 200 types of special taxes and subsidies. The outcome was for the impact of any scheme to be canceled out by the others. The firm failed to react like an obedient puppet when all its strings were pulled from various directions because they were tangled up. This also meant the profit motive ceased to apply, because the financial impact of market success and failure was cushioned by the tailor-made taxes, subsidies, and other interventions in prices and the firm's financial affairs. Instead of a natural environment of free contracts, the firm operated in an artificial setting of bureaucratic decrees.

The arguments against such artifacts do not imply that the state and political movements should be passive bystanders observing the evolution of society. Their activity is required, so long as it reinforces existing healthy trends that arise in a natural way and does not impose artificial constructs on society.

The Democratic Choice of an Economic System

That brings us to the question of *choice* of a system. A distinction was drawn in the introduction between seeking to introduce market socialism instead of capitalism and seeking to introduce it instead of

29. See L. von Mises (1981) and F. A. Hayek (1960), (1989).

classical socialism. All politicians and economists have a self-evident right to recommend market socialism as a replacement for capitalism or a way of reforming it, if that is what they believe, provided they seek to do so by democratic, parliamentary means. A party proposing to introduce market socialism may stand in the elections, and if it wins it can put the necessary legislation through in accordance with the democratic constitution. The fact that I would not vote for such a party myself is irrelevant to my argument—I fully recognize the legitimacy of forming such a party and of its political activity.

But the question of "whence and whither" must be raised again in the case of Eastern Europe. The idea of market socialism did not gain ascendancy through a free competition of ideas. What happened was that the group which had happened to gain power in the Communist party embraced this idea and then imposed it on society. Although the methods used were less brutal than the earlier confiscation of the factories and mass collectivization, the introduction was nonetheless made by government decree. Once again it was a question of "forced happiness." The ruling group considers this will be good for the people, so let them have it.

For a long time many reform economists did not even consider this side of the matter. It seemed to be self-evident that the ruling elite of the party-state should decide. The elite had to be convinced (or its membership altered) for the idea of reform to prevail. One of the gravest shortcomings in the market-socialist blueprint is its failure to enquire whether this is really what the people want.

It is still too early to make general predictions. Majorities were won in the Hungarian, German, and Polish elections by parties that rejected market socialism and sought to introduce a private market economy. What happens in the elections in the other countries which have turned to parliamentary democracy remains to be seen. My guess is that if any party comes out clearly in favor of market socialism, it will fail in free elections to win the majority required to apply its ideas.

This line of argument, by the way, strongly backs up another cardinal point of departure in this study: the sharp difference between the initial positions in the East and in the West. Those in a developed Western country who favor market socialism are normally racked by ethical and political dilemmas. They would like to retain the efficiency of the market economy, but they also demand a more equitable distribution of income and taxation—greater equality. Rightly or wrongly, they hope that some form of market socialism will produce a better compromise between these conflicting sets of values. The tacit assumption behind this line of thinking among Western economists is an axiomatic acceptance of democracy and respect for human rights, including the right to private property.

The debate in the East was about something else; relatively less attention was given to the dilemma of "efficiency versus equity." For a long time the opposing sides merely argued about which kind of socialism was more efficient, taking as axiomatic the absence of democracy, the one-party system, and the harder or softer kinds of totalitarianism. Once this axiom was questioned and doubt cast on the legitimacy of the political structure, it marked the beginning of the end for the system.

The Tutors: Disappointment and Trauma

From introspection, and also from conversations with friends and colleagues, I can state that those who at some stage in their lives changed their opinion on the subjects discussed in this study were not influenced to do so by books or articles. Thinking is strongly affected by metarational factors: values, sentiments, prejudices, and hopes. These act like gates, or at least like filters, either receiving certain influences or rejecting them. The soul and intellect of an individual are either open to an idea or closed to it.

I read Mises and Hayek thirty years ago and rejected their objections to market socialism. Later I read them again in a different frame of mind, and suddenly I became receptive to their arguments. The resistance was gone from my old self, the "naive reformer" who took certain axioms of Eastern European socialism as unquestionable and merely sought greater decentralization instead of overcentralization.

What changed many of our minds was a series of political traumas and disillusionments. With professional experts like economists, the decisive blow was not dealt in many cases by negative experiences in their own areas of competence. Revision of their professional opinions might have come later. First, the foundations of their *philosophy of life* collapsed, usually under the influence of some earthshaking event: the sight of Russian tanks in Budapest, Prague, or Afghanistan, or the experiences related by a friend, on being released from prison. Once this enlightenment has happened, suddenly or gradually, as a result of a psychologically searing experience, the mind immediately opens to the rational arguments as well. A passion to read and reread is aroused.

Works whose ideas had bounced off the walls of prejudice suddenly appear convincing. More superficially or more deeply, people plow up the layers of their own thinking, revising their philosophies and their professional principles. This tilling of the soil is needed before an economist who has had a blind faith can start thinking seriously about professional issues like free entry and market-clearing prices.

This kind of retrospection is a painful process that teaches modesty and intellectual humility. But a little pride can also be taken in remembering that we had the strength at least to struggle with our own prejudices, to open the intellectual gates and to help others to open theirs.

But while admitting the moral virtue in such a gradual awakening, one has to ask whether it was worth painfully seeking the answer to a few very difficult questions if that answer was already known. I am sure it was: there was sense and value in the search.

This ties in with the limits of predictive force in the social sciences, a matter that was touched upon in the section on the compatibility with Walrasian thinking and must be returned to here. The social sciences are capable of giving comparatively reliable predictions only for "small," frequently recurring events. No firm prediction can be given *by scientific means* for "large," non-recurring events. The warnings of a Mises or a Hayek about market socialism are brilliant guesses, but they are not scientifically proved *ex ante*. A vision was confronted by a guess, not a scientific proposition by a scientific repudiation of it. An *ex post* position has now been reached; a large enough body of knowledge has accumulated for assertions to be proved. The economists of countries where an experiment was made in applying market socialism are now in a position to make statements based on firsthand experience. Reports from eyewitnesses and victims have special weight in any trial. It is not the same thing to debate about market socialism in London or Chicago in the 1930s as to debate about it in Budapest, Warsaw, or Moscow today. The second debate has the special weight; it is greater, richer, and in many ways more convincing than the debate in the 1930s.

I spoke just now about the limits of rational convictions and the prejudices that obstruct ideas. But that does not mean people should be left to themselves to go through their own process of learning and disillusionment. The problem still remains. It is still on the agenda where the socialist system persists, which is no small part of the world, including, for instance, China and Vietnam, two countries where experimentation with market socialism continues on a nationwide scale.

In addition, a special rearguard action is being fought to defend market socialist ideas in the postsocialist countries where parliamentary democracy has been introduced. This curious notion, which might be called "anti-Bolshevik market socialism," can be summed up like this: "The Communists could not cope with the state-owned firms. Now we, as the successors in power to the Communists, will show we are capable of managing the state sector well, however large it may be." So state ownership is retained over a far wider sphere than is economically justified, bureaucratic centralization is reintroduced into the management of the state sector, and executive appointments to it are made on political instead of professional grounds. These are phenomena familiar from the period of the socialist system, and their effect will be as damaging now as it was under the leadership of the Communist party.

So the problem continues, which is why it is worth continuing to deal with it. Perhaps there are enough enlightened or potentially enlightened people by now who will listen to what those who have been through the experiments in market socialism have to say. I would like to hope that the experience in Eastern Europe will make it easier for them to avoid the blind alleys and choose the right path.

References

Alchian, Armen A. 1965. "Some Economics of Property Rights." *Il Politico* 30 (4): 816–829.

Alchian, Armen A. 1974. "Foreword." In *The Economics of Property Rights*, edited by E. G. Furubotn and S. Pejovich. Cambridge, Mass.: Ballinger Publishing Company, pp. xiii–xv.

Alchian, Armen A., and Demsetz, Harold. 1972. "Production, Information, Costs, and Economic Organization." *American Economic Review* 62 (5): 777-795.

Arrow, Kenneth J., and Hurwicz, Leonid. 1960. "Decentralization and Computation in Resource Allocation." In *Essays in Economics and Econometrics*. Chapel Hill: University of North Carolina Press, pp. 34–104.

Bardhan, Prahab. 1990. "Some Reflections on Premature Obituaries of Socialism." *Economic and Political Weekly* (India), February 3: 259–262.

Barone, Enrico. [1908] 1935. "The Ministry of Production in the Collectivist State." In *Collectivist Economic Planning*, edited by Friedrich A. Hayek. London: Routledge and Kegan Paul, pp. 245–290.

Brus, Wlodzimierz. [1961] 1972. *The Market in a Socialist Economy*. London: Routledge and Kegan Paul.

Brus, Wlodzimierz, and Laski, Kazimierz. 1989. *From Marx to Market. Socialism in Search of an Economic System.* Oxford: Clarendon Press.

Dewatripont, Michel, and Maskin, Eric. 1990. "Credit and Efficiency in Centralized and Decentralized Economies." Discussion Paper, no. 1512, Cambridge, Mass.: Harvard Institute of Economic Research, Harvard University.

Gorbachev, Mikhail S. 1987. *Perestroika.* New York: Harper and Row.

Hart, Oliver, and Holmström, Bengt R. 1987. "The Theory of Contracts." In *Advances in Economic Theory. Fifth World Congress,* edited by T. Bewly. Cambridge: Cambridge University Press, pp. 71–155.

Hayek, Friedrich A. 1960. *The Constitution of Liberty.* London: Routledge, and Chicago: Chicago University Press.

Hayek, Friedrich A. 1989. *Order—With or Without Design.* London: Centre for Research into Communist Economies.

Hayek, Friedrich A., ed. 1935. *Collectivist Economic Planning.* London: Routledge and Kegan Paul.

Heertje, Arnold, ed. 1981. *Schumpeter's Vision: Capitalism, Socialism and Democracy After Forty Years.* New York: Praeger.

Heilbroner, Robert. 1990. "Analysis and Vision in the History of Modern Economic Thought." *Journal of Economic Literature* 28 (3): 1097–1114.

International Monetary Fund, IBRD, OECD, EBRD. 1990. "The Economy of the USSR: Summary and Recommendations." A study undertaken in response to a request by the Houston Summit, Washington, D.C.

Jasay, Anthony de. 1990. *Market Socialism: A Scrutiny. 'This Square Circle'.* London: Institute of Economic Affairs.

Kidric, Boris. 1985. *Sabrana Dela* (Collected Works). Belgrade: Izdavacki Centar Komunist.

Kolodko, Grzegorz W. 1991. "Polish Hyperinflation and Stabilization 1989–1990." *Most* 1 (1): 9–36.

Kornai, János. [1957] 1959. *Overcentralization in Economic Administration.* Oxford: Oxford University Press.

Kornai, János. 1971. *Anti-Equilibrium.* Amsterdam: North-Holland.

Kornai, János. 1980. *Economics of Shortage.* Amsterdam: North-Holland.

Kornai, János. 1986*a*. "The Soft Budget Constraint." *Kyklos* 39 (1): 3–30.

Kornai, János. 1986*b*. "The Hungarian Reform Process: Visions, Hopes and Reality." *Journal of Economic Literature* 24 (4): 1687–1737.

Kornai, János. 1992. *The Socialist System. The Political Economy of Communism.* Princeton: Princeton University Press, and Oxford: Oxford University Press.

Lange, Oscar. 1936–1937. "On the Economic Theory of Socialism." *Review of Economic Studies* 4 (1, 2): 53–71, 123–142.

Lavoie, Don. 1985. *Rivalry and Central Planning. The Socialist Calculation Debate Reconsidered.* Cambridge: Cambridge University Press.

Le Grand, Julian, and Estrin, Saul, eds. 1989. *Market Socialism*. Oxford: Clarendon Press.

Lerner, Abba P. 1946. *The Economics of Control*. New York: Macmillan.

Liberman, Evsey G. [1962] 1972. "The Plan, Profit and Bonuses." In *Socialist Economics*, edited by A. Nove and D. M. Nuti. Middlesex: Penguin Books, pp. 309–318.

Lipton, David, and Sachs, Jeffrey. 1990*a*. "Creating a Market Economy in Eastern Europe: The Case of Poland." *Brookings Papers on Economic Activity* (1): 75–133.

Lipton, David, and Sachs, Jeffrey. 1990*b*. "Privatization in Eastern Europe: The Case of Poland." *Brookings Papers on Economic Activity* (2): 293–333.

Malinvaud, Edmond. 1967. "Decentralized Procedures for Planning." In *Activity Analysis in the Theory of Growth and Planning*, edited by E. Malinvaud and M. O. L. Bacharach. London: Macmillan, and New York: St. Martin's Press, pp. 170–208.

Marx, Karl. [1867–1894] 1978. *The Capital*. London: Penguin.

Mises, Ludwig von. [1920], 1935. "Economic Calculations in the Socialist Commonwealth." In *Collectivist Economic Planning*, edited by Friedrich A. Hayek. London: Routledge and Kegan Paul, pp. 87–130.

Mises, Ludwig von. 1981. *Socialism*. Indianapolis: Liberty Classics.

Nove, Alec. 1983. *The Economics of Feasible Socialism*. New York: Allen and Unwin.

Nutter, Warren G. 1968. "Markets Without Property: A Grand Illusion." In *Money, the Market and the State*, edited by N. Beadles and L. Drewry. Athens, GA: University of Georgia Press, pp. 137–145.

Organization for Economic Co-operation and Development. 1991. *OECD Economic Surveys: Hungary 1991*. Paris. OECD.

Ortuno-Ortin, Ignacio, Roemer, John E. and Silvestre, Joaquim. 1990. *Market Socialism*. Mimeo. Davis, CA: University of California.

Péter, György. 1954*a*. "Az egyszemélyi felelős vezetésről" (On Management Based on One-Man Responsibility). *Társadalmi Szemle* 9 (8–9): 109–124.

Péter, György. 1954*b*. "A gazdaságosság jelentőségéről és szerepéről a népgazdaság tervszerő irányításában" (On the Importance and Role of Economic Efficiency in the Planned Control of the National Economy). *Közgazdasági Szemle* 1 (3): 300–324.

Péter, György. 1956. "A gazdaságosság és jövedelmezőség jelentősége a tervgazdaságban, I–II" (The Importance of Economic Efficiency and Profitability in the Planned Economy, I–II). *Közgazdasági Szemle* 3 (6, 7–8): 695–711 and 851–869.

Qian, Yingyi, and Xu, Chenggang. 1991. "Innovation and Financial Constraints in Centralized and Decentralized Economies." Mimeo. Cambridge, Mass.: Department of Economics, Harvard University.

Schroeder, Gertrude E. 1988. "Property Rights Issues in Economic Reforms in Socialist Countries." *Studies in Comparative Communism* 21 (2): 175–188.

Schumpeter, Joseph A. [1911] 1968. *The Theory of Economic Development. An Inquiry into Profits, Capital, Credit, Interest and Business Cycles*. Cambridge, Mass.: Harvard University Press.

Schumpeter, Joseph A. 1939. *Business Cycles: A Theoretical, Historical and Statistical Analysis of the Capitalist Progress.* New York: McGraw-Hill.

Schumpeter, Joseph. A. [1942] 1976. *Capitalism, Socialism and Democracy.* New York: Harper and Row.

Schumpeter, Joseph A. 1954. *History of Economic Analysis.* New York: Oxford University Press.

Sik, Ota. 1966. *Economic Planning and Management in Czechoslovakia.* Prague: Orbis.

Stalin, Josef V. 1947. *Problems of Leninism.* Moscow: Foreign Languages Press.

Stiglitz, Joseph E. 1987. "Principal and Agent." In *The New Palgrave. A Dictionary of Economics,* Vol. 3, edited by J. Eatwell, M. Milgate, and P. Newman. London: Macmillan, and New York: The Stockton Press, pp. 966–972.

Sun, Yefang. 1982 (Originally published in the period 1958–1961). "Some Theoretical Issues in Socialistic Economics." In *Social Needs versus Economic Efficiency in China,* edited and translated by K. K. Fung. Armonk: M. E. Sharpe.

Taylor, Fred M. 1929. "The Guidance of Production in a Socialist State." *American Economic Review* 19 (1): 1–80. Reprinted in 1938 in *On the Economic Theory of Socialism* edited by B. E. Lippincott. Minneapolis: University of Minnesota Press.

Temkin, Gabriel. 1989. "On Economic Reform in Socialist Countries: The Debate on Economic Calculation Under Socialism Revisited." *Communist Economies* 1 (1): 31–59.

2 The Affinity between Ownership Forms and Coordination Mechanisms[1]

The world witnesses a great upheaval in socialist countries, where dramatic events have been happening since 1988. The present paper concentrates on evaluating past experience in the hope that a correct understanding of the past will help in devising sound policies for the future. Of course, the number of socialist countries which have engaged in reform in the past is small, and the situation in all socialist or formerly socialist countries is still very unsettled. What can be attempted is nothing more than an outline of a few preliminary conjectures which will have to be tested against future historical developments.

The issues to be discussed in the paper have many political ramifications. Decisions concerning ownership and coordination mechanisms are, of course, strongly linked to the questions concerning power, political institutions, and ideology. Apart from a few short hints, this paper does not elaborate on the political aspects of these topics.[2]

Classical versus Reform Socialism, Reform versus Revolution

Some conceptual clarification is needed. In the following, I distinguish two prototypes of socialism. The first one is *classical socialism*, i.e., the form of socialism that prevailed under Stalin, Mao Zedong, and their disciples in other countries. The second one is *reform socialism*, i.e., the

1. I should like to express my thanks to Mária Kovács, to Carla Krüger, and to Shailendra Raj Mehta for assistance in editing the paper. The support of the Hungarian Academy of Sciences, of Harvard University, of WIDER, and of the Sloan Foundation is gratefully acknowledged.

2. [See my book on the socialist system (Kornai 1992), particularly chapters 3, 4, 7, and 15. *New footnote.*]

new form of socialism that evolved, for instance, under (in chronological order) Tito in Yugoslavia, Kádár in Hungary, Deng Xiaoping in China, and Gorbachev in the Soviet Union; some further countries could be named as well.[3] The reform socialist countries made some steps toward liberalization in the political sphere, somewhat decentralized the control of their state-owned sector, and allowed a somewhat larger scope for the private sector. At the same time, these countries still maintained the fundamental attributes of a socialist system: the Communist party did not share power with any other political force, the state-owned sector still played a dominant role in the economy, and the main coordinator of economic activities was the centralized bureaucracy, even though coordination was effected with the aid of less rigid instruments.

We should also distinguish *reform* and *revolution*. The former aims at major changes in the existing socialist system, but preserves its basic characteristics. The latter starts a transformation that ultimately shifts the country in question away from socialism. Thus the difference between reform and revolution does not lie in the method of transformation (violent versus non-violent change), nor in the speed (slow process versus sudden explosion). The distinguishing criterion is the following: Does the transformation abolish the power monopoly of the Communist party? In this sense, in 1989, a revolution began in (in temporal order) Hungary, Poland, East Germany, Czechoslovakia, and Rumania. East Germany and Czechoslovakia avoided the reform stage and took a leap, by jumping from classical socialism directly to systemic transformation.

In this paper, I am concerned with reform socialism, and do not discuss the problems of "postsocialist" revolutionary systemic transformation.[4] At the time of writing the final version of the paper, reform socialism is still the regime ruling over the two largest countries, the Soviet Union and China, and also a few smaller ones, like Mongolia or Vietnam. For Eastern Europe it is history, yet still so close to the present that it has an extremely strong impact not only on the initial economic conditions of the transformation process, but also on political

3. There is a voluminous literature concerning the description and the analysis of reform processes in the various socialist countries. To mention only a few examples: J. P. Burkett (1989) on *Yugoslavia*, J. Kornai (1986) and L. Antal et al. (1987) on *Hungary*, D. H. Perkins (1988) on *China*, Iu. N. Afanas'ev, ed. (1988), E. A. Hewett (1988), G. E. Schroeder (1987), and N. Shmelev (1987) on the *Soviet Union*.

4. My views on revolutionary transformation are discussed in my 1990 book.

thought and intellectual debates. Therefore, the subject of the paper, common lessons of reform socialism, should be more than timely, as it might provide some orientation in the midst of the breath-taking changes in the socialist world.

Transformation without a Strategy

If we look at the history of the countries mentioned, we find that without exception, reform blueprints or programs were in circulation before the actual period of the reform. In many cases, these blueprints were prepared by scholars. As a matter of fact, for the first example of such an academic proposal for transformation within socialism one can go back as far as Oscar Lange's famous proposal for market socialism and to the debate to which his idea gave rise in the 1930s. Some blueprints were also prepared by the leadership in charge, that is to say by party and government officials in Yugoslavia, in Hungary, in China, in the Soviet Union and in other countries. Finally, there have also been instances of programs published illegally or semi-legally by dissident politicians, such as those by the authors close to the unofficial trade union Solidarity in Poland, as well as by opposition intellectuals in Hungary and in the Soviet Union.

While all these reform proposals are interesting historical documents, and while some of them have exercised a certain influence on the course of events, the reality of the reforming countries never did correspond to any of the blueprints. In fact, even the officially publicized intentions of the party and of the government were usually not consistently realized, and the deviations from the original program were sometimes so large that they bore no resemblance to the initial guidelines. Of course, history stands witness to other cases of discrepancies between intent and outcome: the fate of the French Revolution reflected little of the ideas which the *Encyclopédists* along with Rousseau had been discussing in their works, and the Soviet Union in the 1930s turned out to be a country quite different from the one which Marx or the participants of the revolutions of 1917 had imagined.

It is ironic to note, nevertheless, that major transformations in centrally planned economies go on without being based on a central plan. There is a Chinese adage which talks of "crossing the river by touching the stone." The reform process in socialist economies conforms exactly to this image: whole societies have proceeded to cross the deep water without accurate knowledge about the final direction by a process of moving from one stone to another. The reality of reform in socialist countries is characterized by historical compromises, by movements backwards as well as by movements forwards, by periods of euphoria and of optimism alternating with periods of lost illusions and of frustrations. It also often turns out that, in spite of the best efforts, some changes cannot be preserved. At times, people learn the limits of reformability by, figuratively speaking, running against a stone wall. In any case, the limits of transformability of a society can be accurately gauged only once one begins to transform it.

Under such circumstances it becomes extremely important to observe what evolves *spontaneously* in the transformation process. Marx used the German term "naturwüchsig" (as grown in nature) to characterize spontaneous historical processes. These are phenomena which appear not as a consequence of governmental orders or of administrative pressure but follow the free will of certain social groups.

The study of "naturally grown" changes is all the more important since individual freedom of choice increases as a consequence of reform. True, under the reform socialist system certain restrictions imposed by unchangeable taboos remain. Nevertheless, spontaneous changes reflect to some extent the voluntary decisions and revealed preferences of various social groups.

Exactly this approach distinguishes the present study from many other studies. Most of the work on reform in socialist systems deals with the normative issues, and even in the realm of positive analysis, the intentions and actions of the leadership and the apparatus are discussed. This paper would like to draw the attention to another, not less important, point of view: what is going on spontaneously, not at the orders of the leading groups or even in spite of their orders.

The Evolution of a Private Sector

In this endeavor, our first focus should be on the evolution of a private sector. Let us remind ourselves briefly of the period in which the first reform proposals were elaborated. When, for example, I began to participate in the Eastern European thinking on reform in the years 1954, 1955, and 1956, all of the scholars who took part in the debate were almost exclusively concerned with the questions of reform as it applied to the state-owned sector.[5] Discussions turned around the issues of how to give more autonomy and stronger profit-based incentives to the state-owned firms, of how to decentralize economic administration while, at the same time, maintaining state ownership in all but the most marginal sectors of the economy. These were the views of the radical reformers of those days.

Taking a thirty-year leap in history, it turns out that, quite in accordance with the previous section of this study, history has taken quite a different course from the one outlined in the original blueprints written by academic economists. In all the socialist economies in which reforms have had time to develop, and especially in Hungary, in China, and in Poland, the emergence of a significant private sector is the most important result of the reform in the economy.

The most relevant inroad of private activity in socialist economies occurs through private farming. There exists a variety of forms. Either the land has been reprivatized *de facto* (as, for example, under the Chinese "family responsibility system"), or private farming has never been abolished and survives all kinds of political changes, as for example in Yugoslavia or in Poland. In Hungary, the role of the household plot and of private farming has also increased in the wake of the reform. In addition, typically there also exists some kind of family subcontracting within the agricultural cooperative.

In addition to these private and semiprivate agricultural businesses, we find legal, tax-paying private businesses in various other sectors. A significant private sector has emerged in various branches of the service, transport, and construction industry; to a lesser extent private business operates in manufacturing as well.[6] There appear different forms of income derived from private property, for example, from the renting out of private homes in cities or from privately owned second homes in recreational areas.

In addition to the formal private sector, various types of informal "moonlighting" often appear; unlicensed, and perhaps illegal, but nonetheless tolerated activities proliferate in the service, commerce,

---

5. For the earliest papers advocating a decentralization-based reform in Eastern Europe, see footnote 7 in the first study of this volume.

6. Private business partnerships, owned and operated by a group of people, belong to the private sector, along with businesses owned and operated by single individuals or by a family. In the Soviet Union such partnerships are called "cooperative," although everybody knows that they are in fact private business partnerships.

transport, and construction sectors.[7] Reform economies also experience a significant increase in elaborate do-it-yourself activities, such as the building of one's own house with the help of one or two professionals and some friends.

In some countries, and in some sectors, such as housing and agriculture, it happens that property owned by the state or by some other social organization is sold or leased to individuals.[8] In practice, however, the larger part of the growth of the private sector takes place as a result of entrepreneurial initiative sometimes based on private savings but sometimes almost exclusively on the labor input of the individual.

It must be stressed that the government does not have to convince its citizens to enter the private sector by a propaganda campaign. Usually, after certain prohibitions on private activity are lifted, the private sector begins to grow quite spontaneously with individual enterprises sprouting up like mushrooms in a forest after rainfall. The explosion of private activity is all the more notable as it often follows a period of brutal repression of any form of private ventures. As soon as the repression against private activity is terminated in the reform socialist countries, the private sector immediately begins to expand in a genuinely spontaneous manner. People do not have to be cajoled or coerced in order to choose this way of life.[9] In fact, they are immediately attracted by the higher earnings, by the more direct linkage between effort and reward, and by the greater autonomy which the private sector offers. The third reason—namely the prospect of greater autonomy and freedom in private activity—had particularly strong attraction.

Private activities generate relatively high income because they are able to meet demand left unsatisfied by the state-owned sector. A craftsman, or the owner of a corner grocery store or indeed of a small restaurant is typically in the middle income group in a capitalist, private enterprise economy. But here, in the environment of a chronic

7. About the formal and informal private sector see G. Grossman (1977), I. R. Gábor (1985), C. M. Davis (1988), S. Pomorski (1988), and B. Dallago (1989).

8. In Hungary and Poland it is becoming widespread to sell state-owned property to private individuals and foreign investors. This amounts to a tangible sign that these two countries have stepped over the boundaries of reform socialism and a real system change has started.

9. Perhaps the Soviet Union, and especially the Soviet agricultural sector, is an exception. Here the memory of the terror which accompanied mass collectivization and the "liquidation of kulaks" is so deeply imprinted on the collective conscience that it has been passed on from generation to generation and many individuals are still diffident about starting individual farming or any other kind of private business.

shortage economy the same activities catapult these people into the highest income group, not because they are particularly smart or greedy, but because of the rarity of the service that they provide. The price which they get for their output is just the *market clearing price* in the small segment of the economy, where a genuine market operates. They can be grateful to the state-owned sector and to the fiscal and monetary systems which create supply and demand conditions leading to free market prices significantly higher than the official prices in the state-owned sector.

The dimensions of this growth of private economic activity are even more remarkable if one takes into account the fact that the private sector must adjust to the hostile environment of the half-heartedly reforming socialist economy. Despite some improvements, the daily life of private businesses is still characterized by a multitude of bureaucratic interventions and restrictions. The private sector has limited access to material supply, and almost no access to credits and to foreign exchange. Material, credit, and foreign exchange is often acquired in illegal or semi-legal ways.

A further sign of hostility is the jealousy of people who are suspicious of growing income differentials. This envy of individuals who suddenly come to earn more than others, while it occurs in all systems, is likely to be all the more divisive in a society in which people have been brought up to consider equality to be a major social desideratum. Finally, further difficulties are caused by the absence of legal institutions for the consistent protection of private property and for the enforcement of private contracts, as well as the lack of political movements and associations devoted to the articulation of the private sector's interests. And that leads to the ideological aspects of the issue.

Can one justifiably assume that this small-scale private activity inevitably leads to capitalism? If we were in the Soviet Union at a meeting called upon to decide on the pragmatic question of how many licenses to give to private taxi cab owners, one could not at all object to the argument that private taxi cabs are not genuine capitalist ventures, and that Soviet socialism will not be endangered if a few more such cabs are allowed on the road. Nevertheless, if we want to be objective, it is not possible to dismiss the above question so easily.

Using now the terminology of Marxian political economy, we may classify the overwhelming part of private sector activities in socialist economies as small commodity production. Roughly speaking, the decisive distinction between small commodity production and genuine capitalism in the Marxian sense is that the former uses only the labor input of one individual, together perhaps with that of his family members, whereas the latter uses hired labor regularly and thus becomes exploitative as it seeks to extract the surplus from the employee. In this context, the ideology and practice of socialist countries has been very much influenced by Lenin's frequently quoted dictum that "small production engenders capitalism and the bourgeoisie continuously, daily, hourly, spontaneously, and on a mass scale" (Lenin [1920] (1966), p. 8). In my opinion, Lenin was absolutely right. If a society allows for the existence of a large number of small commodity producers, and if it permits them to accumulate capital and to grow over time, a genuine group of capitalists will sooner or later emerge. To appreciate this fact, the reader is asked to imagine for a moment what would happen if private producers had the same access to credit and to all kinds of inputs as the state-owned enterprise in a socialist economy and, moreover, were to be treated equally by the tax and subsidy system. Without any doubt, the more successful private businesses would begin to accumulate and grow. Thus, the negative answer to the question as to whether small commodity production breeds capitalism in pragmatic discussions of particular cases is already predicated on the assumption that the government will not allow private business to grow beyond a certain critical threshold. In other words, the growth of the private sector in a socialist economy is not only hampered by the excessive red tape of an ubiquitous and omnipotent bureaucracy; the sustained growth of private businesses also runs counter to the ideological premises of the socialist system, and will therefore be held in check by the ruling party and by the government who are not willing to tolerate a significant capitalist sector.

Under reform socialism there are different ways of imposing constraints on the private sector's ability to grow. Sometimes, these constraints simply take the form of legal restrictions (such as, for example, the form of an upper bound on the number of people which may be employed in a legal private enterprise, or of a limit on the amount of capital which may be invested in private businesses). Obstacles to growth may also be incorporated in the tax system. The extent of taxation of a particular activity at a given point in time can vary quite substantially, thus providing the authorities with an additional tool for keeping the private sector under control. For instance, private craftsmen and traders can point out the exact level of taxation up to which they would be able to uphold the venture, and beyond which they would have to abandon it and return to work in the state-owned sector. Of course, these critical reservation thresholds may vary from sector to sector, from period to period, and from business to business. But it is important to note that they exist and that they impose institutional limits on the survival of a private firm. The most powerful upper limit on accumulation is uncertainty and the fear of future nationalization and confiscation. Memories of past repression are alive, and the individual might be scared that he and his children might one day be stigmatized as "bourgeois" or "kulak."

As a consequence of this situation, economies of scale cannot be enjoyed due to the limits on capital accumulation. It might be individually more reasonable in the given political and ideological climate to waste one's profits rather than to put them to productive use. In historical accounts of capitalist economies, we are used to reading about the parsimony of the founders of family businesses who endeavor to bequeath their wealth to future generations. In accordance with the picture painted in Thomas Mann's novel *Buddenbrooks*, we begin to associate wastefulness only with the second and subsequent generations of a family line of capitalists. By contrast, waste in family businesses in reform socialist countries often begins on the very first day of their existence, given that it is quite uncertain whether the venture will have a prolonged existence even within the individual founder's own lifetime.

The social environment of the private sector also results in myopic behavior. The private firm is typically not interested in building up a solid goodwill with its customers for its products or services, because its owners feel that they might not even be in business the following year. Thus, in the extreme, given the overall environment of the sellers' market, private firms may be quite dishonest with their customers so as to reap the largest possible amount of one-time profit. To the extent that consumers are used to the queues and to the shortages in the state-owned sector, it is generally easy for the private firm to keep its customers, even though its employees might hardly be more forthcoming and polite than the employees of its counterpart in the state-owned sector, if there is one. Instead of raising the overall standards of service of the sellers under state ownership in the direction of those of a buyers' market, the standards of a new small private venture drop downward to those of sellers in a chronic shortage economy.

Private ventures have to adapt to the use of bribery, too, in the acquisition of the necessary inputs. Cheating is needed not only to acquire inputs, but also to defend the business against the state. Many individuals joining the private sector are not entrepreneurs, but adventurers. Such is the natural process of selection under the given conditions.

These circumstances set the trap for the social position of the private sector. Daily experience supplies arguments for "anti-capitalist" demagoguery and for popular slogans against profiteering, greediness, and cheating.[10] Such propaganda fuels further restrictions and interventions which lead to further deterioration: to capitalism at its worst.

We therefore face a vicious cycle. The reform socialist system needs the active contribution of a private sector, otherwise it is not able to deliver the goods to the people. Socialism has apparently arrived at a stage in history when it is unable to survive in its pure, strictly non-capitalist fashion and must co-exist with its self-acknowledged arch-enemy not only world wide but within its own borders as well.

The Persistence of Bureaucracy

The central idea of the original reform blueprints had been the abolition of the command economy—that is, the elimination of mandatory output targets and mandatory input quotas. Yugoslavia and Hungary were the only countries which had more or less consistently implemented these proposals in the framework of reform socialism. In the two largest reform socialist countries, China and the Soviet Union, they were realized only partially.

The initial expectation of the reformers had been that, once the administrative system had been abolished, there would be a momentary vacuum which would then be filled by the market mechanism. In other words, bureaucratic commands would be instantaneously replaced by market signals. The underlying assumption of this position was that of a simple complementarity between the two mecha-

10. It is ironic that some politicians and journalists in the reform socialist countries (sometimes even in the "new left" circles within oppositional groups) argue against high prices and "profiteering" on *moral* grounds. It is not recognized that it is inconsistent to declare the desirability of a market and at the same time to refuse the legitimacy of a price generated by the very same market mechanism.

nisms of coordination, namely bureaucratic and market coordination.[11] However, this expectation, which I shared in 1955–56, has turned out to be naive. What actually happened was that the vacuum left by the elimination of administrative commands, and thus by the elimination of *direct* bureaucratic coordination, was filled not by the market, but by other, *indirect* tools of bureaucratic coordination.[12]

The role of the market, which had not been completely eliminated even under the classical socialist planning system, has of course increased in the wake of the reform. However, the role of the bureaucracy continues to remain pervasive, and is asserted in many different ways.[13] To summarize, the role of the bureaucracy remains paramount in the selection and in the promotion of managers, and in the decision-making power with regard to the entry and the exit of firms. And while the bureaucracy has reduced or completely relinquished direct administrative control over the quantities of output and input of state-owned firms, it can still control them through formal state orders and informal requests, and also through administrative price setting and through the extremely strong financial dependence of the firm on its superior organs. Thus the state-owned firm has remained strongly dependent on the various branches of the bureaucracy, on the min-

11. The term "bureaucratic coordination," here, as in my other works, is used in a value-free sense, without the negative connotation implied in many Eastern European writings and speeches. It refers to certain types of controlling and coordinating activities. The main characteristics of this mechanism include the multi-level hierarchical organization of control, the dependence of the subordinate on the superior, and the mandatory or even coercive character of the instructions of the superior.

12. [The later concept first appeared in the works of Kálmán Szabó, Tamás Nagy, and László Antal.

The process of examining the experience gained in the postsocialist economy drew my attention to another phenomenon. After the abolition or collapse of the bureaucratic coordination mechanism (whether this consists of direct or indirect control), a kind of vacuum may occur. Under certain circumstances, an anarchic situation, a confused "no-man's land," may develop in the border area between bureaucratic and market control. (See the seventh study in this volume, p. 179.) *New footnote.*]

13. In the spirit of footnote tenth, a word of explanation is needed concerning the term "bureaucracy." This notion is also used in a value-free way, without implying any negative judgment whatsoever. It denotes the hierarchical apparatus in control of all social and economic affairs and includes not only government officials and managers, but the functionaries of the party and of the mass organizations as well.

In other words, "bureaucracy" refers to a certain *social group* different from other groups in society, and "bureaucratic coordination" refers to a certain *coordination mechanism*, different from other mechanisms, such as, for example, market coordination. Conceptual distinctions notwithstanding there is, of course, close linkage between these two phenomena: the bureaucracy applies bureaucratic coordination methods to govern those who are subject to its power.

istries in charge of production, on foreign trade authorities, on the price control office, on financial bodies, on the police, and so on. The party organizations also intervene frequently in the affairs of the firms. A change has taken place in the form, but not in the intensity of dependence.

In our description of the private sector, we have used the terms "spontaneous" or "naturally grown." Here, we shall emphasize that the persistence of the bureaucracy is a spontaneous and natural outgrowth of the system as well.[14] The Central Committee or the Politburo of the Communist party does not have to decide to maintain as much of the bureaucracy as possible during the process of reform. On the contrary, the bureaucracy may grow *despite* attempts to reduce it, and in the face of dramatic campaigns to get rid of it, such as the one which took place during the cultural revolution in China. The Soviet *perestroika* again set out as its goal the reduction of the size of the bureaucracy; yet, the experience does not allow us to place a lot of confidence in the possibility of checking the natural growth of the bureaucracy, even if drastic methods are employed. A self-reproduction of bureaucracy can be observed in the sense that, if it is eliminated at some place, in one particular form, it will reappear at another place in some other form.

This permanent restoration of bureaucratic control is explained by many factors. One is, of course, all the material advantage associated with bureaucratic positions, namely financial benefits, privileges and access to goods and services in short supply. Even more important is the attraction of power. And here we arrive at a highly political issue again. The relative shares of the role played by bureaucratic and market coordination are not simply a matter of finding the most efficient division of labor between two neutral forms of control. The bureaucracy rules the socialist economy. Allowing the genuine functioning of the market means the voluntary surrender of an important part of bureaucracy's power.

The most important consequences of this situation are the limits imposed on the reformability of the state-owned sector by the system-specific tendency of self-reproduction of the bureaucracy. We might be able to appreciate this point more clearly by considering the question

14. As before, the term "natural" is not used here in the sense of American advertising, where it is a synonym of words such as good, wholesome, and nonartificial. Rather we use it to denote a phenomenon which reproduces without government support, and sometimes even in spite of policies designed to oppose it, simply as a consequence of the social situation.

of the constituency for reform. In the case of greater state tolerance for private economic activity, this constituency is large and well-defined. It consists of all citizens of a socialist country who choose to, or at least would like to able to have the option to work in the private sector, as entrepreneurs or as employees.

On the other hand, nobody is an unqualified winner in the far-reaching decentralization of the state-owned sector. Every person involved with the state-owned sector gains as well as loses as a result of genuine decentralization. Each member of the bureaucratic apparatus may gain more autonomy *vis-à-vis* his superiors, but at the same time may lose power over his subordinates. A reduction in paternalism and a concomitant hardening of the budget constraint[15] entails advantages as well as disadvantages for the managers as well as for the workers of a state-owned firm. They gain in autonomy, but at the same time lose in protection. While it is typically true that people are not in favor of, or are at best indifferent with regard to, the protection of others, they usually like to be protected themselves. In a capitalist economy this ambivalent feeling towards protection is best reflected in the complex attitude towards free trade being evaluated favorably when it allows a company to market its own products in foreign markets with only minimal tariffs, but being less eagerly welcomed when it results in foreign competitors entering the company's domestic markets. In a socialist economy not only the managers but every individual working in the state-owned sector have these schizophrenic feelings with respect to the soft budget constraint, to paternalism, and to protection. While high taxes are disliked, subsidies, even if the firm is not now receiving them, may come in handy in the future, and can therefore not be opposed quite firmly. Shortages, while they inconvenience the firm as a buyer, suit it as a seller.

Thus it turns out that neither the high-level bureaucrats, nor the managers, nor indeed the workers are enthusiastic adherents of competition or of the marketization of the state-owned sector. Some enlightened government officials and intellectuals may come to the conclusion that a hardening of the budget constraint and a decrease in paternalism is needed so as to improve the performance of the economy. However, as far as the public is concerned, there are no strikes or street demonstrations in favor of increasing economic efficiency or decreasing state protection.

15. See footnote 15 in the first study.

As a result, there does not exist a grassroots movement for the decentralization of the state-owned sector. Since on the one hand there is strong inducement to maintain the bureaucratic positions, and on the other hand there is no unambiguous constituency against their maintenance, the final result is the permanent reproduction of bureaucratic coordination.

Alternative Forms of Social Organization

After this discussion of the private sector and of the state-owned sector and of the role of the bureaucracy and of the market under reform socialism, let us now approach the theme of this study from a somewhat more general point of view. Consider figure 2.1.

When referring to state ownership 1, we have in mind the classical case of bureaucratic centralized state ownership, 2 is private ownership, while *A* and *B* refer respectively to bureaucratic and to market coordination.

Two *strong* linkages exist between the ownership form and the coordination mechanism: classical, pre-reform socialist economies which combine state ownership with bureaucratic control, and classical capitalist economies which combine private ownership with market control. These two simple cases might be looked upon as historical benchmark models. It seems quite natural, when economic units based on private ownership operate in the market both as sellers and as buyers, that they would be motivated by the incentives of financial gain and would be highly responsive to costs and to prices. Similarly, economic units under state control are operated by the bureaucracy, using bureaucratic instruments.

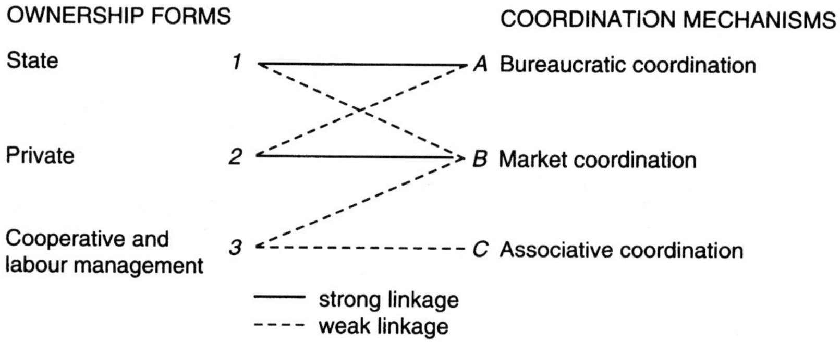

Figure 2.1
Strong and weak linkages

By contrast, we can observe that in the reform socialist economies, the private sector, while mainly controlled by the market, is also subject to bureaucratic control, as symbolized by the dotted line from 2 to *A*. This attempt to impose bureaucratic control on private activities does not and cannot work smoothly due to the basic incongruity of this pair.

In addition, there exist other, generally also inconsistent attempts to coordinate the state-owned sector via market coordination (the dotted line from 1 to *B*). This was the idea at the center of the blueprint of market socialism. However, it turned out not to be possible to decrease the dominant influence of the bureaucracy. The influence of the market on the coordination of state-owned firms is full of frictions, as we have already seen in the earlier sections of this study. In spite of the efforts of reformers to strengthen the linkage of 1 to *B*, there is an inclination to restore the linkage of 1 to *A*: bureaucratic coordination penetrates and pushes out the influence of the market.

To sum up: the relationships between the latter two pairs—namely the relationship between 1 and *B*, and between 2 and *A*—can be characterized as *weak* linkages.

The notions "strong" and "weak" linkages do not imply a value judgement and do not indicate any preference on my part. These are descriptive categories. In accordance with the general philosophy of the study, a linkage between an ownership form and a coordination mechanism is strong if it emerges spontaneously and prevails in spite of resistance and countermeasures. It is based on a natural affinity and a cohesion between certain types of ownership forms and certain types of coordination mechanisms respectively. The adjective "weak" refers to linkages, which are to some extent artificial and not sufficiently strong to resist the impact of the stronger linkage. Weak linkages are pushed aside by the strong ones time and again, whether the intellectual and political leaders of reform socialism like it or not.[16]

What is the case with the other forms of social organization? First, let us turn to the issue of ownership. In row 3, where figure 2.1 refers to cooperatives and labor management, we must emphasize the nonprivate, but also the nonbureaucratic character of social ownership,

16. There are many other combinations of 1, 2, *A*, and *B* worth considering. For example, if in an economy the private sector is strong and stable, and the linkage of 2 to *B* is the dominant one, a certain segment of the economy can be successfully subjected to the linkage of 1 to *B*. In other words, in a basically private market economy the state-owned sector can adjust to the rules of the market.

such as that found in genuine communes or in instances of genuine workers' management.[17] The idea of cooperative socialism has long been part of socialist thinking. As for coordination mechanism of type C, the term associative mechanisms is the collective name of a set of potential mechanisms. It is probably easiest to define the set in a negative way, as any mechanism of coordination which operates neither through the bureaucracy nor through the market, but which is based on self-governance, on free associations, on reciprocity, on altruism or on mutual voluntary adjustment. The literature on socialism is rich in proposals which suggest that socialist society be based on cooperative ownership, and on nonmarket, nonbureaucratic associative coordination. In referring to this tradition of thought Marx coined the somewhat derogatory term "Utopian Socialism." Early representatives of this line of thinking have been Proudhon, Fourier (to an extent), Owen, and others.

The literature does not always couple the property form of cooperatives and self-government (3) and associative mechanisms (C). Some authors place the emphasis on 3, others on C, while in some cases, the two are considered together. Ideas of this kind come up frequently in the context of the reform discussions in socialist countries.[18] The whole Yugoslav experience constitutes an attempt, albeit a highly imperfect one, to move socialism away from the exclusive reliance on state or private ownership and on the bureaucracy or on the market, i.e., in the direction of 3 + C linkage. The Chinese cultural revolution may be looked upon as an attempt to smash the bureaucracy and to proceed to a non-bureaucratic kind of socialism without the introduction of market elements. But neither of these two great historical experiments leads to conclusive results. In both cases the transformation was forced upon society by the political leadership and although at the beginning

17. In accordance with the definitions used in the present paper, private business partnerships in the Soviet Union cannot be regarded genuine cooperatives. They belong to property form 2 and not to form 3.

18. Of course, cooperative ownership can be linked not only to coordination mechanisms of type C, but to the market mechanism as well. For example, Yugoslavia experimented with a coupling of ownership form 3 (self-management) with both coordination mechanisms *B* and with mechanism *C* (market and "associative" coordination). Large segments of the economy were coordinated in the usual way by the market mechanism. At the same time, so-called "social compacts" were arranged to establish direct contacts between the representatives of producers and of consumers; they were expected to voluntarily make mutual adjustments. While the official policy alternated in the emphasis given to mechanisms *B* and *C*, in fact bureaucratic coordination mechanism *A* was prevailing all the time, and was in a latent fashion the dominant force.

the initiative from the top had enthusiastic support among at least a part of the population, it was subsequently institutionalized and forced through, without countenancing any deviation from the central party line. Therefore the fact that something resembling ownership form 3 was the dominant form in Yugoslavia or that the rhetoric of Mao's Cultural Revolution reasserted principles similar to coordination mechanism C does not allow us to reach any conclusions concerning the true strength of these forms.

Let us apply instead the criterion proposed previously and look at whether cooperative ownership and associative coordination grow *spontaneously and naturally* during the reform process of socialist systems. This question is meaningful, because the establishment of genuine voluntary cooperatives, voluntary adjustments and other forms of associative coordination are not prohibited in these countries. Small cooperatives are far better tolerated by the system than private economic activities. And altruism and non-commercialized reciprocity are of course legal in any system.

However, we can observe that, while 3 and C forms exist and did exist even at the peak of bureaucratic centralization, these forms have not experienced a spectacular growth after the command system had been abolished. When beside centralized state-ownership other forms were permitted, only private ownership gained ground rapidly. While the elimination of direct bureaucratic control left a momentary vacuum, this vacuum has been filled mainly by indirect bureaucratic control, as well as with some form of market coordination. Cooperative ownership and associative coordination play only an auxiliary role at most.[19]

Let us sum up our *general conclusions* concerning the strengths or weaknesses of the forms of social organization. While ownership forms 1 and 2 are robust, 3 has few followers. Similarly, while coordination forms *A* and *B* are widely applied, C operates only in a rather restricted area of affairs. And in contrast to the strong linkages between 1 and *A*, and between 2 and *B*, all other potential linkages from 1, 2, and 3 on the ownership side to *A*, *B*, and C on the coordination mechanism side are weak. (Figure 2.1 shows with dotted lines only four of the potentially weak linkages. There are, of course, others.)

---

19. Ownership forms 3 and coordination mechanisms C are associated in many writings with certain political ideas such as administrative decentralization of government activities, the increased role of local governments, participatory democracy and self-governance, corporative ideas of various sorts, and so on. Again the discussion of these aspects is beyond the limits of the present study.

The validity of conjectures concerning the strength or weakness of certain ownership forms, of coordination mechanisms and of linkages between ownership forms and coordination mechanism is an *empirical* matter. As indicated in the introductory paragraphs, the present study does not provide empirical evidence. However, let me mention that the validity of the above general conclusions can be tested. These conjectures can be accepted, modified or rejected by inference from empirical studies reported in the available literature or conducted in the future. In any case, the issue of the validity of empirically testable conjectures must be strictly separated from the normative issue: political and moral preferences over the set of alternative forms of ownership and coordination mechanisms.

It must be admitted that the observations concerning the weakness of some forms and linkages, drawn from a small sample observed over a brief period. Perhaps twenty or thirty years from now, researchers might be able to observe that this tendency was stopped and that history took an alternative route. History is always unpredictable. But as long as no contrary evidence is provided by experience, it is worth while to keep in mind the observations concerning the strength or weakness of the alternative ownership forms and coordination mechanisms.

It is fully understandable that various social groups and intellectual currents advocate a wider role for property forms 3, coordination mechanisms C, and their various linkages. These efforts may have beneficial effects, provided that those who make such suggestions do not nourish false hopes and do not strive for the dominance of nonstate and nonprivate ownership, and of the nonbureaucratic and nonmarketized coordination. It would be intellectually dishonest to hide the weakness of these forms, and the observation that they can play at most auxiliary roles alongside the strong forms.

About Normative Implications

No search for a third form of ownership and/or for a third form of coordination mechanism allows one to evade the real tough choices. Hence, we really need to decide what the relative importance of the two robust forms of ownership—state versus private—will be. Closely allied to this will be the choice concerning the relative shares of the two robust coordination mechanisms: that is, bureaucratic versus market coordination.

Here a *caveat* is needed. In the discussion of reform ideas it has not infrequently been observed that critical propositions generated by the positive (descriptive) analysis of an existing socialist system acquired a *normative twist*. The logical structure of this normative twist is as follows: "If you say that the phenomenon *A* has harmful effects, then it implies a value judgement and a prescriptive suggestion as well: the elimination of phenomenon *A* eliminates the harmful effects. Therefore phenomenon *A* should be eliminated." This train of thought is logically false and also dangerous. Even if one can prove that phenomenon *A* has harmful effects, it does *not* follow from this proposition, that (1) the elimination of phenomenon *A* is at all feasible under the given conditions, and (2) that the elimination of phenomenon *A* is a sufficient condition for the elimination of the harmful consequences.

And now we can return to the ideas elaborated upon in the present study. I would like to avoid normative twists to my positive analysis. The positive (descriptive) statements to the effect that both state and private ownership are robust forms, and that each of them has a strong linkage either to bureaucratic or to market coordination does *not* imply a clear economic policy position on these forms. These positive statements do not imply that reform socialist society must give up state ownership and shift to private ownership, or the opposite suggestion—give up private ownership and establish the dominance of state ownership. Nor does the study suggest that we are faced with an "either-or" type of binary choice between mutually exclusive forms: *either* state ownership cum bureaucratic coordination, *or* private ownership cum market coordination. The ideas presented in the study can, however, be construed to entail the following:

1. State and private ownership can coexist within the same society. Yet in the political, social, and ideological environment of reform socialism this is an uneasy symbiosis, loaded with many dysfunctional features.

2. The position on the actual shares of state and private ownership, and the associated position on the combination of bureaucratic and market coordination are both dependent on the *value system* of those taking the position (would it be an individual, a movement, a party, or an association). One's attitude towards state ownership or towards private ownership is not based on strict economic or efficiency considerations. It is strongly influenced by political, ideological, ethical, and emotional attractions or aversions.

The study does not comment on these value judgements, nor on the political and ethical criteria underlying the possible choices.[20] What it tries to do is much more modest: it offers *conditional predictions* based on the theoretical conjectures about the strengths and weaknesses of various possible linkages between ownership forms and coordination mechanisms.

This study merely warns: let us not have illusions and false expectations. Once one arrives at a large share for state ownership, one gets a "package deal," and the package then inevitably contains a large dose of bureaucratic coordination. Another warning is also needed: if one really wants a larger and continuously growing share for market coordination, one must *ipso facto,* accept a larger share for private ownership and for individual activities. But a desired coordination mechanism, (say market) does not come about without a significant backing of the appropriate ownership form (say private ownership). Likewise, one cannot get the desired ownership form (say public) without getting its associated form of coordination (say bureaucratic coordination). Such is the *Realpolitik* of reforms and socioeconomic changes in the socialist system.

Market socialism is an illusion. The usual slogans demanding state ownership cum market entail a misunderstanding or engender a naive, false expectation which will certainly be disproved by the bitter track record of experimentation with half-reforms. We might even say that in various reform socialist countries some economists and policy makers have used this catchphrase as a tool of mass manipulation, or, to apply a less pejorative formulation, as an educational instrument. ("After a long period of telling $2 \times 2 = 8$, it is reasonable to say at first $2 \times 2 = 6$. Declaring immediately that $2 \times 2 = 4$ causes too much of a shock.") But then, must every socialist country tread the painful path of gradual disenchantment? Is it really hopeless to expect that the latecomers to the reform process might learn from the disappointments of those who have gone before them?

3. Those who really want a larger role for the market, must allow more room for formal and informal private activities, for free entry and for exit, for competition, for individual entrepreneurship and for private property. Only a radical extension of the private sector creates favorable conditions for the marketization of the whole economy.

20. I have stated my position on these questions in my 1990 book. I emphasized the necessity for fast private-sector development and for the continuous increase in its share. This study remains in the domain of positive analysis.

Movement in that direction—namely in the direction of the extension of the private sector—is the most important yardstick of economic reform. Without such movement reform slogans are only a lip-service to decentralization and market coordination.

I think that notwithstanding the change of system taking place in Eastern Europe, it is still timely to rethink the questions analyzed above. There are extremely strong illusions about the ideas of market socialism among many highly influential persons, especially economic leaders and academic economists. Many hope that the state-owned firms can be, after all, transformed into genuine market-oriented organizations. I think that Gáspár Miklós Tamás was right in pointing out that this idea is one of the various kinds of Third Road notions.[21] I believe that only those who face the failure of reform socialism and also a deeper explanation of this failure can form unbiased views on the practical economic policy tasks of the system change and on the transition to the new system. One element in this deeper explanation is the rethinking of the questions: what ownership forms and coordination mechanisms are compatible with each other and also have affinity with each other, and which are basically incompatible.

References

Afanas'ev, Iuri N., ed. 1988. *Inogo ne dano* (There Is No Other Way). Moscow: Progress.

Antal, László, Bokros, Lajos, Csillag, István, Lengyel, László, and Matolcsy, György. 1987. "Change and Reform." *Acta Oeconomica* 38 (3–4): 187–213.

Burkett, John P. 1989. "The Yugoslav Economy and Market Socialism." In *Comparative Economic Systems: Models and Cases,* edited by M. Bornstein. Homewood, IL and Boston, Mass.: Irwin, pp. 234–258.

Dallago, Bruno. 1989. "The Underground Economy in the West and East: A Comparative Approach." In *Comparative Economic Systems: Models and Cases,* edited by M. Bornstein. Homewood, IL, and Boston, Mass.: Irwin, pp. 463–484.

Davis, Christopher M. 1988. "The Second Economy in Disequilibrium and Shortage Models of Centrally Planned Economies." Berkeley-Duke Occasional Papers on the Second Economy in the USSR, no. 12, July.

Gábor, István R. 1985. "The Major Domains of the Second Economy." In *Labour Market and Second Economy in Hungary,* edited by P. Galasi and Gy. Sziráczky. Frankfurt and New York: Campus, pp. 133–178.

Grossman, Gregory. 1977. "The 'Second Economy' of the USSR." *Problems of Communism* 26 (5): 25–40.

21. See G. M. Tamás (1989).

Hewett, Ed. A. 1988. *Reforming the Soviet Economy. Equality versus Efficiency*. Washington, DC: The Brookings Institution.

Kornai, János. 1986. "The Hungarian Reform Process: Visions, Hopes and Reality." *Journal of Economic Literature* 24 (4): 1687–1737.

Kornai, János. [1989] 1990. *The Road to a Free Economy. Shifting from a Socialist System: The Example of Hungary*. New York: W. W. Norton.

Kornai, János. 1992. *The Socialist System. The Political Economy of Communism*. Princeton: Princeton University Press, and Oxford: Oxford University Press.

Lenin, Vladimir Ilych. [1920] 1966. *Left-wing Communism, an Infantile Disorder*. Moscow: Progress Publishers.

Perkins, Dwight Heald. 1988. "Reforming China's Economic System." *Journal of Economic Literature* 26 (2): 601–645.

Pomorski, Stanislaw. 1988. "Privatization of the Soviet Economy under Gorbachev I: Notes on the 1986 Law on Individual Enterprise." Berkeley-Duke Occasional Papers on the Soviet Economy in the USSR, no. 13, October.

Schroeder, Gertrude E. 1987. "Anatomy of Gorbachev's Economic Reform." *Soviet Economy* 3 (3): 219–241.

Shmelev, Nikolai. 1987. "Avansy i Dolgi" (Credits and Debts). *Novyi Mir* June, 6: 142–158.

Tamás, Gáspár Miklós. "A Kornai-bomba" (The Kornai bomb). *Heti Világgazdaság* November 11, 11 (45): 66.

3 The Soviet Union's Road to a Free Economy: Comments of an Outside Observer[1]

The transition to a market economy is an incredibly difficult task. The job can only be done and the great problems that arise can only be resolved in each country by those living *in* the society concerned. It is inevitable that the situation can be understood only to a limited extent by an *outsider*. That warns me to be modest; no one can be sure whether his or her advice is applicable or points in the best possible direction. I immediately state this emphatically at the outset, but I shall not add repeated warnings and reservations to my proposals later. To all the recommendations in my study the general comment applies that they must be taken critically; Soviet economists must formulate their own views on the basis of their own far greater local knowledge.

I am not a "Sovietologist." In trying to grasp the Soviet Union's problems and the choices before it, I draw on two kinds of sources.

As a Hungarian I have studied all that has happened in my own country at close quarters. Hungary is small by comparison with the Soviet Union, but it can rightly be considered a laboratory where some very important experiments were conducted. In this respect it has moved far ahead of the Soviet economy in recent decades. The first hesitant, interrupted, and mercilessly suppressed experiments aimed at a radical transformation of society took place in the period 1953–1956. Dismantling of the old-style command economy then recommenced in 1968. Finally came the great political turning point in 1989, with the formation of the institutions of political democracy, followed

---

1. I owe thanks to the Rector of Leningrad University, Professor S. L. Merkuriev, and his colleagues for their kind hospitality. I express my gratitude to Brian McLean and Julianna Parti for their precise and fluent translation.

This lecture was given shortly before Leningrad's name was changed to St. Petersburg. Apart from the city reverting to its old name since then, the Soviet Union has ceased to exist and many other great changes have occurred in the political and economic fields.

by free elections and an open, declared transition towards the kind of market economy in which private ownership will become the dominant property form. I think a through familiarity with Hungary's historical experience is very instructive for all countries seeking to advance in a similar direction.[2]

Another part of my knowledge comes from the fact that I have specialized in comparing economic systems. I deal primarily with the comparison of East and West, capitalism and socialism. This I do not do merely by studying professional literature and statistics. Half of my time in the last decade has been spent in the socialist world (more recently the postsocialist world), and the other half in the capitalist world. One of my workplaces is the Hungarian Academy of Sciences and the other the American Harvard University. This "commuter" lifestyle has enabled me to gain experience of both systems *from within*, by living under them.

In 1989, before the completion of the political change and the free elections, I wrote a book about Hungary called *A Passionate Pamphlet in the Cause of Economic Transition*. This later appeared in English in a somewhat expanded form as *The Road to a Free Economy* (1990*a*).[3] I was delighted that the book also became available to readers in Russian.[4] My belief is that much of the book's message also applies to the Soviet Union's case, when adjusted, of course, to the conditions there. This study is connected with the book. I sum up its content briefly, adding a few ideas inspired by experience gained since it was written.[5] I would

2. Works on the history of the Hungarian economic reforms available in English include L. Antal (1979), T. Bauer (1983), I. T. Berend (1990), P. Hare, H. K. Radice, and N. Swain, eds. (1981), J. Kornai (1983), (1986), [1989] (1990*a*), J. M. Kovács (1990), G. Révész (1990), and L. Szamuely (1982), (1984).

3. [This study can be considered to some extent as a short summary of the *Road to a Free Economy* [1989] (1990*a*). It differs from it in certain respects, however. For instance, it puts my view on the question of shock therapy more plainly. Some of the recommendations are less radical, e.g., on the progressivity of the personal income tax schedule, or speed of introduction of convertibility. *New footnote.*]

4. The book appeared in Russian on three occasions; first in a limited exclusive edition, then in four installments in the very widespread and popular periodical *EKO*, and finally in a large edition from the publishers *Ekonomika* (1990*b*).

5. A great influence on my ideas was exerted by the experiences of the Polish stabilization, and in connection with these the conversations I had with Professor Jeffrey Sachs, to whom I would like to express my thanks here. I learned much from the first radical programs of the Soviet transition, which are generally associated with the names of S. Shatalin and G. Yavlinsky, with several other Soviet and foreign economists also taking part in the elaboration of them. See the so-called Shatalin Plan under Working Group (1990) and the volume edited by G. Allison and G. Yavlinsky (1991). The proposals put

like to emphasize particularly the proposals I consider of prime importance from the point of view of Soviet practice at present.

The study consists of two main parts. The first two sections contain warnings: they discuss which are the blind alleys that should be avoided in my opinion. The remaining sections of the study present my proposals.

Reform Socialism

I draw a distinction between two "prototypes" of the socialist system. To make them more graphic, I attach the names of party leaders to the two types. One is *classical socialism*; the socialism of Stalin and Brezhnev (Soviet Union), Mao Zedong (China), Honecker (East Germany), Husák (Czechoslovakia), and Ceausescu (Romania). The other is *reform socialism*: the socialism of Tito (Yugoslavia), Kádár (Hungary), Deng Xiaoping (China), and Gorbachev (Soviet Union).[6] [. . .]

The reform is an effort to combine socialism and capitalism to some extent. The idea is for the following facets of classical socialism to remain: (1) the ruling role of the Communist party, but somewhat mitigating the repression and allowing a degree of freedom for alternative views; (2) the pervasive role of state control and the subordination of the economy to the bureaucracy; (3) the predominance of state ownership. The following elements of capitalism should concurrently appear: (4) market coordination as the main (or one of the major) integrators of the economy—this embraces far-reaching decentralization, a high degree of autonomy for the firm, and partial liberation of prices; (5) the development of the private sector, although confined within very narrow limits. [. . .]

The reform had useful consequences, but it failed to attain its fundamental objectives; it was incapable of convincing and permanent good economic results. [. . .]

The *microeconomy* did not gain a truly market-economic character. This connects with several unfavorable *macroeconomic* phenomena.

---

forward in this study conform with other stabilization programs to a large extent, but differ from them on a few essential points.

6. [In this section of the Leningrad lecture that formed the basis of the study I dealt with questions that are covered in much greater detail in the first study in this volume. To avoid repetition, this written version presents only in a heavily abbreviated form thoughts that I expressed at much greater length in the lecture. Even so, I have been unable to avoid a measure of duplication between the two studies. *New footnote.*]

There is a runaway in nominal wages. Although the firm is not really autonomous, its partial independence is enough to produce a reckless rise in wages divorced from productivity growth. The banking system distributes loans irresponsibly and does not insist on them being repaid. In fact credit becomes one of the main instruments for salvaging firms on the brink of financial ruin. Fiscal discipline loosens. On one side, there is a growth in subsidies to loss-making production and exports and in price subsidies for various consumer goods and services. Meanwhile there is unjustifiably generous financing of state investments that yield a poor return or an actual loss. Huge sums are consumed in maintaining the armed forces and further rearmament. On the other side, there is laxity in collecting state revenues. The ever greater discrepancy between expenditure and revenue raises the budget deficit, which is covered by taking up foreign loans or printing money, *i.e.*, by inflationary means.

Three dangerous *macro disequilibria* appear: a chronic, worsening shortage, accelerating inflation, and growing indebtedness. These three problems appear in differing proportions in each country and period. The threefold problem used to be called the "Polish syndrome," because that is where it arose in its most extreme form. But Poland has embarked on radical changes since then. These days it is more apposite to call it the "Soviet syndrome," for it is the Soviet Union where the three negative phenomena are developing in parallel and in combination to the most oppressive degree.

Perestroika brought an end to the brutal oppression of classical socialism, but it also loosened its tight discipline and coherence. Meanwhile it proved unable to create a true market discipline in its place, for which laws passed by a legitimate parliament and market competition would have been required. What is needed are real private owners who take costs and profit seriously because they affect their own pockets, and who cannot rely on the state invariably bailing them out of any financial trouble.

The market-socialist experiment that has taken place in the Soviet Union so far has been incomplete and inconsistent, since it was unbacked by radical change, either on the political scene or in property relations. It is a system that falls between two stools: it is not viable socialism (because it cannot operate permanently without firm repression and limitation of civil liberties) and it is not a modern capitalist market economy either. Failure is inevitable.

The Romantic Third Road

Market socialism, as mentioned before, is itself an attempt of a "Third Road" kind; it has been tried out in several countries, including the Soviet Union, and it did not work. However, there is another intellectual trend one might call the Romantic Third Road which has never been tried out anywhere. It appears only in writing, or more frequently in conversation, mainly among writers, politicians, and social scientists. There are also some economists whose ideas can be placed here.

Although the trend is not uniform, I will try to pick out a few common traits in their ideas.

All kinds of socialist systems ruled by the Communist party must be rejected—not just classical socialism, but socialism that experiments with market reforms as well. Capitalism must be dismissed as well, including its modern Western forms, because the profiteering, commercialism, and degenerate morality that flourish under it are repulsive.

So what kind of society must be aimed at? The answers vary according to the roots and outlook of the respondent:

- There must be a return to the pure and natural life of the village.
- A truly communal life must be created. This entails communal ownership. A great many versions of this are put forward in the discussions: the village community, the peasant community, genuinely voluntary cooperative ownership, and so on.
- Although it can be considered a version of the previous item, special mention must be made of the idea that worker communities must be established and ownership of the factories given to them. To this is connected the demand for workers' self-management.
- There should be direct relations between producers and consumers; the profiteers and speculators of commerce must be eliminated.
- There should be discipline, but it should rest on tradition, on the commandments of religion. Some people want an autocratic ruler—a king or a tsar—to impose order in accordance with age-old tradition. Others oppose autocratic rule, rejecting the idea of discipline based on respect and coercion. Their ideas come close to the old and more up-to-date forms of anarchism and anti-étatism, advocating a voluntary discipline complemented by a kind of "direct democracy" that avoids the forms of modern Western parliamentarianism and the multiparty system.

I am afraid that the list just given is too orderly. In reality there is a tangle of ideas that are unclarified and emotionally inspired rather than rationally ordered.

Let me try without prejudice to assess these views. In fact, the only view that I reject on *ethical* grounds is autocratic rule: discipline is not worth it *at that price*. Liberty and human rights are things of such value that they cannot be subordinated to other desires—for instance, the demand for order and discipline.

All the other aspirations are not repugnant in themselves to my mind; I respect people's desire for honesty, community life, and liberation from bureaucracy and profiteering. My prime objection is a pragmatic one: we seem to be presented only with a collection of desires, not with a realistic constructive program. The First System was not imposed on people by the force of the state. There was no Politburo or government to declare in earlier centuries: "Let there be capitalism." The capitalist market economy developed by evolution as the combined outcome of millions of voluntary individual decisions. Although the state has promoted this evolution with its laws and apparatus, the capitalist economy is basically built up "from below"; the entrepreneurs decide about accumulation and the expansion of production.

The position was different with the Second System, which was established by the force of the state. Each of its institutions was brought into being "from above."

Adherents of the Third System need to consider: Why do the forms and patterns of behavior they favor not appear on a mass scale and come to predominate? And if people do not choose this Third Road even in places where there has been freedom of choice so far, why do they expect people to choose precisely this in our region? Or if people do not choose it of their own accord, should it be the system imposed upon them at this time?

Churchill said that democracy was a bad system, but no one had yet found a better one. The same can be said of the capitalist market economy: it is a bad system, but no one has yet discovered anything better. There are many versions of it: the individualistic North American and the more egalitarian Scandinavian models differ from each other, but both form a capitalist market economy. This system too could do with fundamental repairs through reforms, but however much it is repaired, it will be far from perfect. The *real choice* is between the socialist system that has existed hitherto and the Western type of capitalist market economy. The choice must be made without illusions: the socialist system cannot really be repaired, and the capitalist system will have many repulsive attributes even in its repaired form. Yet, basically, these days we must choose the relatively better of the two. Third Road views are an effort to sidestep that choice, but I do not believe they offer a road that can be followed or an alternative that can be realized.

Reform and Revolution

Having explored the two blind alleys, let us turn to the road that leads to a free economy. A short clarification of terms is required first of all, concerning the distinction between reform and revolution. There are many different current definitions, but for my part I use the following in this study and my other works: While reform yields important changes, it retains the fundamentals of the system concerned. Revolution, on the other hand, changes the fundamentals radically, so bringing about a *change of system*.

Thus the distinction between reform and revolution in this vocabulary is *not* whether it takes place slowly and steadily or explosively and rapidly. A reform may be swift and a revolution may be gradual. Moreover, the distinction is *not* that a reform is peaceful and a revolution violent and bloody. The process of reform may also be induced by bloody uprisings, and those impeding it may use violence against the reformers; a revolution, on the other hand, may take place without bloodshed. The difference lies in how superficial or deep the change is. To use a Hegelian expression, revolution brings a qualitative change.

Applying these definitions, it can be stated that *perestroika* was not a revolution but a reform, despite the many assertions to the contrary in the Soviet debates on the matter. What is now required in the Soviet Union is a real revolution, a change in the fundamental characteristics of the system. If that does not occur, the problems will worsen and the crisis will continue and, in fact, deepen.

It is clear from these definitions that what I advocate is the need for a revolution, not an explosive rapidity of change. I am not recommending an uprising or any other violent action. The more smoothly and peaceably it takes place, the better. In terms of my value judgments, the most attractive solution is the kind of "velvet revolution" that took place in Prague. Revolution in my vocabulary means this and only this: radical events that make no concessions and consistently alter the bases of the system are required. It means *only* this, but it is no small thing, of course. The country's citizens need a new system if they want to prosper.

The title of my study contains the expression "free economy," not simply market economy, because the former is more comprehensive and contains more elements. Let me briefly sum up the main criteria for a free economy.

- A political system with free competition of ideas, freedom of speech, freedom of the press, freedom of assembly, and freedom of association. These freedoms contain in themselves the abolition of the one-party system, freedom for alternative parties to organize, and free parliamentary elections.
- An economic system that guarantees the right of free enterprise and freedom of entry into economic life.
- Freedom of property belongs among the liberties that need to be respected. Private property must be protected; legal guarantees must be given that it will not be confiscated. The economy must be led towards property relations in which private ownership is the predominant property form.
- The role of the state must be reduced, with the authorities subject to control by the law, parliament, and publicity.
- The market must be the main (although not the exclusive) coordinator of the economic processes.

The New Political Era: Democratic Consensus

An essential condition for solving the economic problems is a fundamental change of the *political* system. I am an economist, but I have to emphasize that the primary problem is political and not economic.

I make no comment on the present situation or on what will happen in the coming days. I do not feel competent to do so. I shall describe instead a hypothetical political situation, the beginning of a *new political era*. The main factors would be the following:

1. Several parties form and compete with each other. A fair election campaign takes place, followed by a fair multiparty election. A new legitimate parliament gets down to work. A new government is formed and can count on strong parliamentary support.

2. A satisfactory agreement is reached between the federative organizations and the republics, which the latter accept. Viable cooperation develops among the republics. The division of spheres of authority, rights, and obligations is clearly defined. It may be that several republics secede. It can be assumed that most of the present territory of the Soviet Union will continue to form a common economic area in the future.

3. An agreement is reached on the role of the army, which comes under civilian supervision.

4. Reconstruction and the program of transition towards a free economy receive widespread support. A consensus develops, in two senses. On the one hand, there is overwhelming majority support in parliament for the economic program, and on the other, it receives support both from the employees and the employers, the latter including the entrepreneurs of the private sector as well.

From now on I will call the political position summed up in those four points the *democratic consensus*.

The government of the democratic consensus would have political, legal, and moral grounds for addressing the people like this: We want to open a new chapter in the country's history. We cannot promise that life for everyone will improve swiftly or markedly. Great difficulties can be expected, with much suffering for many people. But we are capable of leading the country towards a better system under which growth along a better path will begin in a few years, bringing an improvement in the standard of living.

I regard what I have just outlined as a historic, nonrecurrent opportunity, but not as a *prognosis*, for it is by no means certain that the situation will really develop in this way. What I have put forward is a *desire*: this is how I would like to see the political situation for this long-suffering people develop. Although a great deal of trouble and deprivation would still accompany this desired situation, it would entail relatively less suffering than any other and bring a resolution of the economic crisis relatively sooner.

There is a historic, nonrecurrent opportunity, but this opportunity can be missed. The situation may become far worse: bloody conflicts may break out, the changes may be held up, and the troubles may be aggravated by domestic political strife and the lack of agreement between the interested parties. The painful but vital measures may be deferred by a leadership that shrinks from the sacrifices and tries to prevaricate instead. Measured in historical terms, this will only delay the radical turn, not take the edge off it, but procrastination that continues for several years is undesirable because it will demand sacrifices that might have been avoided.

The rest of the study sums up the economic tasks ahead, to each of which a label is attached.

Some of the proposals are *conditional*. This means that their feasibility is strongly dependent on the political situation; for it to succeed completely, a democratic consensus must develop.

The other proposals are *unconditional*. Even if a democratic consensus fails to develop, there is still a good chance of implementing them and they will still contribute to improving the economic situation.

This categorization also shows that I am not arguing for an "all-or-nothing" strategy. I am not claiming that *either* the optimal political conditions are achieved, in which case everything can be accomplished, *or* the position on the political front is the worse than desired, in which case everything is hopeless. A great many useful changes can be made in either case, but a new political era will be required for a real breakthrough.

My proposals are grouped under three themes: (1) macrostabilization and liberalization, (2) the transformation of property relations, and (3) social welfare policy.

I have not tried to make my proposals "original" in an academic sense: I do not come up with some hitherto secret magic cure for all the ills. Economists have been debating these matters all over the world for a long time. On most of them there is no general agreement, but I would like at least to convey which of the alternative views I subscribe to myself.

Macrostabilization and Liberalization

I am convinced of the need for a large-scale package of measures for stabilizing and liberalizing the Soviet economy.[7] This is absolutely nec-

7. This idea was proposed for the Hungarian economy in my book [1989] (1990*a*). Practical implementation of the stabilization package for the Polish economy is associated primarily with L. Balcerowicz. A great influence on the Polish stabilization package was exerted by the work of J. Sachs; the ideas and early experiences on this are summarized in his articles written jointly with D. Lipton (1990*a*), (1990*b*). Many other economists support this strategy. See, for example, O. Blanchard et al. (1991) and S. Fischer and A. Gelb (1990).

essary: in my view it is impossible to set the Soviet economy to rights without one.

The expression "shock-therapy" is widespread in this context. It is a very unfortunate expression, and to the extent that a name can do damage this one has certainly done so by scaring many people away. The expression was taken from psychiatry, where the shock itself is thought to have a healing effect. In economic stabilization, however, it has nothing of the kind. To stick to the medical analogy, the shock is not the actual therapy, because it is an undesirable, but in some cases inescapable side effect. If the job can be done without administering a "shock" to people, that is all to the good. It is worth aiming to minimize the upheaval and pain.

In fact I employ a medical metaphor in my own writings, advocating surgery for stabilization. This, in my view, is a better way of conveying that this is a quick, radical intervention, to be preceded by presurgical treatment and followed by after-care.

The expression "package" conveys that it consists of a set of measures closely dependent on each other. If single measures were divorced from the package and introduced by themselves, the effect would be doubtful or perhaps even detrimental. It is a condition for success that the measures be introduced at about the same time, or condensed into a short period, and harmonized with each other in detail.

The main components of the package, in my view, should be the following:

1. Elimination of the state budget deficit. This in itself is a complex task, of which only a few elements will be noted out here.

Effective steps must be taken towards eliminating subsidies (both price subsidies and subsidies to loss-making firms). Even if all subsidies cannot be eliminated in a single stage, a large-scale partial dismantling of subsidies must be accomplished straight away in the first stage and a clear timetable worked out for complete elimination of them.

Another vital measure is a drastic cut in military spending.

At the same time, tax revenues must be raised. Sooner or later it will be necessary to devise an up-to-date tax system that includes value-added tax and personal income tax. However, I feel the first step should be to standardize turnover taxes and raise their average rate.

Under no circumstances can the budget deficit be covered anymore by credits from the central bank, since that continuously fuels inflation. If the measures listed prove insufficient, foreign or domestic loans will be necessary.

2. A tight, restrictive monetary policy is required, with tight control on credit. If the banking system continues to distribute credits indiscriminately, the stabilization will be gravely endangered.

3. Care must be taken to ensure wage discipline. It is extremely important for the employees and the unions representing them to behave in a self-restrained and responsible way. This was one of the things I was thinking of when I talked about the need for the democratic consensus. But it must be added that the fate of the stabilization cannot be entrusted exclusively to voluntary self-restraint. Punitive taxes, using an appropriate fiscal formula, must be levied on firms that fail to impose wage discipline, causing nominal wages to run away by comparison with the tend in productivity.

4. All prices must be freed. The chance of certain firms abusing their monopoly position must be prevented by antimonopoly legislation and adequate state supervision.

5. The ruble must be drastically devalued. An exchange rate must be set that corresponds realistically with the market conversion rate between hard currencies and the ruble and can then be sustained over a longer period.

Stabilization of a shaken currency invariably entails changing every price, every exchange rate and interest rate, every wage, and the nominal value of every quantitative index at once. There must be some "fixed point" to hang onto. For this the literature on stabilization uses the expression "nominal anchor"; it is something to which the tossing ship of the economy can be chained. A wide variety of economic quantities may appear as applicants in various kinds of stabilization—for instance, the money supply, the average wage level, or a fixed foreign exchange rate. I share the view of other economists that the best candidate for nominal anchor during the process of stabilization in Eastern Europe and the Soviet Union today is a predetermined foreign exchange rate. This will concurrently lighten task no. 4, the liberalization of prices. At least for products and services that are items of foreign trade on the world market, the starting point for the calculation must be the world-market price multiplied by the stable foreign exchange rate. The domestic price may differ from this due to the relations between supply and demand, but it is a calculation from which a start can be made, so that the new price system need not be conjured out of thin air.

6. When and how the domestic currency should be made convertible is a matter of debate. My proposal, in agreement with many other economists, is that the first stabilization package should already con-

tain substantial steps towards convertibility, even if all the complex criteria for it cannot be satisfied immediately in every respect. I would draw special attention to two interrelated measures. One is to legalize private foreign exchange dealings. It is needless and dangerous to force them underground. The public should be able to place foreign exchange in their possession as deposits in foreign exchange accounts without restriction or enquiries into the source of the money. The other measure required is an undertaking from the state banking system to convert foreign exchange without limitation at the stable foreign exchange rate. This is just what turns this rate into an "anchor." Everyone understands—state-owned firms, the private sector, individuals, and foreign business people—that the money has a stable value, because they can always obtain hard currency for domestic money at the fixed exchange rate.

There are numerous conditions to satisfy, of course, before convertibility can be applied in reality, not just declared. Some of them will be mentioned later, but there is another condition that ties in with task no. 5 above: the correct foreign exchange rate. It is hard to gauge the figure. If a "miss" cannot be helped, it is better to undervalue the domestic currency than overvalue it. Let imports be a trifle too costly and exports disproportionately profitable; though this places a greater burden on the public, it enhances the stabilizing effect.

7. A final very important task is to liberalize foreign trade, including imports. Foreign goods flowing into the country improve the supply, while the competition encourages domestic producers to perform better. What is more, foreign prices are imported along with the foreign goods; as mentioned earlier, this is highly important in a situation where a previously absurd and irrational system of prices has to be replaced swiftly with a realistic system of market prices.

There is a whole range of requirements for the success of the stabilization surgery.

Above all there must be painstaking preparation. The partial measures must accord with each other; careful calculations must be used to work out the harmony between a few of the most important macroindices.

Prime importance attaches to creating the requisite political conditions, the state referred to earlier in the study as democratic consensus. Among the factors behind inflation are inflationary expectations; in other words, the participants in the economy expect the inflation to continue. This expectation is a self-fulfilling prophecy. It must be dispelled and replaced with a new expectation, so that the public, the firms, and the economic leaders believe the situation will change and inflation will be curbed. For such a belief to take hold, the words of politicians and the promises of the government must gain credibility, which is not something created by command; it must be based on political legitimacy and trust. Without such trust, credibility, and consensus, the stabilization program will crumble away under the effect of obstruction and a crisis of confidence.

Also required from the outset is at least a minimal private sector. There must be in operation a formal and informal private sector able, in the weeks of the change over, to plug the gaps left by the state sector in the supply to the general public, and deliver the main staple articles from the producer to the consumer. This will be returned to later.

Reserves are required. On the one hand, there must be reserves of goods, above all stocks of foodstuffs that appear in the stores in the first hours of the stabilization operation and engender confidence in a better future. On the other hand, there must be foreign exchange reserves to ensure that convertibility can be maintained. These also allow quick auxiliary imports to be made if there are problems with supply.

The stabilization operation must rest fundamentally on the country's own resources, but it is desirable to have substantial Western aid to lighten the burden. The most favorable forms for this assistance are contributions to a stabilizing foreign exchange reserve and to goods stocks in the form of import credits.

Even if all these conditions are satisfied and the government decides to perform the stabilization surgery, there will still be an enormous upheaval. On the one hand, considerable results can be achieved. It can be expected (after an initial surge of price rises) that the currently rising rate of inflation will be curbed, and also that one of the gravest chronic ailments of the socialist system—shortage—will be overcome in wide areas of the economy. On the other hand, alongside with the partial successes, great difficulties must be expected: with a fall in production in numerous sectors and the appearance of unemployment that continues to grow for some time. Even when accomplished, the stabilization achievements will be very hard to defend.

Unfortunately, there are other possible scenarios that cannot be ignored: many of the conditions listed may be lacking. I fear it is impossible here to give any simple prescription. If certain elements in the "package" summed up under the seven heads above are introduced individually (or slowly), they may well do more harm than good. Economic politicians cannot be given a blank check inviting them to set about any of the seven tasks they fancy, at any pace or in any order, just so as to get things under way. That would be a dangerous game that could discredit the stabilization plans altogether.[8]

But I do not say either that it is a case of "all or nothing." To take just two examples, any progress in reducing the budget deficit or curbing the supply of credit can be beneficial. All an adviser can do is to weigh the advantages and drawbacks of single partial measures on a case-by-case basis. The Soviet Union today is at any rate in a situation where no partial measure can substitute for a large and drastic package of measures.

Transformation of Property Relations

The main direction of the changes is clear: it is toward building an economy in which the majority of social production derives from enterprises in private ownership. Let me say a few words first of all about the ultimate position.

It can be expected that the private sector will not be an absolute ruler, any more than it is in developed Western countries. A smaller share of the firms will remain in public (state or municipal) ownership. It is still too early to decide exactly where the line will be drawn. That will emerge from the competition between the various property forms, with attention being paid to international experience. Here again, the will of the public must be exerted through parliament; what is to remain in state ownership and what is to be privatized must be decided by legislation.

8. [Very radical changes are generally known to have been made in Russia early in 1992, and one or two of these resemble the package of proposals mentioned in the study. Also generally known is the presence of many unfavorable, worrying tendencies in the Russian economy. My view nonetheless is that the grave situation of the Russian economy in 1992–94 does *not* prove that recommendations made in this study in 1990 were faulty at the time. I stated in the study the political and economic conditions for the success of the surgery for stabilization, underlining especially the need for the political institutions and power relations to be in a state that I term one of democratic consensus, and for the private sector to attain a critical minimum weight in the economy. Unfortunately, the stabilization measures of 1992 took place at a time when these requisite conditions were lacking. The recommendations I put forward were *conditional.* Since the conditions were not fulfilled, historical experience does not allow a conclusive assessment of my recommendations to be made.

What took place was an eventuality the study warned against: only some of the radical measures were introduced and even these lacked the requisite conditions. Since the process was distorted and only half-accomplished, the stabilization program became widely discredited. *New footnote.*]

As in advanced capitalist countries, the private sector will not present a uniform picture. Small, medium-sized, large, and even gigantic firms will operate side by side. There will certainly be an increase in the relative weight of small and medium-sized firms, because production in the Soviet economy, as in the other socialist countries, has been excessively concentrated.

Private firms of various types in terms of their legal form will exist side by side: joint-stock companies in which all or most of the shares are in private hands and listed on the stock exchange, limited-liability companies (companies not listed on the stock exchange), personal enterprises, and so on. It is worth remembering that—with the United States and Britain as exceptions—the joint-stock companies listed on the stock exchange in most developed countries account for only the smaller proportion of aggregate production, in spite of their large role.

The transition cannot achieve this terminal situation in a short period of time. On this matter I take issue with many of my Western and Eastern European colleagues, who urge "rapid privatization." Let there be no misunderstanding—I too want the process to take place as soon as possible. But a desire is one thing and a realistic chance of attaining it another. The government may decide about convertibility or the modification of the foreign exchange rate and having made up its mind accomplish it in a short space of time. But the government cannot decide to "introduce capitalism"; it cannot appoint entrepreneurs by decree. The word itself sheds light on the matter: private enterprise assumes that people undertake risky investment voluntarily in the hope of making a profit. Once they have done so, some of them will go bankrupt, while others accumulate wealth and expand their undertakings. In other words, this is an *evolutionary* process that wise government measures can speed up and stupid measures or indifference can slow down. Whatever the case, it will take several years to run its course.

To use the qualification mentioned earlier, development of the private sector is an unconditional task, unlike macrostabilization, which is a conditional task (at least in its most advantageous "packaged" form). Turning immediately to the partial tasks, most of them can be embarked on at any time, even if some of the conditions for a democratic consensus are lacking. And it would be a good idea if some of the energies currently expended on political battles were transferred to these tasks instead. That is not to deny, of course, that radical political change and the creation of a democratic consensus would greatly boost the development of the private sector as well.

Let us list the component tasks:

1. The "legal infrastructure" for the operation of the private economy must be created. Here are a few examples of the legislation indispensably required: a law on contract, a company law, a law on foreign investment, a bankruptcy law, a banking law, and a labor law. Even if these subjects have been covered by earlier laws and decrees, the legislation must be redrafted in line with the requirements of a modern market economy.

2. It is desirable for the changes in the law to be accompanied by a reeducation of public opinion. Appreciation and respect for private property and business undertakings must be developed and prejudices overcome. Here a great deal depends on the politicians and on the press and television.

3. Private business activity was largely banned earlier on, and even since the beginning of the reforms private enterprise has only been permitted under exceptional circumstances within narrow limits. A significant part of the private sector has been forced underground and been operating as a "shadow economy." It is time to change the proportions between what is permitted, what is restricted, and what is banned. The point of departure should be freedom to pursue all private activity; "free enterprise" should become a fundamental right. This right can then be restricted, but only where important public interests dictate. The restrictions should be laid down in carefully drafted legislation, not subject to the whims and ill-will of bureaucrats.

4. It follows from the previous points that harassment of private entrepreneurs by the police, the authorities, and the political organizations must cease. The private sector cannot be expected to accumulate unless it feels that its property is totally secure.

5. The foundation of private enterprises must be encouraged. Apart from moral and political inducements, they need credit on favorable terms; the state should lighten the credit system's task by offering guarantees for these "start-up" loans; it should also give tax concessions for private investments.

6. Great importance attaches to what is known in several Eastern European countries as "small-scale privatization." This covers the sale

of stores, restaurants, small hotels, small factories, vehicles, housing, and agricultural small holdings to private owners, either individuals or partnerships. I have only mentioned transactions that could be entered into by a buyer with a relatively small stock of capital. Special long-term credit and repayment schemes must be devised and generous finance must be made available for small-scale privatization.

In many cases it is justified to break up a large state-owned firm into smaller parts, thus making it amenable to small-scale privatization. It is not right to do this, of course, where advantages of mass production, the economies of scale provided by a large factory, would be lost. But as mentioned before, the socialist economy is excessively concentrated; the size of many gigantic firms is economically unjustified. Breaking them up into smaller units will have a beneficial effect.

Tasks 5 and 6 are closely connected. A new private firm may in fact start life by buying an asset owned by the state, or a private firm that has come into being by some other means may purchase state property at a later stage in its development as a way of expanding its factory.

7. The property rights in large state-owned firms that (a) it is not advisable to retain in state ownership, (b) it is not desirable to break up into smaller units, and (c) are economically viable must be transferred into private hands. There is a lot of debate about the most effective way of doing so.

The main instrument in my view should be to transform these firms into joint-stock companies and *sell* their shares. The buyer may be either domestic or foreign. It can prove useful for managers and employees to take part in the privatization program; it is worth encouraging them to take up a percentage of the shares by offering suitable credit schemes, for instance. Once the market economy has normalized, a significant proportion of the general public will be willing to hold some of the savings in the form of shares. Equity will also be purchased by various large institutions (e.g., insurance companies and private foundations).

Many people support the idea of a *free* distribution of shares, either to the employees of the firms concerned or to the whole population through a system of coupons or vouchers. For my part I do not feel this is an expedient solution to the problem. At most I would give property free of charge to certain institutions (for instance, decentralized pension funds) as a way of supplying them with initial operating capital. A detailed account of the arguments for and against would exceed the bounds of this study, and so I will merely draw my Soviet colleagues' attention to the literature on the subject.[9] In any case correct planning of Soviet privatization will be made easier by having the early experiences in Eastern Europe available by the time it comes onto the agenda. The strategies chosen differ from country to country: Germany and Hungary have basically opted for sales, while free distribution on a mass scale is being prepared in Czechoslovakia and Poland. It will be instructive to compare the results.

8. All the tasks mentioned so far tie in with a forceful development of the financial sector. There is a need for decentralization of the banking system and for the development of private pension funds and insurance companies (alongside the social security system). A modern market economy includes a great many other kinds of financial institutions such as investment and mutual funds, venture capital funds that can finance high-risk new undertakings, financial institutions specializing in housing investments, and so on.

While emphasizing the multiplicity of the paths and instruments, I would like to pick out from the many partial tasks one that I consider to be the most important of all: *the evolution of a new middle class*, the emergence of a million entrepreneurs on a small and medium scale. By entering the private sector, this new stratum, along with its employees, whose earnings will normally become appreciably higher as well, can become a bulwark for the new system in the cities and the countryside alike. I would measure the speed of the transition primarily by the rate at which this stratum grows. The degree to which the growth of this entrepreneur stratum is promoted also constitutes one of the major measures of economic success for the new democratic governments.

Social Welfare Policy

All active participants in the new democratic political era must strive from the first day to accomplish the tasks of the transition in a humane way. This too is among the "unconditional tasks"; whether the conditions favoring the changes emerge or not, all believers in the new democratic political order and an efficient market economy must do

9. I state my own position in the fourth study of this volume. To my knowledge, the idea of a free transfer of property rights was first advanced in an article by J. Lewandowski and J. Szomburg (1989); see also R. Frydman and A. Rapaczynski (1990) and D. Lipton and J. Sachs (1990*b*).

everything they can in their own field to alleviate the grave problems and suffering that accompany the transformation of society.

Politicians can win popularity with populist rhetoric at most for a time, until it emerges that they are doing nothing to help with the problems. I do not want to disguise the fact that implementation of the program outlined in the earlier parts of this study is accompanied by sacrifices of many kinds. Production in many sectors falls, producing unemployment. Relative prices and wages are readjusted, reducing the real income of many people. Masses of people will be afflicted by the freed prices and raised taxes and compensated for them only in part. As the real market becomes dominant in the economy, insecurity increases as well in many respects: businesses fail and jobs are no longer secure. All this happens at a time when the country is down at heel, its reserves exhausted.

So what is the minimum that can and must be ensured even under these circumstances?

First of all, unemployment must be openly recognized as a permanent concomitant of life. That means setting up a system of unemployment benefits, after responsible consideration of the country's financial potentials, augmented by better organization of labor exchanges and retraining schemes.

Apart from that, a welfare system must be developed to give at least temporary help to those of the needy whose reintegration takes time and permanent support to those incapable of helping themselves.

Under socialism there were large, cumbersome, overcentralized systems of redistribution in operation; these allocated housing and dispensed health care and pensions. There is a great need for decentralization in this area, and also for private institutions to take part in the provision alongside the institutions of the state. But the transformation must be accomplished in a way that does not cause a further trauma to people already shaken during the stabilization process. A gradual, very tactful approach is needed here.

I notice social welfare policy being relegated into the background in many Eastern European countries, which impedes the development of the democratic consensus. I sincerely hope that in the Soviet Union they will learn from this experience and try to avoid committing the same error.

The need is not just for new state regulations and new institutions, but for a new public morality. Too great a role was played in our earlier lives by a state that was both repressive and paternalistic; people expected it to take care of them. With the advent of the market economy, the idea of individual liberty and autonomy becomes the center of the system of values. The chief commandment for all active people is to help themselves, not wait idly for the state to decide instead of them and do something on their behalf. But this prime imperative should be complemented by another: that society must assist those in need of help, both by voluntarily and spontaneously organized solidarity and by state means.

References

Allison, G., and Yavlinsky, G., eds. 1991. "Window of Opportunity: Joint Program for Western Cooperation in the Soviet Transformation to Democracy and the Market Economy." Mimeo. Cambridge: Joint Working Group of Harvard University, and Moscow: Center for Economic and Political Research.

Antal, László. 1979. "Development—with Some Digression. The Hungarian Economic Mechanism in the Seventies." *Acta Oeconomica* 23 (3–4): 257–273.

Bauer, Tamás. 1983. "The Hungarian Alternative to Soviet-Type Planning." *Journal of Comparative Economics* 7 (3): 304–316.

Berend, Iván T. 1990. *The Hungarian Economic Reform*. Cambridge: Cambridge University Press.

Blanchard, Oliver, Dornbusch, Rudiger, Krugman, Paul, Layard, Richard, and Summers, Lawrence. 1991. *Reform in Eastern Europe*. Cambridge, Mass.: MIT Press.

Fischer, Stanley, and Gelb, Alan. 1990. "Issues in Socialist Economy Reform." Working Paper WPS 565. Washington, D.C.: World Bank.

Frydman, Roman, and Rapaczynski, Andrzej. 1990. "Markets and Institutions in Large Scale Privatizations." *Economic Research Report*. New York: New York University, pp. 90–420.

Hare, Paul, Radice, Hugo K., and Swain, Nigel, eds. 1981. *Hungary: A Decade of Economic Reform*. London and Boston: Allen and Unwin.

Kornai, János. 1983. "Comments on the Present State and Prospects of the Hungarian Economic Reform." *Journal of Comparative Economics* 7 (3): 225–252.

Kornai, János. 1986. "The Hungarian Reform Process: Visions, Hopes and Reality." *Journal of Economic Literature* 24 (4): 1687–1737.

Kornai, János. [1989] 1990*a*. *The Road to a Free Economy. Shifting from a Socialist System: The Example of Hungary*. New York: W. W. Norton.

Kornai, János. 1990*b*. *Put k svobodnoi ekonomike. Strastnoe slovo v zashitu ekonomicheskih preobrazovanii* (The Road to a Free Economy). Moscow: Ekonomika.

Kovács, János Mátyás. 1990. "Reform Economics: The Classification Gap." *Daedalus* 119 (1): 215–248.

Lewandowski, Janusz, and Szomburg, Jan. 1989. "Property Reform as a Basis for Social and Economic Reform." *Communist Economies* 1 (3): 257–268.

Lipton, David, and Sachs, Jeffrey. 1990*a*. "Creating a Market Economy in Eastern Europe: The Case of Poland." *Brookings Papers on Economic Activity* (1): 75–133.

Lipton, David, and Sachs, Jeffrey. 1990*b*. "Privatization in Eastern Europe: The Case of Poland." *Brookings Papers on Economic Activity* (2): 293–333.

Révész, Gábor. 1990. *Perestroika in Eastern Europe: Hungary's Economic Transformation, 1945–1988*. Boulder: Westview Press.

Szamuely, László. 1982. "The First Wave of the Mechanism Debate in Hungary (1954–1957)." *Acta Oeconomica* 29 (1–2): 1–24.

Szamuely, László. 1984. "The Second Wave of the Economic Mechanism Debate and the 1968 Reform in Hungary." *Acta Oeconomica* 33 (1–2): 43–67.

Working Group formed by a joint decision of Mikhail S. Gorbachev and Boris N. Yeltsin. 1990 (August). "Transition to the Market. Part 1. The Concept and Program" (The Shatalin Plan). Mimeo. Moscow: Avkhanagels'koe: Cultural Initiative Foundation.

4 The Principles of Privatization in Eastern Europe[1]

A wide-ranging debate on privatization in Eastern Europe is taking place, both in the region itself and abroad, among Western experts. The debate, of course, is not confined to men and women of science. Since privatization is among the fundamental issues of the postsocialist transition, governments, parties, international organizations, and the business world must take a position on it. A hundred different views have been expressed so far and a hundred different specific programs have been put forward for resolving the problems in practice.[2] I make no attempt here to formulate any hundred-and-first program, although I do put forward my own views.[3] My main purpose is to help readers conduct a methodical analysis of the problem. I outline an intellectual structure allowing people to assemble the body of information they possess and confront the alternative views encountered with each other before formulating a position of their own.

The word "privatization," which features in the title, is used in two senses. In the narrower sense it means the transfer of assets hitherto owned by the state into private hands. The broader interpretation covers the property relations in the economy *as a whole*, so that privatization of the economy must be understood to mean that the share of the

1. The Hungarian text of the study was translated by Brian McLean and Julianna Parti, to whom I am grateful for their excellent work. I also thank Mária Kovács and Carla Krüger for their assistance in gathering the literature on the subject.

2. There is a very extensive literature on the subject. I have selected here just a few of the studies in English which deal with Eastern European privatization: S. Fischer and A. Gelb (1990), R. Frydman and A. Rapaczynski (1990), D. Lipton and J. Sachs (1990), J. Levandowski and J. Szomburg (1989), and M. Hinds (1990). An excellent survey of the polemic is provided by D. Stark (1990).

3. I first formulated my own proposal in a book [1989] (1990). This study further develops and expands the ideas I put forward on privatization, in the light of the subsequent debates and practical experiences. My earlier proposals on some questions are corrected in this study, where I feel this is necessary.

private sector grows until it ultimately becomes the dominant economic sector. This study is concerned with the concept of privatization in that broader sense.

The title mentions Eastern Europe, and in the main the study deals with the group of small countries embarking on the road of postsocialist transition. However, I believe that most of the problems discussed in the study resemble those in the Soviet Union as well.

The first chapter deals with the values fostered during privatization, the second with the evolutionary nature of the transformation and the role of the state, and the third and fourth chapters with the main forms of private ownership. Finally, the fifth chapter deals with the pace of privatization.

I Values

Some of those taking part in the international debate put forward their practical proposals on privatization without clearly answering some crucial questions: What purposes do they want the process to serve? What values do they seek to implement? What criteria do they intend to apply to the decision?

I share the philosophy of those who argue that the ends and the means must be clearly distinguished in any analysis of practical tasks.[4] Lucid clarification of the criteria for judgement is also required for any subsequent appraisal of processes after they have taken place. Rather than attempting to detail all the values taken into account, I only mention the ones I consider the most important to the subject. I classify these under four *aspects*.

1. *The sociological aspect, in longer, historical terms.* What is the new democracy's direction of movement in a society inherited from the socialist system?

Socialism in its classical, Stalinist form gave rise to a society which was governed bureaucratically and organized hierarchically. Nationalization extended beyond firms in production to cover practically every activity, so that every able-bodied person, with a few exceptions, became an employee of the state.

In countries like my own—Hungary—where reforms had begun many years ago, there had been a movement away from that ultimate

4. This is one of the methodological ideas that run as a *Leitmotif* through J. Tinbergen's works. See J. Tinbergen (1952), for instance.

form of *étatism* before democracy arrived in 1989–1990. I shall not deal here with such transitional states, but turn straightaway to the longer-term prospects offered by the process.

1-a. It would be desirable for the structure of society to resemble in its main features the structure in the most highly developed capitalist countries. A broad stratum of independent, autonomous business people and entrepreneurs should emerge. Rather than the vast majority of the property being concentrated in the hands of just a small group, there should also be a broad middle class that includes the masses of owners of small and medium-sized enterprises. Society should undergo *embourgeoisement*.[5] The bureaucratic, hierarchical stratification of society should be widely superseded by stratification according to property. In other words, the hyperactive, overgrown role of the state in the economy should be reduced, even though the economic activity of the state will remain considerable.

All this transformation in the structure of society should be coupled with the modernization of production and the other activities of society, through the spread of up-to-date technologies and life-styles.

This "Western-style" image of society is seen as an attainable goal by many Eastern Europeans who think about the prospects of transforming society, but it is not, of course, the sole course envisaged, even among those opposed to the concept of society espoused by the earlier socialist system.

1-b. Some people are put off by modern-day Western Europe and North America, with their business mentality, commercialism, profit-mongering, and oversized and overcrowded modern cities, the environmental damage caused by industrial civilization, and many other drawbacks. So instead they tend towards an image of another, romantically "unsullied" society. Those subscribing to this kind of Third Road" *Weltanschauung* are attracted by the proximity of nature in a village, by the peace of a small town, and by the simplicity of small-scale agricultural and industrial economies.

1-c. There is another "Third Road" image of society where the intention is to blend capitalism with plebeian-*cum*-socialistic ideas. The goal becomes a "people's capitalism" that would turn all citizens into proprietors.

All these images of future society have direct implications for the way the process of privatization is judged. For my part, I favor an

5. See I. Szelényi (1988).

orientation towards the "Western-style" social structure 1-a, even though I am aware that it has many bad features. I am ready to condemn these and advocate efforts to diminish them, but I am also aware that these bad features will inevitably appear. Those who subscribe to "Western-style" social development must accept its warts and all. I do not consider the Third Road images of the future just mentioned either practically attainable or desirable.

2. *The economic aspect.* This does not form a single criterion; a variety of economic interests can be taken into account.

2-a. The most important economic criterion in my view is to arrive at forms of ownership that induce efficient production. One of the most damaging features of the bureaucratic state ownership prevailing under the socialist system was that it gave little incentive to efficiency, and, in fact, frequently encouraged waste. One of privatization's missions must be to bring about a close and overt linkage between the direct financial interest of owners on the one hand and market performance and profit on the other.

Let me pick out three other economic requirements which are also worth taking into consideration.

2-b. The privatization process should help to reinforce the security of private property.

2-c. The fiscal motive: privatization can help to increase state revenue through the proceeds from the sale of state-owned property, the relief of budgetary expenditure of subsidizing loss-making state-owned firms, and the opportunities of finding new sources of tax revenue.

2-d. The monetary motive: the effects of some forms of privatization are anti-inflationary; they help to eliminate the "monetary overhang" of unspent purchasing power. Other forms have the precisely opposite effect of increasing inflationary pressure.

3. *The aspect of political power.* Though scholars concerned with criteria of economic rationality or of ethics may be averse to considering this aspect, the fact must be faced that privatization of any kind is a political issue. Governing political parties and groups want to reinforce and preserve their power, while those in opposition see the issue through the lens of their aspirations to form a government. So one cannot ignore the problem of how popular, deservedly or undeservedly, any privatization program will be.

3-a. Among the factors considered by those who want to return property confiscated by the state to its earlier owners is the political weight of the group it benefits, or: how many votes can be won at the next election.

3-b. Those who support employee ownership would like to win the political support of this broad stratum in society.

3-c. Finally, advocates of giving free shares or vouchers to all citizens count on the idea being popular with the public as a whole.

I will return to this question later. Let me confine myself here to a single observation. Those who seek political popularity through some scheme or other often forget to examine carefully and critically whether those whose approval they expect really *are* enthusiastic about the idea. I could hardly find a convincing public-opinion survey on the subject. For my part I still have doubts, although I must admit that my skepticism is based on insufficiently reliable impressions. Those who receive the property may be disillusioned and angry, not politically grateful, to find what they receive is less than they expected and were promised, and that the process is slow and cumbersome.

4. *The aspect of distributive ethics.* This system of criteria is another highly complex one, full of inner contradictions. The ethical principles considered here are confined to those connected directly with the distribution of income and wealth.

4-a. Those who suffered losses under the previous system must be wholly or partly *compensated* for them during privatization. Some take the view that, where possible, the actual items of property confiscated should be returned if they still exist in their original physical form. Others support the idea that the compensation should merely be in money or securities. Several versions of the latter approach are conceivable, with various restrictions on redemption and the degree of transferability.

A range of difficult questions arises in this respect. What kind of injuries deserve redress? Should compensation be confined to the economic damage sustained through confiscation, or should it cover losses of other kinds as well, ranging from cases of unjust imprisonment or execution to those who lost their jobs or were denied the chance to continue their education or to travel abroad? And what should be the earliest qualifying date? Should it be when the communists came to power, or has the time now come to redress the injuries of those who received no compensation under the socialist system for losses sustained in the Second World War and the period of fascist rule, for instance?

Ultimately, those who espouse the ethical arguments for reprivatization want to apply the principle of just recompensing. An economic argument, listed under 2-b, can also be brought forward in support of reprivatization: restoring the old property relations is a tangible demonstration of the idea that private property is sacrosanct. But this argument can be countered with another that likewise rests on criterion 2-b: the protracted process of reprivatization may undermine the security of property relations based on the *status quo*. A building or business claimed by a former owner may already be in private ownership.

Reprivatization can also conflict with other economic criteria. It robs the treasury of income or actually involves extra public expenditure (criterion 2-c). If those entitled to compensation are given securities and these can be traded, many will sell them in order to spend the proceeds straight away on the consumer goods market. That means this procedure will increase the inflationary pressure (criterion 2-d).

A further comment needs making on the programs for compensation through reprivatization. An attempt is made by their supporters to give the impression that the *state* is granting the compensation to a certain section of the public. But what is the state in this context but the sum of all the taxpayers? Compensation by way of reprivatization is a *redistributive* action that transfers wealth to the beneficiaries of the compensation from the pockets of non-beneficiary, taxpaying citizens. There is no question of those who gained at the time from confiscation now recompensing those who suffered losses from it. The members of the *present* generation receiving no compensation have also lost, suffering like everyone else from all the consequences of the economic losses and backwardness caused by the previous system.

4-b. It can be argued on grounds of *moral entitlement* that a specific group has a right to some part of the state or other communal wealth in view of their social position. "Let the land belong to those who till it." "Let factories belong to those who work there." "Let state-owned flats belong to those who live in them." Even if the debate is confined to the ethical plane, it can be objected that the rest of society also contributed to creating these assets. Do today's tillers of good land, today's workers in a profitable factory, or today's tenants of attractive, spacious apartments really deserve more valuable property than those less fortunate? In the last resort, the slogans quoted are redistributive principles that favor some groups in society at the expense of the rest.

4-c. There are demands for *fairness* and *equality*. This principle is voiced chiefly by those who want to divide part of the property of the state among all citizens. The question of whether this program clashes with the other criteria is discussed later on. Let us remain for the time being within the logic of ethical arguments.

The old system failed to fulfil its egalitarian promises: democracy inherits a society marked by unequal distribution of material wealth and intellectual capital. Compared with these initial conditions, little is changed if rich and poor, well educated and unschooled, healthy and sick alike receive a modest free gift. Moreover, the free gift will soon be sold by those in need and bought cheaply by those who are clever and have the capital to buy it. Sincere advocates of a more equal distribution of income and wealth should campaign in the fields of fiscal policy, welfare policy and education, health and housing policy, where the scope for furthering their objectives is greater.

Privatization is intended to introduce a capitalist market economy. Although the market and capitalist property have many useful qualities, above all the stimulation to efficient economic activity, fairness and equality are not among their virtues. They not only reward good work but also good fortune, and they penalize not just bad work but also ill-fortune. While they are useful to society as a whole by encouraging exploitation of good fortune and resistance to ill-fortune, they are not "just." I think it is ethically paradoxical to mix slogans of fairness and equality into a program of capitalist privatization.

Mention has been made of a range of criteria whose appraisal can serve as a basis for arriving at a position on the question of privatization. Some of these are compatible and complement one another. But there are also values which conflict with each other in this particular context. Short-term economic interests may clash with the long-term interests behind the transformation of society. Ethical considerations may run up against sociological or economic requirements.

The value judgements on which my own view rests have emerged to some extent in what I have said already, but I will summarize them here briefly. Even though I am an economist, it is aspect 1, the long-term sociological criterion, that I rate as decisive, and I also opt for alternative 1-a, as I consider the emergence of a broad stratum of entrepreneurs and business people and widespread *embourgeoisement* to be of paramount importance. I accordingly place the strongest emphasis of the economic arguments on 2-a: privatization must be accomplished in a way that gives the strongest incentive to efficient production. Although the other economic criteria are also important, I rate them as subordinate to the one I have mentioned. I acknowledge the fact that aspects of political power also apply, but they do not influence me in my choice of values. I am not indifferent to the moral aspects of distribution, but I would refrain from applying them in the context of privatization.

Naturally, I respect the right of others to choose values different from my own. What I would like to recommend to statesmen, legislators, the specialists who suggest legislation and the journalists who monitor and criticize the plans and their execution is this: let them analyze and make public the choice of values that justify the privatization programs they support. Let them face up to the conflicts of values and the "trade-offs" between conflicting requirements, and admit it openly if they jettison one value in favor of another. Let them refrain from pretending that the practical proposal they prefer is a neutral one that would further all the values for consideration equally well.

II The Transformation's Evolutionary Nature and the Role of the State

A view widely spread is that state institutions should play a very large part in privatization. Such a view can be found in governmental circles. In Hungary, for instance, a central authority called the State Property Agency tried for a long time to concentrate almost every act of privatization in its own hands. A similar kind of centralization could be observed in Germany.

There is also strong emphasis on the role of the state in the views put forward by many foreign experts, who certainly cannot be accused of wanting to increase their own power. I myself have heard the following proposal: the Soviet Union should quickly establish twenty investment funds by state decree. The managers to head them should be appointed by the government, with the advice of experts from abroad. The funds should be assigned the shares in the firms formerly owned by the state, and the stock in the investment companies should then be distributed free to all citizens.

I think the inordinate state centralization of Hungary's privatization and the notion of forming investment funds by state decree to manage private property are good illustrations of what Hayek termed a "constructivist" formation.[6] They are artificially created, whereas the vitality of capitalist development is a result from the fact that its viable institutions arise naturally, without being forced.

6. See F. A. Hayek (1960) and (1973, chapter 1).

During the period of Stalinist collectivization in the Soviet Union, it was possible to eliminate the class of well-to-do farmers, the *kulaks*, by state decree. But no state decree can create a class of well-to-do farmers; that will emerge only by a process of historical development. The state can decide to implement confiscation, but no state resolution can appoint a Ford, a Rockefeller or a DuPont. The selection of the class of owners in a capitalist economy takes place by a process of evolution. And it is an evolutionary process that selects among the institutions and organizations which emerge, causing the ones that are not functioning well under the prevailing circumstances to wither away, and choosing as survivors the ones truly fit for their task.[7]

The Polish economist J. Kowalik coined the ironic term "étatist liberalism" for the curious school of thought that suggests pursuing liberal objectives (private property, individual autonomy, consumer sovereignty) by artificially creating organizations contrived by officialdom, and aims at controlling the transformation of society by bureaucratic state coercion and administrative measures.

What the state should primarily be expected to do is to stand aside from the development of the private sector and ensure that its own agencies remove the bureaucratic obstacles. There are a number of feasible state measures that go beyond this and actively assist in the privatization process, and these are discussed later. But governments should not be expected to replace the spontaneous, decentralized, organic growth process of the private economy by a web of bureaucratic, excessively regulatory measures and a hive of zealous activity by state officials.

III Types of Owners

A. *Personal owners.* First let me give a few examples, to make this concept clear.

A-1. A family farm or a family undertaking in another branch of the economy, which does not employ outside labor apart from family members more than occasionally.

A-2. A small or medium-sized firm where ownership and management have not been separated and the owner remains in charge.

7. The idea that the market performs a natural selection among organizations already appeared in J. A. Schumpeter [1911] (1968) and was later elaborated upon in more detail by A. A. Alchian (1974). Schumpeter's idea of selection is strongly emphasized in connection with the transformation of the socialist countries in the works of P. Murrell (1990*a*), (1990*b*).

A-3. A newly founded firm in Schumpeter's sense, managed by the entrepreneur establishing it and normally employing borrowed capital, not the entrepreneur's own.[8]

A-4. A joint-stock company of any size in which an individual or group of individuals has a dominant shareholding. This need not necessarily be a majority of the shares; a holding of 20–30% is often sufficient to give the dominant owner (or group of owners) a decisive say in the choice and supervision of management and in major financial matters and investment decisions.[9] Dominance of this kind can emerge so long as the other shareholders are sufficiently passive, which can be the case, for instance, if ownership of the shares is fragmented. The situation may be similar if the rest of the shares are held by the state, and the state refrains voluntarily from active intervention in the firm's affairs.

A-5. A firm in which the former chief executive officer or a group of managers have become owners, or at least dominant shareholders, through a management buy-out.

I have not conducted a rigorous classification of mutually exclusive cases, merely listed examples, and these may overlap in some feature or other. The examples can cover small, medium-sized, and large firms alike. They may take legal forms that entail unlimited liability or liability limited to various degrees, and range from a family farm to modern joint-stock companies. So what, in the end, do these cases have in common? The presence of a live, "visible," "tangible" person or group of persons at the head of the firm. This individual, family, or group has a strong and direct proprietorial interest, so that the size of the firm's profits or losses affects the owner's pocket. In addition, the owner either runs the firm directly or plays a dominant role in hiring and firing the managers and overseeing what they do.

A *personal owner* can enter the stage of the postsocialist economy in two ways. One is by setting up a brand new undertaking. The other is

8. "The original nucleus of means has been but rarely acquired by the entrepreneur's own saving activity . . ." writes J. A. Schumpeter [1949] (1989, p. 266), and goes on to catalogue the various sources of finance, including the credit system. One of the sources "was tapping the savings of other people and 'created credit' . . . 'Credit creation' introduces banks and quasi-banking activities. . . ." In this study and several others, Schumpeter analyzes the connection between the credit system and entrepreneurs in detail.

9. The term *noyau stable* (stable core) has become widespread, following French literature. See J. Friedmann (1989).

by buying part or all of an existing state-owned firm. The two methods are often combined: a state asset is bought by an existing private firm.

I believe this personal owner to be the key figure in Eastern European privatization. Let me recall the first chapter of this study, which I ended by outlining my own selection of values. It is compatible with this selection to assert that the appearance of personal owners on a mass scale will ensure to the greatest extent the desired transformation of society, the *embourgeoisement* (criterion 1-a), and the incentive to efficiency (criterion 2-a). Moreover, if one constituent of this process is the purchase of state assets, it will also satisfy the fiscal and monetary criteria (2-c and 2-d). It can be stated, therefore, that the vaster the area in which ownership and control pass into the hands of personal owners, the more successfully privatization will proceed. One of the most encouraging features of the transformation in Eastern Europe is the perceptible advance of this evolution.[10]

There is a widespread notion that an upper limit on privatization by purchase is set by the amount of savings accumulated by the general public. Comparisons of the savings at the public's disposal with the value of the state's wealth are used to arrive at alarming forecasts. The conclusion reached is that it could be 50 or 100 years before the public has managed to buy up the state's wealth. So there is no other solution: the property of the state can only be reduced quickly by distributing state assets free of charge.

In my view this line of argument relies on false premises. The purchasing power intended by the public for investment (including the purchase of state property) can be multiplied several times by suitable credit and deferred-payment schemes.[11] The proportion of the down-payment to the credit or deferred payments can be as little as 1:10 or 1:20. This proportion is what determines right from the start how

10. Statistics in the Eastern European countries have reached a critical situation. All previous statistics were based earlier on detailed information provided by the large state-owned firms. Their proportion is shrinking. At the same time, the statistical offices are not equipped, neither organizationally nor methodologically, to observe and measure the activity of the private sector, least of all under circumstances in which the private sector tries to disguise as much of its activities as possible in order to escape taxation. So it is impossible to give reliable estimates for the scales of expansion of various types of private ownership as a whole.

11. Here again I draw attention to Schumpeter's statement on the relation between the entrepreneur and the credit system, quoted in footnote 8. Schumpeter attributed such importance to this that he incorporated it into the *definition* of capitalism he formulated: "Capitalism is that form of private property economy in which innovations are carried out by means of borrowed money" (1939, vol. I, p. 223).

much of the state's wealth can be bought by those wanting to go into business with the savings they initially possess. In addition, the process can speed up as soon as some of the businesses start to show a profit and a greater propensity to invest. Above all, it depends on the domestic and foreign banks and other financial intermediaries what range of attractive credit and deferred-payment schemes they offer. Moreover, the main way foreign governments and international financial and economic organizations ready to help can contribute to building up the private sector in Eastern Europe is by setting up financing and backing schemes of this kind. To some extent special "venture-capital" institutions will have to be established, for there is no denying that special risks are attached to lending money to new private businesses in a postsocialist economy. But these risks can be reduced by an appropriate mortgage system to ensure that the property reverts to the lender if there is a default on the payments. Alternatively, the lender can be a co-owner from the outset. And if the state really wants to be active, it should go about it by offering at least partial credit guarantees that lessen the lender's risk. The majority of private entrepreneurs will, in any case, be more reliable borrowers than many inviable state-owned firms repeatedly bailed out even though they default on their loans.

As long as the credit and deferred-payment schemes are devised with sufficient caution, they will not entail a risk of inflation. In fact, the debt repayments and interest will siphon some of the potential consumer spending away from the entrepreneurs (criterion 2-d).

It is worth drawing particular attention to the question of management buy-outs. The public is ambivalent towards them. It is pleased that experts, rather than dilettantes, take over the factory, but displeased to see members of the *"nomenclatura"* under the old regime transmuted into born-again capitalists. In my view it is not worth legally prohibiting something that will inevitably occur. It is more expedient to bring the occurrence into the open and place it under the supervision of the public, the law, and the appropriate authorities. Clarification of the moral and business rules for management buy-outs is needed, including the normal credit terms. Let a manager or group of managers capable of buying a business property from the state according to these rules do so by legal means.

Special attention should be paid to the question of peasants wanting to farm privately, private small-scale industry and trading, and small business as a whole. It is quite common in the developed market economies for these groups to receive credit on favorable terms, and possibly longer or shorter-term tax reductions. This is appropriate in Eastern Europe as well, particularly now, when the aim is to set these groups on their feet and encourage new small businesses on a mass scale. One factor in criterion 1-a is the creation of a broad middle class; an important ingredient in that process is the speeding up of the development of small and medium-sized firms.

This ties in with another range of problems: how to overcome the distortion in the size distribution of firms. Excessive concentration took place in the socialist economy. Whereas the larger proportion of employment in most Western and Southern European countries is in firms with less than 500 employees, small and medium-sized firms in most Eastern European countries were wound up on a mass scale or artificially merged.[12] The need for a healthier size distribution is among the reasons for giving favorable consideration to credit applications from small and medium-sized businesses.

B. *Employee ownership.* I am thinking here of the form in which the shares in a state-owned firm which has been converted into a joint-stock company are taken up by its employees. The most commonly used term for this in Anglo-Saxon writings is employee stock-ownership plan (ESOP). The idea comes in a number of variants; in some the employees receive all the shares, and in others only a smaller proportion. The proposals also vary on the conditions under which the employees receive the shares, ranging from entirely free distribution to price and payment conditions that are more favorable than the market terms. Finally, various suggestions have been put forward on what limits to place on the sale of the shares, for instance, restricting transferability either temporarily or permanently.

The decision makers are influenced primarily by the political criteria when they consider this form of ownership. So long as the politicians have convinced themselves through reliable research into public opinion that there is a real call for employee stock ownership, and that employees actually demand it, I see no particular danger in accepting some moderate version of it, i.e., in offering the employees, on favorable terms, a fairly small proportion, say 10–20% of the shares in a firm

12. É. Ehrlich (1985), using data for 1970, made a comparison between the size distributions of industrial firms in a group of Western European capitalist and Eastern European socialist countries. According to her calculation, only 32% of those employed in capitalist industry worked in firms with more than 500 employees, while 66% of those in socialist industry did so.

due to be privatized. In my view it is more practical to offer the shares for sale to the employees at a large discount than to give them away for nothing.

In the case of a smaller firm, it is also conceivable for all the shares to pass into the hands of the employees, in other words, for the form of ownership of the firm in question to come close to a partnership or a true cooperative.

The consistent (or perhaps I should say extreme) advocates of employee ownership go much further. They would like all state-owned firms (or as many as possible) to assume this form of ownership entirely, irrespective of their size. Many of them couple this proposal with the idea of transfer free of charge. They put forward two main arguments for their position. One is criterion 2-a: an employee who is also an owner will have a stronger incentive to produce efficiently. For my part I do not see proof of this. On the contrary, if employees choose their own managers, the managers become dependent on their own subordinates, which can undermine wage and labor discipline. Sufficient evidence for this assumption is provided by the experience with workers' self-management in Eastern Europe, particularly Yugoslavia.

The other argument advanced for comprehensive employee ownership is to choose criterion 4-b from the aspect of distributive ethics: let the factory belong to those who work in it. My counterarguments have been expressed in the chapter on value criteria.

I would expect the various forms of employee ownership to gain a similar position to the one they have in the developed Western European and North American countries sooner or later, in other words, that they will represent a respectable proportion, but they will fall far short of becoming the dominant form.

C. *Institutional ownership.* This large group of property forms needs dividing into sub-groups before I can comment properly on the alternative ideas put forward.

C-1. Banks and other banking institutions. Some of the postsocialist economies inherited from the socialist economy a two-tier banking system in which there were already commercial banks alongside the central bank. Certain postsocialist countries, which entered the postsocialist period directly, skipping the period of reform within socialism, still inherited the monobank system, and are now obliged to set up a network of commercial banks. But whichever of the starting positions pertains, the banking sector has the following characteristics at the beginning of postsocialist transition:

The sole owner of the banks is the state. There may have developed what is known as "cross-ownership," under which state-owned firms outside the banking sector are shareholders in the banks, sharing ownership with the institutions nominated for the task by the state administration, and conversely, a bank may hold shares in a state-owned firm which has been converted into a joint-stock company.[13] But cross-ownership remains merely an indirect form of state ownership, and is no substitute for privatization.

The various organizations making up the banking sector of Eastern Europe are engaged in a quite narrow range of activities. Developed market economies possess a great many financial institutions that do not qualify as "banks" according to the strict legal and economic criteria in force, such as credit-card companies, venture-capital companies, investment funds, mutual funds, saving-and-loan associations, exchange bureaus, and so on. There are strong reasons why postsocialist economies need to develop a banking system with a similarly varied and multiple profile.

Some of these bank-like financial intermediaries (which cannot be called "banks" in the strict sense) may appear in private-ownership form from the outset. A major role in the development of the new quasi-banking institutions can be played by foreign capital.

The development of genuine private banks, particularly large private banks, seems more difficult, even though their activity is clearly essential to a modern market economy. On the one hand, foreign banks can be expected to open branches in the Eastern European countries, and of course these will be true private banks. It is possible that one or two institutions performing quasi-banking functions that were privately-owned from the start may be converted into real banks. Alongside all these developments, the privatization of the currently state-owned commercial banks will take place. Particularly in the beginning, this will presumably mean only partial private ownership and mainly foreign involvement.

Privatization of the banking sector in the broad sense will not take place all at once. It will take some time before private property

13. Cross-ownership was discussed in my book [1989] (1990). Detailed descriptions of the phenomenon, based on experiences in Hungary, can be found in the studies of M. Móra (1991) and É. Voszka (1991); these had not yet reached me at the time this lecture was delivered.

becomes the dominant ownership form. Several factors will play a part in this.

One bottleneck is shortage of expertise, experience, and up-to-date technical equipment. One only has to remember that these are countries where even payment by check has yet to spread among the population and in trade and services. Another example of backwardness is that consumer credit is used only sporadically in these economies.

Another requirement for development is the creation of requisite legislation, and, beside that, success in building up a system of state regulation and supervision of the banking sector. It would be desirable if state intervention were not on a scale as to stifle individual initiative, but at the same time the sector cannot be left to its own devices. The security of depositors and the financial stability of the country both require legal, insurance and supervisory guarantees.

The subject so far has been privatization of the banking sector itself. However, this ties in closely with the privatization of other parts of the economy. Reference is often made by debaters on the subject to the German (erstwhile West German) and Japanese examples, where a sizeable proportion of industrial shares is in the hands of large banks. On these grounds the recommendation is presented that a considerable proportion of the shares in the state-owned firms should already have been handed over to the Eastern European banks.

Not much will be achieved, in my view, if this idea is applied prematurely and hastily; it will be ineffective chiefly in terms of criteria 1-a and 2-a, which I consider the most important. It will not produce a true owner with a strong interest in increasing efficiency. There are many cases at present where a large state-owned firm making heavy losses is closely tied up with a large state-owned bank, which may be a shareholder and is usually its main creditor. If that is the case, the bank and the firm share an interest in seeing the firm bailed out and artificially sustained. The danger is that if a bank, under the present property relations, is also a shareholder in large joint-stock companies, it will fail to apply business criteria adequately.

Another danger is that the state-owned banks will remain the "politicized" institutions they were before. The parties in government will, at any time, treat them as their own backyard, and try to plant their own people in leading positions. This is also a warning against the plan to turn the banks in their present state into factory owners, through a deed of gift by the state, even though the banks themselves are owned by the state.

My view is that it will become desirable at a later stage for the ownership relations to develop along the lines just mentioned in connection with the Japanese and German examples. As the weight of domestic and foreign private ownership increases among the owners of a bank or a quasi-banking institution,[14] they can become partial owners of formerly state-owned non-financial firms. The more a bank or other bank-like financial institution operates on a truly commercial basis and is dominated by private ownership, the more it can be expected to satisfy criterion 2-a: to exercise strict control over the firm it owns and take a truly proprietorial attitude. In other words, as privatization of the banking sector advances as an organic process, so, at the same rate, can whole blocks of shares and portfolios of holdings in various firms previously owned by the state pass into the ownership of the banks. For instance, such blocks and portfolios could form part of the state's capital contribution to joint ventures formed in the banking sector.

C-2. Pension funds. The pension funds have become one of the main holders of corporate shares in several developed capitalist countries. Notable in this respect is Britain, where more than half the shares are in the hands of the pension system.[15] Many participants in the privatization debate recommend that the pension funds in Eastern Europe assume a similar ownership role. So the problem must be discussed in a little more detail.

The provision of pensions was a task of the state under the socialist system. Pension contributions were paid in as tax and pensions were a liability on the state budget. Even where pension provision was in the hands of a separate institution and the sum received in pension contributions was nominally treated as a separate fund, any surplus in the fund was utilized in practice by the state and the state covered any deficit. Although the real value of pensions was always quite low, and further reduced by the effects of inflation, the nominal sum was guaranteed by law. No other decentralized pension system operated in the socialist economy.

---

14. Let me repeat here something emphasized earlier: the key issue is not the percentage of the shares in some private owner's hands, but whether or not the private owner has a decisive say. It is possible that a reputed foreign bank might become the dominant owner of a Hungarian bank even though it is only a minority shareholder.

15. According to M. E. Schaffer (1990), 32% of British shares were in the hands of pension funds in 1987 and 25% in the hands of insurance companies. As for the role of pension funds and insurance companies, Schaffer's proposals resemble in many respects the idea put forward in this study.

Radical alteration of the pension system came onto the agenda during the postsocialist transition, but the final forms it will take have yet to be developed in many Eastern European countries. The pension systems of the developed capitalist countries are not uniform in any case, and no consensus has emerged in Eastern Europe on which Western country's pattern to follow. Although it is not a task for this study to take a position on this, the role of pension funds cannot be avoided in connection with institutional shareholdings. I therefore start out from the following assumptions.

Sooner or later a mixed system emerges. One of its segments is a state scheme with the task of guaranteeing a pension on at least a subsistence level for those qualifying for it. Of course a guaranteed state pension above this minimum level can be laid down by law, but this must only be done in the knowledge that the ultimate financial source is taxation, or social security contributions gathered in the same way as taxation.

The other segment of the pension system is private in nature, and its primary source of funding is the payment of voluntary contributions. Their cost is shared between employers and employees according to legal stipulations and labor contracts. The network of pension funds is decentralized, and it can be joined by both nonprofit organizations, whose sole task is to provide their members with pensions, and profit-oriented insurance companies, which undertake to pay annuities similar to pensions.

The revenue and expenditure of the state segment rest on compulsory legal stipulations. Membership of the private segment, on the other hand, is voluntary. Employers and employees are free to decide whether to join or not. In the case of a developed decentralized pension system, every employer or employee can choose between several kinds of private pension schemes.

There is no way of telling beforehand exactly what the future pension system in Eastern Europe will be like, but it seems quite realistic to assume that it will resemble the system just outlined. It is also clear that the transition to a mixed system (containing a private segment) can only be gradual, for the starting point differs among generations. Those already on pension or approaching pensionable age no longer have a choice; they must be provided with a guaranteed pension. The longer the life expectancy for individuals, the more possible it becomes, in this respect as well, to offer them freedom of choice. They may decide at their own risk whether or not to devote part of their savings to some private pension scheme or other. It will clearly be a long time before a mature, responsible, decentralized pension-fund sector develops. This also belongs to the type of process I termed organic development.

Let us now return to the question of shares. Numerous private pension funds in the West invest the capital accumulated from contributions in shares and other securities.[16] The funds employ professional managers who try to build up the most favorable portfolios, paying close attention to the interests of their members. Although they are able to control all purchases and sales of this enormous fortune, they can only assert their influence indirectly, by buying certain securities and selling others. Their transactions influence market prices, which are then reflected in the valuation of the companies. This ultimately has a disciplinary effect on company managers, as a sharp drop in the valuation of their company sheds a bad light on their while a conspicuous rise in valuation is evidence, of varying accuracy, of their success. In all events, this kind of ownership only partially satisfies criterion 2-a: to provide an inducement to company managers and effective control over them.

Starting out from the value premises put forward in the first chapter, the conclusions in relation to privatization are obvious: it is worth aiming to turn the decentralized pension funds into shareholders. There is no need to rely exclusively on their investing part of their accumulated contributions in shares at some future date. The establishment of non-profit, private pension funds could be helped in the first place if each were assigned a portfolio of previously state-owned shares as a constituent of their initial capital. The transfer can even be free of charge, for there is an implicit offset: they are taking over some of the pension commitments which have hitherto been borne exclusively by the state budget.

Legislation is needed, of course, to lay down the conditions for such transfers. Care must also be taken to provide them with portfolios of shares which can be expected to have a positive yield. Otherwise the transaction will be fraudulent, for the ones who suffer will be the pensioners whose pension expectations include the prospective yield from the fund's shareholdings.

16. Many pension funds in the United States, for instance, leave it to the contributors to decide what proportions of their contributions are to be invested on the stock market, the bond market, and the money market.

Moreover, the difference between pensions from the state and pensions from the private segment must be made clear to the voluntary members of the decentralized pension systems. There is a degree of exposure in either case. Pensioners in the state segment are at the mercy of those who devise and apply the legislation on pensions provisions, while pensioners in the private segment are exposed to the fluctuations of the security market and to the degree of success with which the private pension fund manages its securities.

The value premises also show what plans should be rejected. The idea has come up that the state pension system should receive shares before any decentralization and privatization of the pension system takes place. In Hungary, for instance, the transfer has actually begun. This, in my opinion, is a superficial move, from which no particular benefit can be expected. The centralized, state pension system is a branch of the state bureaucracy, and so it should be. But if its function is to provide pensions guaranteed by law, its sources of income should not be exposed to the fluctuations of the stock market or the fortunate or unfortunate trends in corporate profits.

C-3. Insurance companies. Here the situation is very similar to the case of the pension system, and so the conclusions can be drawn straight away by referring to the previous point.

So long as the insurance companies are large, oligopolistic institutions exclusively owned by the state, it is only a superficial measure to transfer shares to them. The result is just another form of "cross-ownership" discussed earlier, since one state-owned institution becomes an owner of another.

The value premises I have made suggest that it is worth supporting a partial privatization of the insurance system. The system might contain state and private segments operating side by side, and the latter include both nonprofit and profit-oriented insurers. The private insurance companies should be encouraged to invest some of their accumulated capital in shares. With suitable legal guarantees and supervision, the state could hand share portfolios over to nonprofit private insurers, even free of charge, as a way of encouraging their establishment and consolidation. This again is a kind of ownership transfer where there is an implicit offset: the private insurance sector which emerges by a process of organic development can steadily take over some of the commitments of the guaranteed state insurance system.[17]

17. Let me draw special attention to the need for this transfer of commitments to be conducted fairly. Under no circumstances should the individual citizen (in case C-2 the pen-

C-4. Cultural and education institutions, charitable societies and foundations, churches. The list contains the kind of institutions which in a developed market economy may invest some of their accumulated savings in shares or other securities. The same will no doubt apply in Eastern Europe. The tighter the bonds tying the leaders of such an institution to the institution itself, the stronger its traditions, and the greater the responsibility they feel for the performance of its functions and for its financial position, the more they can be relied upon to be good custodians of the wealth placed in their charge. For that to happen, of course, such institutions must find financial managers who can perform the task of handling their securities professionally.

Here again one has a group of potential buyers of state property: these institutions can be expected to purchase shares. But the process can be speeded up as well. My value premises do not advance any argument against such institutions receiving share portfolios even free of charge. The only requirements are suitable legislative and supervisory guarantees. And one must ascertain, of course, that there are the vital social conditions to ensure that the institution receiving the gift of state property will really be a good custodians, because those running it have the institution's interests at heart.

C-5. Local governments. Some of the wealth of the state previously managed centrally is likely to be transferred into the hands of local government authorities. This is a necessary and desirable trend, since it promotes the decentralization of power, but it clearly does not mean privatization. A municipality is part of the state, and so once again, the property is passing from one arm of the state to another. It is worth mentioning this because the cases covered by C-1 to C-4, which can really imply privatization are frequently confused in debate with Case C-5, which is merely decentralization within the state, not privatization at all.[18]

---

sioner and in case C-3 the sick or other insured person) suffer losses. Nor should it happen that the state segment hastens to shed its commitments, arguing that the private segment has now received free shares, if in fact such shares do not yet ensure enough income to cover the outgoing pensions and insurance claims. In this respect particular attention, foresight, and caution are required to guard private citizens, already troubled by uncertainties, from further worry.

18. It is another matter that the transfer of some of the state wealth previously handled centrally to the ownership of local authorities may speed up the privatization. This effect only ensues, of course, if the local authority is legally authorized to place property in its possession in private hands, and if it has an economic incentive to do so as well. Also important may be whether the elected local authority officers and councillors think their assistance to privatization will be popular with their voters.

Having come to the end of the discussion of institutional forms of ownership, there are some further general observations to be made. It is inadvisable to create the institutional forms of truly private ownership in a bureaucratic way, by state decree, all at once. And apart from being inexpedient, it is not usually possible in any case. Such institutions will arise through processes of evolution. The speed with which they develop depends on several factors, for instance the inclination of domestic and foreign capital to invest in them (C-1, C-3), and the availability of domestic and foreign professional staff capable of managing institutional share portfolios (C-1, C-2, C-3, and C-4). But it also depends on the activities of the state's legislators and executive apparatus: on how fast the right legal frameworks and supervisory institutions develop, how much initiative the bureaucracy shows in bringing the requisite new institutions into being, and finally to what extent there is a free transfer of state property to create the initial capital for the organizations serving as institutional owners.

D. *Anonymous shareholders.* An important part in modern, mature capitalism is played by anonymous shareholders who do not themselves possess enough capital to make themselves heard directly at the general meeting of a joint-stock company, but are able to vote with their feet. If they do not have enough confidence in the future profitability of a firm in comparison with the profitability of alternate investments, they sell their shares, or in the opposite case, they buy shares. The trend in the demand, supply, and price of the shares then exerts indirect influence on both the major shareholders represented at the general meeting and the management of the company. This indirect influence is applied through a broad network of intermediaries: the stock exchange, the brokers, and the banks and other financial institutions dealing with the purchase and sale of shares.

These institutions of ownership are beginning to appear in the Eastern European economies as well. Stock exchanges already function in the capitals of a few countries and they issue reports on the turnover and daily prices of the publicly traded shares. But all this is still in its infancy. It will take time before this form of ownership, along with the primary and secondary markets for securities, becomes widespread by a process of organic development. A great many things are needed for this to happen: expertise and routine, confidence, a large corpus of competent staff, the right legal regulations, effective state supervision, and so on.

Let us take a look into the more distant future. One can expect the role of joint-stock companies and the distribution of their ownership to develop in a similar direction to the one in the developed capitalist countries. So what are the characteristics of the situation there?

In a range of European countries where the capitalist market economy has operated continuously, without the interruption of the socialist system, only part of the total productive wealth operates in the corporate sector, composed of joint-stock companies, and only a proportion of the corporate sector is accounted for by companies whose shares are publicly traded.[19] This proportion is smaller in continental Europe than in the United States or the United Kingdom.

Some people are prepared to invest their savings in shares voluntarily. But others will not take the associated risk and prefer other kinds of investment. That is one explanation for the concentration in the distribution of share ownership. In the United States, for instance, the Securities and Exchange Commission has demonstrated that 87% of the population on the lower level of income distribution owns only 1% of the shares, while those in higher income brackets own 99%. Within this group, the richest 1% own 80% of the shares, and the very richest 0.1% own 40% of the shares.[20]

So real capitalism is not "people's capitalism." In the light of the American figures, it seems a curious idea to turn all citizens into shareholders overnight by a free distribution of shares. To use Hayek's terminology again, this is a "constructivist" idea, artificial, contrived, and therefore quite alien to the real development of capitalism. I do not think the whole population treasures an inward desire to own a little piece of share capital. Moreover, there is a danger that the expert, honest and adequately supervised institutions and staff required for a primary and a secondary market in shares for such a giant extent will be absent.[21]

---

19. This should be understood to mean the shares which are quoted and traded on the stock exchange.

20. The figures are from J. O. Light and W. L. White (1979, p. 338).

21. [Although investment funds are mentioned in the study as "bank-like organizations" that deserve development, the services they offer small investors are not dealt with in detail here. Such funds play an important part in "voucher schemes" for privatization based on free distribution, as they do in the Czech Republic and Russia. Instead of buying specific shares for themselves, voucher-holders can opt to buy units in an investment fund, which has a capital strength many times greater with which to buy shares in many companies. The problem is whether the investment funds are capable of playing an active part as owners in the supervision and governance of the companies. This can hardly be expected, due to very wide spread of company share in their portfolios.

For my part I can expect only one benefit to come from mass share-distribution campaigns, and that is a drastic reduction in the proportion of state ownership. That may facilitate the expansion of a dominant group inside a joint-stock company, because it will no longer be confronted with a predominant state owner. This advantage in itself should not be underestimated, but one cannot expect too much of it either. Ownership of share or voucher allocations for every citizen will do little to further the two purpose to which I gave particular emphasis in the chapter on value criteria: development of broad strata of entrepreneurs and business people (objective 1-a), and strengthening of the incentive toward efficiency (objective 2-a). At the same time, I fear there will be negative effects for the other economic criteria. The state treasury, hard-pressed in any case, loses the potential income from sales (criterion 2-c). Some recipients of the gift soon pass on their shares or vouchers and appear on the consumer market with the proceeds, which raises the inflationary pressure (criterion 2-d). In all events, this is a trade-off in which the advantages of speeding up privatization are opposed by drawbacks which merit serious consideration.

It seems there will not be a general, free distribution of shares or vouchers in East Germany or Hungary, but implementation of such ideas are quite far advanced in Poland and Czechoslovakia. Experience may refute the skepticism expressed above, in which case I am prepared to review my position.

As mentioned before, the justifications given for schemes which distribute shares or vouchers to all citizens free of charge include arguments based on distributive ethics as well: this is considered to be a start for the new capitalism that is fair and offers equal opportunities (objective 4-c). I have put forward some of my counter-arguments already. I would now like to add a further observation after the survey of institutional forms of ownership. Those who really want to improve the equality of opportunity and approve of distributing state property free of charge should press for the donation of truly profit-yielding shares to charities, health and educational institutes, foundations offering scholarships and other similar, non-state, autonomous institutions.

It is worth stressing, however, that the foundation and healthy development of investment funds can be extremely useful. They are indispensable on the modern capital market because of their ability to pool the capital of many small investors who would shrink from the responsibility of choosing, buying, and selling shares alone. *New footnote.*]

This would really help to improve the position of those way down on the distribution scale of income and wealth, and would do so more effectively than a hand-out of shares or vouchers to rich and poor alike.

At this point it is worth summing up briefly my point of view on free distribution, which has been touched upon at several points in the study. There is, in my opinion, a case for a gratuitous transfer of part of the wealth formerly owned by state to new private owners. The following can be included among them: private, non-profit pension and insurance institutions, cultural and educational institutions, charitable societies, foundations, and churches. In effect, the discount price of shares purchased by employees also contains a gift element. These transfers should only be made under specified conditions. (The conditions have been mentioned in this study.) I do not see a justification for any distribution of gifts beyond that.[22]

IV Domestic and Foreign Ownership

The question arises with all forms of ownership and institutions discussed so far as to whether the owner is domestic or foreign. Let me first put forward two extreme points of view. One is a position of narrow minded nationalism and xenophobia, whose exponents want to exclude all foreign imports of capital, seeing in them a threat to national independence and the specific national character of the emerging economy.

This position, in my view, causes serious damage. Eastern Europe has a huge need for foreign support in all forms. It is particularly important to have direct foreign investment of capital in all sectors of the economy, but most of all in the financial sector. It is desirable that foreign capital should take part in the purchase of the firms formerly owned by the state. Where the property is bought by a serious foreign firm, it enters as a real owner, fulfilling the requirements of criterion 2-a, that there should be an incentive towards efficiency and strict control over management.

I also do not agree with the other extreme: the position that the proportion of foreign capital in any sector is quite immaterial. The econo-

22. In my book [1989] (1990), I rejected the idea of granting all citizens free shares or other securities, and did not touch on other forms of free transfer at all. So my present position corrects my earlier one on an important point, because I now support a few forms of free transfer indicated to be both feasible and desirable.

my contains key positions which are expedient to keep in national hands, because they are indispensable to sovereignty. It is worth ensuring, through a circumspect policy, that the source of all capital investments from abroad should not be concentrated in a single country, but spread among various countries. This gives the recipient country more scope for manoeuvre and so reinforces its independence. Apart from those considerations, there is a need for the country's own citizens to take part in the forming of a large business class, as that will strengthen the domestic base for a market economy founded on private property. Among the requirements of criterion 1-a, transformation of society in the direction of *embourgeoisement*, is that capitalism should strike root primarily in domestic soil.

V The Pace of Privatization

Those who take part in the debates on privatization are frequently asked whether they recommend fast or slow privatization. I think the question is phrased in the wrong way. No one would call himself an advocate of slowness. If I may add a subjective comment here, I myself am particularly put out if people call me an advocate of slow privatization.

What the debate should be about is not the speed but the choice of values, the role assigned to the state, and the assessment of the importance of the various forms of ownership and types of owner. Once anyone takes a position on these points at issue, the speed to be expected arises *as a result* of that decision.

I would like to declare that I am a believer in the process of privatization proceeding as fast as possible. But I do not think that it can be accelerated by some artful trick. I do not believe that finding some clever organizational form plus bureaucratic aggressiveness in enforcement are sufficient conditions for fast privatization.

The key issue, in my view, is not the pace at which the wealth hitherto owned by the state is transferred into private hands. The most important thing is the pace at which the private sector grows, (i) in the form of newly established firms, or (ii) through the transfer of state wealth, or by combinations of both these forms.

The following calculation is easy to check. Let us assume that at the start of the privatization process, the state sector accounts for 75% of the actual GDP and the private sector for 25%.[23] Production by the pri-

23. This includes the informal private sector not considered in the official statistics.

vate sector then rises by 25% a year and production by the state-owned sector falls by 10% a year. Under those conditions, the private sector will dominate production at the end of the fourth year. Privatization in the broader sense depends on the difference in pace between the two processes, and above all on the vitality of the private sector, not on how cunning a way can be found of transferring state-owned shares into private hands.[24]

There are grounds for optimism in that. The course of privatization is not ultimately set by the wisdom or stupidity, the strength or weakness of Eastern European governments, opposition forces, foreign governments, international organizations, or advisers at home or abroad. At most, they may slow down or speed up the events. The process is directed by an irresistible inner force: the inherent motivation of the present and future private owners.

References

Alchian, Armen A. 1950. "Uncertainty, Evolution, and Economic Theory." *Journal of Political Economy* 58 (93): 211–221.

Alchian, Armen A. 1974. "Foreword." In *The Economics of Property Rights*, edited by E. G. Furubotn and S. Pejovich. Cambridge, Mass.: Ballinger Publishing Company, pp. xiii–xv.

Ehrlich, Éva. 1985. "The Size Structure of Manufacturing Establishments and Enterprises: An International Comparison." *Journal of Comparative Economics* 9 (3): 267–295.

Fischer, Stanley, and Gelb, Alan. 1990. "Issues in Socialist Economy Reform." Working Paper WPS 565. Washington, D.C.: World Bank.

Friedmann, Jacques. 1989. "Sur l'expérience de privatisation et sur les noyaux stables." *Commentaire*, pp. 11–18.

Frydman, Roman, and Rapaczynski, Andrzej. 1990. "Markets and Institutions in Large Scale Privatizations." *Economic Research Report*. New York: New York University, pp. 90–420.

Hayek, Friedrich A. 1960. *The Constitution of Liberty*. London: Routledge and Kegan, and Chicago: Chicago University Press.

24. [The calculation was optimistic in that it assumed there would be growth, or at worst stagnation in aggregate production. To expect private-sector production to grow by 25% from one year to the next is unrealistic in case of a general recession. In the event a general recession has ensued in every postsocialist country. (See the seventh study.) Disregarding this, although the numerical results of the calculation have not proved correct, I still consider the qualitative conclusion to be valid: how quickly the private sector becomes dominant depends on the difference in growth rate between the two sectors. *New footnote.*]

Hayek, Friedrich A. 1973. *Legislation and Liberty*. Chicago: Chicago University Press.

Hinds, Manuel. 1990. *Issues in the Introduction of Market Forces in Eastern European Socialist Countries*. Mimeo. Washington, D.C.: World Bank.

Kornai, János. [1989], 1990. *The Road to a Free Economy. Shifting from a Socialist System: The Example of Hungary*. New York: W. W. Norton.

Lewandowski, Janusz, and Szomburg, Jan. 1989. "Property Reform as a Basis for Social and Economic Reform." *Communist Economies* 1 (3): 257–268.

Light, J. O., and White, William L. 1979. *The Financial System*. Homewood, Ill.: R. D. Irwin.

Lipton, David, and Sachs, Jeffrey. 1990. "Privatization in Eastern Europe: The Case of Poland." *Brookings Papers on Economic Activity* (2): 293–333.

Móra, Mária. 1991. "The (Pseudo)-Privatization of State-Owned Enterprise." *Acta Oeconomica* 43: 37–58.

Murrell, Peter. 1990*a*. *The Nature of Socialist Economies: Lessons from Eastern European Foreign Trade*. Princeton: Princeton University Press.

Murrell, Peter. 1990*b*. *An Evolutionary Perspective on Reform of the Eastern European Economies*. Mimeo. College Park: University of Maryland.

Schaffer, Mark E. 1990. *On the Use of Pension Funds in the Privatization of Polish State-Owned Enterprises*. Mimeo. London: London School of Economics.

Schumpeter, Joseph A. [1911] 1968. *The Theory of Economic Development. An Inquiry into Profits, Capital, Credit, Interest and Business Cycles*. Cambridge, Mass.: Harvard University Press.

Schumpeter, Joseph A. 1939. *Business Cycles: A Theoretical, Historical and Statistical Analysis of the Capitalist Progress*. New York: McGraw-Hill.

Schumpeter, Joseph A. 1949. "Economic Theory and Entrepreneurial History." In *Change and the Entrepreneur*. Cambridge, Mass: Research Center in Entrepreneurial History, Harvard University, pp. 63–84. Reprinted in J. A. Schumpeter, *Essays*. New Brunswick and Oxford: R.V. Clemence, 1989, pp. 253–271.

Stark, David. 1990. "Privatization in Hungary: From Plan to Market or From Plan to Clan?" *East European Politics and Societies* 4 (3): 351–392.

Szelényi, Iván. 1988. *Socialist Entrepreneurs: Embourgeoisement in Rural Hungary*. Madison: University of Wisconsin Press.

Tinbergen, Jan. 1952. *On the Theory of Economic Policy*. Amsterdam: North-Holland.

Voszka, Éva. 1991. "Tulajdonreform vagy privatizáció?," (Reform of Ownership or Privatization?). *Közgazdasági Szemle* 38 (6): 117–133.

5

The Postsocialist Transition and the State: Reflections in the Light of Hungarian Fiscal Problems[1]

I deal here with only one of the innumerable problems that arise during the transformation of the postsocialist countries: the role of the state in the economy. My treatment is based on the experiences of Hungary, but I believe the problems I discuss are quite general and will arise sooner or later in all postsocialist countries, though they may vary in intensity and form. Although my illustrations are from Hungary, the study is not intended to offer an overall survey of the Hungarian economy. One feature, perhaps, is worth noting: while several countries in the region face grave economic problems and may even be threatened by chaos, the transition in Hungary is taking place under orderly conditions, and there are signs of promising economic development.

I The Suggestions in Western Writings

Of course, the first trip that academic economists like ourselves make in search of guidance is to the library, where the body of writing on the division of labor between the state and the market is certainly abundant, even embarrassingly so.

Many economists in the postsocialist region, disillusioned with central planning, are prone to make an uncritical, mythical cult of the

1. Great assistance was given to me by Eszter Erdélyi, Mária Móra, László Muraközy, Mária Zita Petschnig, Anna Seleny, István György Tóth, and Alexandra Vacroux in gathering the materials for this study and the information that serves as the background for the analysis, and I take this opportunity to thank them for their support. I am grateful to Brian McLean and Julianna Parti for translating the text, which was originally written in Hungarian. I received valuable comments on the first draft of the study from Francis M. Bator, Tamás Bauer, Zsuzsa Dániel, Martin S. Feldstein, George Kopits, Álmos Kovács, Michael Marrese, and László Urbán. Of course, the author alone bears the responsibility for any errors that remain. The research was supported by the Hungarian National Scientific Research Foundation (OTKA).

market. One effective cure for this disorder is to read Western writings on the shortcomings of the market mechanism. They convincingly prove the existence of several fundamental problems to which the market alone has no reassuring solution: for example, preserving the macroequilibrium of the economy, ensuring a fair distribution of income, accounting for the effect of externalities, supplying an adequate quantity of public goods, and limiting the power of monopolies. The writers suggest that, where market failure occurs, the state should actively intervene.[2]

There is another strand of Western literature, however, that persuasively shows how political action, politicians, and bureaucrats, perhaps even more significantly than the market, can fail to coordinate the economy. This doubt, voiced long ago by the Austrian school and then reformulated in the arguments of public-choice theory, has induced economists to reconsider the problem.[3] Are those who intervene in the economy in the state's name intent only on serving the public interest? The question strikes a strong chord in anyone who has lived under the socialist system. Similarly relevant is the analysis critical of the welfare state for imposing a high level of redistribution that dulls the incentive for investment, innovation, and enterprise.[4]

However, when an Eastern European economist comes out of the library, he stops in confusion. He is still unfamiliar with capitalism from within; he would like to rely on the professional literature, but at least at first glance it seems to be giving him strongly conflicting directions. What should he be fighting for after all: a more or a less active state?

This confusion can be contained to some extent by studying the literature more thoroughly. The normative proposals to be drawn from the theoretical literature are always *conditional*. The conditions under which the arguments apply are either stated explicitly or implied. Any

2. Earlier summaries of the theories of market failure can be found in the works of F. M. Bator (1958) and W. J. Baumol (1965). For a present-day survey, see J. E. Stiglitz et al. (1989). As research progresses, light is shed on the shortcomings of an unfettered market in more and more areas. Consideration, for instance, of imperfect competition and economies of scale leads to several alterations in the earlier concept vindicating free trade and suggests that, under certain conditions, the state may be justified in playing a more active role. An overall account of the wide-ranging research that followed the pioneering work by P. R. Krugman, E. Helpman, and others can be found in Helpman (1990).

3. See J. Buchanan and G. Tullock (1962) and W. A. Niskanen (1971).

4. See e.g., A. Lindbeck (1988). An account of left- and right-wing criticisms of the welfare state is given by C. Offe (1984).

Western expert giving advice to a postsocialist economy or any economist in a postsocialist country using Western literature when reaching his position has a duty to clarify these assumptions very carefully before citing "authoritative" Western economic writings. Let me mention just two typical assumptions.

1. The cited literature refers to a mature market and a stable, deeply rooted, and well-established democratic state that operates in the advanced capitalist countries of our time. The trouble is that the market and state in Hungary and the other postsocialist countries differ from this situation in several respects: the private sector is still immature, and the democratic institutions are weak and not yet fully developed.
2. The literature assigns roles to the state and to the market assuming a capitalist system with permanent or slowly changing institutions and operating under robust rules of behavior. In contrast, the postsocialist system is in the midst of a revolutionary transformation: institutions vanish at breathtaking speed, others are just appearing, the legal system is changing at a very rapid rate by historical standards, and the behavior of every player in the economy keeps changing accordingly. So, a special kind of dynamic analysis is needed.

II The Political and Governmental Spheres in Postsocialist Hungary

Let me try to outline briefly, in almost telegraphic style, the characteristics of the political and governmental sphere in Hungary today.[5] I do not give a similar description of the present state of the market here, because this will emerge in the later part of the study.

Although a measure of political liberalization had begun earlier, the turning point in Hungary came in 1989–1990. The Communist party's monopoly over government ended, other parties became free to organize, and free elections were held for the first time in 43 years.

5. Rather than using an overall, comprehensive definition of "the state," I will try to break the political sphere down into its components. Different approaches to this can be distinguished in political science, among them functionalist models, the public-choice theory of economics referred to earlier, analyses that examine the conflicts between groups and classes, and the various institutionalist approaches. In my view, these are, for the most part, complementary, rather than mutually exclusive explanations, and I have tried to draw on the ideas of all the trends in this study. Summaries can be found in the works of J. D. Aberbach, R. D. Putnam, and B. A. Rockman (1981) and P. A. Hall (1986).

A government with a parliamentary majority was formed. The main roadblock to the development of a market economy, the political domination of a Communist party that had liquidated or sought to liquidate capitalism, was removed by this radical change in the structure of power.

The legislature, executive administration, and judiciary were only formally separate under the socialist system. In fact, the officials filling all the posts in each branch were selected by the Communist party, which directed their activities. The separation of the branches of state power only became institutionalized after the political turning point.

Parliament is now mastering its new role. The myriad of rules required for a constitutional state evolved in the developed democracies over a long historical period, while in Hungary the most essential laws are being drafted at a forced pace. The sluggishness and constant delay with which the government drafts legislation and the rate at which Parliament can cope with its legislative load form one of the most distressing bottlenecks in the advance toward a modern market economy. Most members of Parliament are political novices: they do not have enough time or a sufficiently large staff of experts and advisers to conduct a thorough study of the bills, let alone to devise legislative proposals of their own. Therefore, Parliament cannot really be said to be supervising the work of the administration closely. The courts too are inexperienced in imposing law and order on a market economy.

Before the political turning point came, the anticommunist forces were united in the face of a common enemy. This cooperation between them has been replaced by bitter political clashes between the governing and opposition parties, and even within the governing coalition. There is nothing surprising about it, as the same phenomenon occurs under all parliamentary systems. However, the absence of a broad political consensus almost precludes the possibility of resolving the grave problems on the agenda, such as curbing inflation, bringing about budgetary stability, and restructuring production, because they all involve unpopular measures that require serious sacrifices. When the political rivalry for power becomes acute, politicians aim to maximize their electoral chances, not a "social welfare function."

According to the normative theory of a classical democracy, there should be a clear demarcation line between the politicians directly responsible to the electorate and the bureaucracy that loyally serves each successive constitutional government, regardless of political program. Political appointments and "civil service" positions should be clearly distinguished by law or respected convention. In the post-socialist political system, this distinction is not yet made unambiguously. The governing parties of today have thoroughly learned the oft-quoted slogan of Vladimir Ilyich Lenin: the question of power is the fundamental question. Political loyalty is a far more important criterion than competence when a great many posts are to be filled.

The bureaucracy has greater expertise in Hungary than in other postsocialist countries because the partial reforms commenced in 1968 induced it to adapt to the requirements of a market economy. Yet it has nothing like the knowledge or experience required to perform the administrative tasks of a modern capitalist economy. The change of system, moreover, puts the bureaucrats' livelihoods at risk: who knows who will be dismissed when? Servility spreads. Many of the more-talented specialists leave the state service for more lucrative and secure jobs in the private sector. State discipline is lax due to inexperience and uncertainty, and there is a great friction in the process of enforcing the laws and state regulations.[6]

We are dealing neither with the philosopher-statesmen of Plato, who rise above all selfish criteria, nor with the expert, law-abiding, punctilious bureaucracy of Max Weber. Nor are we dealing with the political decision-makers described in studies of welfare economics, who exclusively serve the public interest. Therefore, any economist arguing that market forces should be curtailed must soberly consider that *this* is the kind of state to which he now wishes to assign a function, and this is the kind of state it will remain for some time to come.

The only components of the political sphere discussed so far have been the organizations of the state and the political parties. Two other important phenomena that can affect the operation of both the state and the market must be mentioned.

First, it is inestimably important that the press, often called the fourth arm of government in the mechanism of checks and balances, is now free in Hungary.[7] Anyone trying to abuse the state's power or to mismanage the state's money runs a risk of being exposed in the press.

6. T. Skocpol (1985) pointed out the "capacity" of the state, defined as its actual ability to perform specific tasks, is an important determining factor of state activity. The scarcity of this capacity, which I mentioned in connection with the drafting and enacting of legislation, also hinders law enforcement.

7. The increasing freedom of the press ties in with the fact that a sizable proportion of the press has passed into private ownership.

Second, what political scientists call the "civil society," the public's capacity to organize itself, is steadily awakening. Organizations embodying certain strata, groups, and occupations are forming in succession and are making their voices heard. Such special-interest groups are often referred to disparagingly in the United States and can certainly play a detrimental part as well, but the citizens of a country where all kinds of voluntary and spontaneous association were persecuted are better place to value the advantage of people's freedom to associate and apply political pressure. It must be added that, in the economic sphere, the expression of civil society remains obscure. The rearguard actions of the unions surviving from the old order, combined with the weakness of the new unions, leave employees without a mature and effective system of representation. The employers' organizations are immature as well. In other words, the kind of European extraparliamentary representative associations capable of overriding narrow professional interests and negotiating with each other with a sense of responsibility for the nation have yet to develop or gain strength. There is a danger, therefore, of populist organizations winning over large numbers of people and impeding the process of political and economic consolidation. This is one of the vulnerable points in the new democracy, for such populist movements can prevent the conclusion of a "social contract" among broad layers of society willing to show moderation in order to help overcome the economic difficulties.[8]

My general position on the division of labor between the state and the market is supported strongly by the current situation in Hungary's political and governmental sphere. (In fact, I could call it my prejudice, since my opinion is clearly based on a value judgment.) I am ready to ask for government intervention so long as it is clear in the case concerned that the market left to itself will decide badly and there is a very strong likelihood that state intervention will improve matters. I must be convinced that the authority concerned is in expert, impartial, and honest hands, and that in this particular case it is really possible to ensure a public scrutiny which will force the state to act wisely. However, if I am in doubt about which to leave the decision to, an ill-operating market or an ill-operating state, and I can only make a random choice, my instincts tell me to choose the market. One factor here

8. In 1990, one small group in Hungary, the taxi drivers, who were well organized through their radio links, managed to cripple the capital with a blockade to protest a rise in gasoline prices. Many employees were sympathetic to the taxi drivers, with whom members of the government negotiated before television cameras.

is certainly that I am an Eastern European, for my compatriots and I have been disappointed very often by the state, and our confidence is not easily restored. This preference will be the underlying philosophy of the rest of the study.

III Four Fiscal Problems

Socialism before the reforms was marked by totalitarian power, in other words, by a hyperactive state which sought to control all activity in society. Although the process of partial reform that began in 1968 produced some reduction in the role of the state in many respects, the new democratic system has still inherited "big government."[9]

The weight and scale of the state can be measured in several ways, one of the most important measures being the ratio of the government budget to GDP. Table 5.1 shows that the government in Hungary withdraws and redistributes more than 60% of GDP, whereas the typical proportion in Western Europe is 40-45%, and it is even lower, in

Table 5.1
Summary of general government operations: International comparison

Country	Year	Revenue (as a percentage of GDP)	Expenditure (as a percentage of GDP)
Austria	(1988)	46.9	49.7
Canada	(1989)	40.3	43.9
Denmark	(1989)	59.6	59.4
France	(1989)	46.2	47.8
Greece	(1988)	32.7	46.3
Netherlands	(1989)	51.1	56.6
Portugal	(1988)	40.7	45.0
Spain	(1987)	35.0	38.6
Sweden	(1988)	59.1	56.9
United States	(1988)	34.3	36.5
West Germany	(1989)	45.7	45.9
Hungary	**(1989)**	**61.3**	**63.7**

Source: Compiled by G. Kopits and L. Muraközy, based on International Monetary Fund (1990).
Note: The data refer to consolidated general government revenues and expenditures (i.e., they include revenues and expenditures of central and local governments and extrabudgetary funds).

9. The role of the state under the socialist system is dealt with in my 1992 book.

fact, in countries with a level of development similar to Hungary's. Table 5.2 does not register any clearly perceptible tendency toward a decline in this ratio, which is stubbornly stuck at a size close to 60%.[10]

As the subtitle of this study suggests, I am primarily concerned here with fiscal questions. What policy would be required in order to reduce the proportion of production withdrawn and spent by the state? Given political, social, and economic conditions, what is the probability of a policy producing "smaller government?" For reasons of space, I do not even intend to cover the whole sphere of fiscal problems.[11] I will discuss the following four topics: administrative expendi-

Table 5.2
Summary of Hungarian general government operations

Year	Revenue	Expenditure	Deficit (-) or surplus (+)
		(as a percentage of GDP)	
1981	61.0	63.9	-3.2
1982	59.1	61.2	-2.1
1983	60.9	62.0	-1.1
1984	60.8	59.4	1.4
1985	60.0	61.2	-1.1
1986	63.2	66.0	-2.9
1987	60.3	64.1	-3.9
1988	63.7	63.6	0.0
1989	61.3	63.7	-2.5
1990	57.9	57.4	0.5
1991	55.3	57.8	-2.7

Sources: Compiled by L. Muraközy. Figures for the period 1981–1990 are based on International Monetary Fund (1991); 1991: Data given by Pénzügyminisztérium (Ministry of Finance, Hungary).
Note: The data refer to consolidated general government revenues and expenditures. (For their explanation, see the note to table 5.1.)

10. [The figures for 1990 and 1991 in table 5.2 have been given in a corrected form, making use of more recent figures and of the debate going on in the professional press. See I. Kovács (1993) and Cs. Laszló (1993). *New footnote.*]

11. Let me mention specifically two subjects that are omitted from this study even though they tie in closely with a discussion of the role of the state. One is the restoration of macroequilibrium and macro management of the economy in general; the other is the role of the state in the privatization of firms hitherto under state ownership. Discussion of them has been avoided not because I consider them unimportant, but because there is already a wealth of literature analyzing them both. I have also attempted to discuss them myself, for instance in my [1989] 1990 book and in the fourth study in this volume. I prefer in this study to bring up a few questions that have received less attention so far.

tures, assistance to loss-making firms and unemployment benefits, taxation of the private sector, and welfare expenditures. Although all four topics are connected with the budget, I would like to go beyond the scope of public finance in the narrow sense and examine each problem in its political, social, and general economic context; and to that extent the subject of my study falls under the category of *political economy*.

A. Administrative Expenditures

Demands for cuts in administrative spending are heard in every budget debate in every parliament in the world. They are particularly apposite in Hungary, where spending on general public services and public order and safety in 1990 was equivalent to 8.8% of GDP, which is inadmissibly high. For comparison's sake, the same item accounted for 5.5% of GDP in 1988 in West Germany, 5.1% in Chile, and 4.4% in Denmark.[12] The government of the new democracy promises to cut such expenditures year after year, and the opposition, rightly, calls for a far more vigorous reduction in the overall size of the budget.

Two opposing trends can be observed. On the one hand, earlier administrative expenditures have ceased or decreased, while on the other, new administrative expenses have appeared. Let me give four examples.

1. The vast bureaucracy of the Communist party, which almost duplicated the state apparatus in size, has been disbanded. At the same time, a new professional political apparatus, made up of the employees of all the parties and the staff assisting all the members of national and local assemblies, has been formed.

2. Many institutions of the centralized planned economy are being eliminated; for example, the planning and price offices have shut down, and several ministries that previously controlled production amalgamated, with a smaller combined staff. The new system, however, requires some new agencies: offices for privatization, bank regulation, insurance regulation, monitoring the observance of anti-monopoly legislation, an agency dealing with small business, an auditor-general's office to supervise the financial affairs of the state bureaucracy, and so on.

12. Calculated by L. Muraközy based on data from the International Monetary Fund (1990).

3. The secret police, a pillar of the old system, has been disbanded, but there is a demand for more police to combat an appalling increase in common crime. Among the reasons for the crime wave are the dissolution of the nationwide network of informers, the easing of the obligation to register changes of residence with the police, and the opening of the borders, which makes drug trafficking easier. In other words, the increase in crime is partly explained by the harmful side-effects of a healthy process, namely the abolition of the police state.

4. Under the old system, many disputes were settled arbitrarily by the party secretary or by some administrative organization, but in a constitutional state this becomes mainly the task of the courts. As the private sector and the prestige of the law increase, so does the number of court cases.[13] The backlog of undecided cases will continue to grow unless the present staff of the courts is enlarged.

To sum up point A, an effort must be made to cut back administrative expenses, but high hopes cannot be placed on this effort contributing to a substantial reduction of the budget: GDP ratio in the near future.

B. Assistance to Loss-Making Firms and Unemployment Benefits

It is apparent from table 5.3 that the subsidies and transfers to firms in Hungary have been showing a tendency to fall for a long time (unlike those in Czechoslovakia and Bulgaria, also shown in the table, where they tended to grow before the political changes). However, a further, more vigorous dismantling of assistance brings up some sensitive problems that require detailed analysis.

The socialist system produced a curious phenomenon which I termed in my earlier writings the syndrome of the *soft budget constraint*.[14] In this situation the firm's spending is not strictly constrained by its financial position or, ultimately, in a dynamic context, by its revenues. Even if it should land in serious financial difficulties, make steady losses, and become insolvent, it can count on help from the state. Such a firm will be given tax concessions or allowed to postpone

---

13. The Budapest courts received 9,000 new civil cases in 1988 and 16,400 in 1990. The numbers of requests for payment injunctions received by the courts in the same two years were 31,000 and 64,000, respectively (statement by the president of the Metropolitan Judiciary in the daily paper *Népszabadság*, November 23, 1991).
14. For an explanation of the concept, see footnote 15 in the first study.

Table 5.3
Subsidies and transfers to firms: International comparison

Year	Bulgaria	Czechoslovakia	Hungary
	(as percentage of GDP)		
Total current expenditures:			
1985	48	51	53
1989	52	55	57
Subsidies and transfers to firms:			
1985	13	15	21
1989	15	19	16

Source: G. Kopits (1991, pp. 22–23).
Notes: Subsidies and transfers to firms include product-specific price subsidies, explicit interest-rate subsidies, and debt servicing on behalf of firms and institutions. Subsidies and transfers constitute one component of total current expenditures (*i.e.*, the data in the first lines of the table).

payment of its taxes, it will receive a subsidy, or it will gain access to soft loans. It is quite safe in building into its expectations a state bailout to ensure its survival. This softness of the budget constraint has a number of baneful consequences, among them that it leads to toleration of inefficiency, postponement of adjustment to demand, and mistaken investment decisions.

It is a widely accepted view that this harmful phenomenon is incompatible with a market economy, so that in the postsocialist transition period the budget constraint on state-owned firms must be hardened at last. The question is: to what extent will this requirement receive only lip service and to what extent will it be acted upon? No clear answer can be given because at present there are conflicting tendencies at work, and it is unclear which of them will prevail.

The situation of firms varies, and so does their behavior.[15] Some have moved toward privatization, converting themselves into joint-stock companies or planning to do so in the near future, and have negotiated with prospective Hungarian or foreign private owners. However, I wish to focus attention here on the ones that have not yet taken any practical steps towards privatization. Some of these have adapted quite successfully to the new situation, but others are facing serious problems, and in the latter cases the typical attitude is to try and muddle through. That means on the physical or real side of pro-

15. On the position of loss-making state-owned firms, see the article by M. Móra (1991) and the more detailed study (Móra, 1990) on which it is based.

duction that they utilize stocks hoarded under the shortage economy without replacing them, neglect maintenance and renewal, and perhaps sell off a plant or an office building. There is continual disinvestment; in other words, the firm eats itself up by consuming its own assets. Parallel events occur on the monetary side, where the steady losses increase the firm's indebtedness. It no longer makes punctual or full payments of its taxes and social-security contributions, or of the interest and repayments on its debts to the commercial banks.[16] Most commonly of all, the firm stops paying the bills of the firms that supply its inputs. There is no voluntary credit contract in any of these cases: the debtor is forcing the creditor to lend by refusing to pay. This brings me to the other side of the problem: how the creditor reacts to this kind of behavior by the firm.[17]

Softness of the budget constraint actually means that the involuntary creditor tolerates the debtor's default. In postsocialist Hungary, the present situation is ambivalent, as mentioned earlier, because the accustomed tolerance continues to be shown in some of the cases, but the opposite also occurs. Already there are, albeit infrequently, instances of the tax or social-security authorities or the banks taking measures to wind up a debtor firm. More commonly, the suppliers initiate liquidation proceedings against firms that are unable to pay their bills.[18]

Although firms had also been liquidated earlier, that constituted *administrative selection*, because the death sentence or the reprieve came from the bureaucracy. Now one can see the first signs of *natural selection*. The latter, once it really develops to the full, will take place as a decentralized market process. Instead of matters of life and death being decided by an arm of the state, proceedings against defaulting debtors will be taken by creditors acting in their own best financial interest.

In fact, there has been liquidation legislation on the statute books in Hungary for some time, and the legal framework for the exit of insolvent firms was available in other respects as well. These were not taken advantage of before, but it now seems as if there is a movement

16. The sum of the first two debts (unpaid taxes and social-security contributions) in mid-1991 was greater than the entire budget deficit planned for 1992.

17. Hardening the budget constraint is partly a *fiscal* matter, since it is closely related to state subsidies and to taxation. However, the problem is far more complicated in nature than that, and so I must go beyond the subject-matter of this study outlined earlier, for instance by touching briefly on aspects of *monetary* policy as well.

18. See K. Lányi, ed. (1991, p. 64).

to do so. A surge of liquidations in the state sector is forecast for 1992, and if it takes place, it will be accurate to say that the budget constraint has hardened.

How this change should be appraised is the subject of much debate. For my part, I consider it painful but healthy. Let me recall Joseph A. Schumpeter's well-known concept of *creative destruction*.[19] Renewal and reorganization of production, technical progress, and innovation are normally accompanied by destruction of the old product lines, organizations, and institutions. This cleansing is essential for development. For a number of reasons, the socialist system was incapable of it. The old industrial dinosaurs, the distended, sluggish, clumsy giants, survived, and the softness of the budget constraint served as the financial mechanism for warding off creative destruction; but the destruction has now begun, in the form of various corrective measures. Five closely connected processes can be cited:

1. Anti-inflationary monetary policy inevitably entails a contraction of production. In some cases this means the total closure of firms, and in others it means curtailment of production. The Schumpeterian interpretation of the business cycle seems to be justified in this context; a macro recession accelerates natural selection and the destruction that clears the decks for creation. There was no way that the planned economy, with its drive for continual expansion and forced growth, could perform this selection.

2. There is a restructuring in the sectoral composition of production. The share of manufacturing in total output is falling, and the share of services is rising. This involves a halt or cut in the activity of certain manufacturing firms.

3. Closely related to the previous process is the restructuring of exports. The collapse of the Comecon market has brought dire problems for firms that specialized in supplying it and prove to be incapable of satisfying the demands of new markets.

4. Restructuring takes place in the size distribution of firms. There was an excessive concentration of production under the socialist system in Hungary, as there was in the other socialist countries. Firms were oversized, even in branches where there were no economies of

19. J. A. Schumpeter [1911] (1968) wrote about the benefits of destroying loss-makers in his first classical work. The expression "creative destruction" was introduced in his 1942 book (see J. A. Schumpeter, 1976, pp. 81–88). The Schumpeterian aspect of the transition process is emphasized in the work of P. Murrell (1990).

scale to justify it. Moreover, small undertakings were almost completely eliminated under pre-reform classical socialism, and too little scope was left for medium-sized firms. Part of the corrective process consists of closing a good many firms that are oversized to the point of being inviable and cannot be broken down into smaller units.

5. The majority of the bureaucratically controlled state-owned firms under the socialist system operated at a low level of efficiency. Unemployment on the job was widespread. Efficiency has to improve as a result of the corrective process. Even if the volume of production were to stay the same, it could be achieved with a far smaller workforce.

All five corrective processes have serious side effects: jobs are eliminated on a massive scale. However, some of these processes (numbers 2–4) create as well as destroy: they provide new jobs, mainly in the private sector, and primarily in the small and medium-sized segments. This will be discussed again later. All that needs to be said in advance is that the creation of new jobs is failing to keep pace with the loss of old ones. Therefore, unemployment rises. This is a shattering experience under any system, but it is doubly painful under postsocialism, for people in Hungary's part of the world have been used not only to full employment but to absolute job security and even a chronic shortage of labor for a long time. Table 5.4 presents a short time-series. May 1990 was the particular moment in history when the number of unemployed persons exceeded the number of vacancies for the first time and the labor market switched over from a state of excess demand to one of excess supply. The rate of unemployment reached 7.3% in November 1991, which is quite high even for countries accustomed to unemployment. Unfortunately, according to the forecasts, a further rise in unemployment can be expected.[20]

What should the government do under the circumstances? Before trying to answer that question, let me say just a few words on what it should *not* try to do. It should not, in my opinion, yield to the pressure to relax monetary policy at the macro level and use casually dispersed loans and export subsidies, rashly raised nominal incomes, and budget-financed grand investments to whip up aggregate demand, particularly not in the state sector. The Hungarian inflation rate, which has

20. On the present state of the Hungarian labor market and unemployment, see the studies by J. Köllő (1990, 1991).

Table 5.4
Vacancies and unemployment in Hungary

Months		Number of registered vacancies	Number of registered unemployed persons
1990			
	January	37,711	23,426
	February	38,335	30,055
	March	34,048	33,682
	April	35,191	33,353
	May	37,938	38,155
	June	37,859	43,506
	July	36,222	50,292
	August	33,732	51,670
	September	26,969	56,115
	October	22,763	60,997
	November	17,150	69,982
	December	16,815	79,521
1991			
	January	12,949	100,526
	February	14,721	128,386
	March	13,583	144,840
	April	16,478	167,407
	May	14,919	165,022
	June	14,860	185,554
	July	15,186	216,568
	August	14,124	251,084
	September	15,351	292,756
	October	15,389	317,692
	November	13,021	351,285

Source: Reports of the Országos Munkaügyi Központ (National Labor Center, Hungary), 1990–1991.

been curbed with great difficulty and still lingers around 35% in 1991, would suddenly take off, with frightening consequences.

Another warning is needed, concerning the micro level. Now, amid the first signs that the budget constraint on firms is hardening, the government should not relapse into softening it again. I am convinced that it is better to accept the serious problem of unemployment openly (giving effective assistance, of course, to those losing their jobs) than to continue the policy of trying to cover up the superfluity of many inefficient workplaces by artificially sustaining terminally ill firms and perpetuating unemployment on the job. The danger of a relapse into the earlier soft-budget-constraint syndrome persists even under the present political conditions. The image of a politician intervening to bail out a firm in financial trouble is not unknown in the United States; nor is the prospect of interest groups lobbying for a protectionist policy to favor some sector or another. Another danger is that some of the banks may be ready to grant soft loans irresponsibly, calculating that their survival will be ensured no matter what, even in the last resort, at the taxpayer's expense. This attitude, recently observed in the Savings-and-Loan sector and parts of the banking system in the United States, is prevalent and deeply embedded in the postsocialist economy and its financial sphere.

It is desirable for many reasons that the ownership of the overwhelming majority of formerly state-owned firms should pass into private hands; but let no one think that the problem just outlined, the task of "creative destruction," can be comfortably solved by privatization. No buyer, domestic or foreign, willingly purchases a hopelessly insolvent firm with a view to carrying on its operations. At most there will be a buyer for the physical assets and human capital that belong to the firm. In some other instances, it will not be clear from the outset whether the privatized firm has any chance of financial recovery. If it does not succeed, the new owners (be they individual shareholders, mutual funds or other institutional owners) will no doubt shut it down as soon as it becomes apparent that the firm cannot operate at a profit. This is no less bitter a pill for those concerned, and it may be even more brutal than if the liquidation had preceded the privatization. Another possibility is that, after the privatization, the employers and employees of the private firm together may set about salvaging it by lobbying the connections they have built up under the new regime. This possibility brings us back to the starting point, the softness of the budget constraint.

I will now turn to the advisable measures. A *one-time, temporary* subsidy or loan could be granted to firms that the government wishes to give a last chance, just in case they can adapt to actual market conditions after all. However, it must be strictly stipulated that the subsidy is to be phased out and that the loan will not be repeated if the adaptation does not succeed. I feel somewhat uncertain about raising this possibility at all, because there remains the danger that all the phenomena that emerged in connection with the soft budget constraint may arise here as well.

The state must establish an adequate system of unemployment insurance. This should provide temporary assistance to cushion the shock, but it should not be allowed to weaken the incentive for the jobless to seek work and be prepared to adjust to the demand for labor. One favorable feature of the economic transformation in Hungary is that the organization of unemployment insurance was begun much earlier than in other postsocialist countries. The present system, however, leaves much to be desired; the amount, duration, and conditions of the benefit are all questionable.

The insurance must be accompanied by the organization of employment exchanges and retraining. This is undoubtedly a task for the state. It is laudable that it has begun in Hungary, although performance thus far leaves much room for improvement.

Finally, there is the most important task: job creation, primarily in the private sector. This leads to the problem discussed in the next section.

To sum up point B, the policy of hardening the budget constraint sets a *fiscal trap*. On the one hand, the state budget reduces expenditures by withdrawing subsides for state-owned firms that are incapable for surviving. The tougher fiscal discipline applied to state-owned firms should bring about an increase in tax revenues, assuming that firms will be capable of paying taxes at all. On the other hand, the hardening of the budget constraint may cause economic activity to contract more sharply, thereby reducing the tax base and, therefore, budgetary revenue. Meanwhile, spending on unemployment benefits represents a growing burden on the budget.[21] There is no way of

21. Unemployment benefits in Hungary are paid out of an extrabudgetary insurance fund formed out of contributions from employers and employees. This separate handling is expedient, but it does not alter the fact that this is *ultimately* a fiscal problem in two senses. Contributions to the fund are compulsory, not voluntary, and a kind of tax. If the fund should fall into deficit, the state budget guarantees to make it up out of other tax revenue.

predicting the net result of these conflicting trends accurately: will they improve or aggravate the overall fiscal situation? I consider a deterioration to be the more likely outcome in the next few years, but I think nonetheless that the grave short-term drawbacks must be accepted in order to gain the longer-term, lasting advantages: the development to be expected from the "creative destruction."

C. The Taxation of the Private Sector

Perhaps the most important tendency in the process of the transition is the very fast growth of the private sector. Mention was made in the last section of the destructive side of Schumpeter's "creative destruction." The mushrooming of new private enterprise forms perhaps the most conspicuous manifestation of the other side, creation. The private sector is the most likely source of mass job creation, the introduction of innovations, better supply to the consumer, and the winning of new export markets.

Unfortunately, given the system of statistical records in Hungary (and in the other postsocialist countries), for the time being it is not possible to measure the expansion of the private sector.[22] Expert estimates vary, but most of them fall inside the range of 25–35% for the private sector's contribution to GDP.[23]

Part of the private sector operates within the framework laid down by law. The tax authorities had records of 111,700 economic organizations in August 1991.[24] For comparison's sake, one should recall that a decade earlier there were some 3,000 large state-owned firms and a few thousand other large, quasi-state agricultural cooperatives in operation. The number of registered private undertakings has certainly grown very rapidly.

Private businesses have appeared in particularly large numbers in the service sector and in domestic and foreign trade. The latter obser-

22. Researchers are trying to gain a picture of the true extent of the private sector through confidential interviews, but they run up against great difficulties. N. Esti (1991, p. 23) writes in her report on a survey of private entrepreneurs that when questions were asked about income in the interviews, "it occurred on several occasions that an entrepreneur who had been patient so far declared the interview to be over at that point." In the main it was precisely those doing well who refused to respond.

23. The production of the private sector is compared here with the true GDP, in which both officially recorded production and the unrecorded contribution of informal private undertakings are included.

24. See Pénzügyminisztérium (1991, p. 848).

vation is supported by table 5.5. It is worth noting the appearance between 1989 and 1991 of more than 4,500 exporters that were not exporting at all in 1989. The change is still more conspicuous if a comparison is made with the earlier periods. In the prereform, classical socialist economy, the entire foreign trade turnover was monopolized by about two dozen giant, state-owned foreign trade firms.

Alongside the legal private undertakings there is a very extensive semilegal segment. This informal economy existed even under prereform classical socialism and grew very fast during the reform process. Defining real crime as black and undertakings that meticulously observe all the laws and regulations as white, the sphere I would like to mention here can be depicted as various shades of gray. Since the political turning point, there has been a considerable expansion of the "gray segment," to which a variety of kinds of activity belong. These include "moonlighting," the activity of people who have one foot still in the state sector, but who have stepped into the private sector with the other. There are others whose entire working time is spent in the private sector, but they evade the legal regulations. Many officially registered private undertakings operate partly in the white and partly in the gray segment.[25]

Table 5.5
Hungarian firms engaging in hard-currency exports

Size classes	Number of firms		Volume of trade (million $)	
	1989	1990	1989	1990
> $10 million	136	158	4,422	5,268
$0.5-10 million	668	1,115	1,700	2,554
< $0.5 million	1,899	5,108	172	347
Total	**2,703**	**6,381**	**6,294**	**8,169**

Source: K. Lányi and G. Oblath, eds. (1991, p. 76), based on the figures drawn from the data bank of KOPINT-DATORG.

25. A further indicator of the growth of the informal and formal private sector is the rapid increase in the hard-currency bank deposits of individuals. The source of such deposits is not asked of the depositors, but it is widely believed that a large part originates in private business activities, like exports or services to tourists in Hungary.

In the first nine months of 1991, the net increment of individuals' hard-currency deposits (called "net unrequited transfers" in official statistics) contributed 40% of the total positive balance of the current account (National Bank of Hungary, 1991, p. 24).

However varied the forms of gray activity may be, they have one feature in common: they involve *invisible earnings* that the tax authorities are unable to get their hands on. Which brings me to the fiscal side of the problem.

It was comparatively simple under the classical socialist system for the financial authorities to "get hold" of a large state-owned firm. The business accounts were easily checked, and the monobank simply deducted the sum due to the budget from the firm's account. These days, as I have mentioned, it is not easy to collect money even from state-owned firms. As far as the private sector is concerned, the "dark gray" part of it entirely evades its tax obligations and the "light gray" part evades at least some of them. This is not confined to personal income tax and corporate profits tax, for it extends to total or partial evasion of value-added tax, social-security contributions and all other kinds of payroll tax. It seems that as Hungary moves towards a market economy, citizens and authorities have adopted an "Italian style" attitude to taxation, rather than a Dutch or Swedish one, in which people dutifully pay their taxes.

This evaporation of tax revenues is one of the gravest obstacles to budgetary equilibrium. This situation, moreover, turns into the most serious infringement of the principle that taxation should be fair. The main factor in progressivity is not the formula used to decide the rates of taxation on visible earnings. The highest degree of regressivity results from the fact that the direct burdens of taxation are placed on visible earnings, while invisible earnings escape being taxed at all.

One task under these conditions is clearly to improve the efficiency of tax collection, which involves a great many things: more in situ inspections, more frequent and thorough audits and accounting requirements, and legal action when rules are broken.[26] This task creates one of the great political and economic dilemmas. On the one hand, both fiscal and fairness criteria demand forceful tax collection, but on the other, it must be recognized pragmatically that a large proportion of the new business people are emerging into the twilight world of a curious "early capitalism." Nothing will be gained here by brutal crackdowns or harassment of private entrepreneurs. That would only push some people deeper into illegality and discourage others from private enterprise altogether.

26. See M. C. de Jantscher, C. Silvani, and C. L. Vehorn (1991).

The measures against those breaking the law must be strict but within the bounds of legality and the norms of a civilized constitutional state, and as a complement there must be a range of changes to make it *advantageous* to abide by the law. A growing proportion of the private sector must be guided to legality by combinations of stick and carrot, as in the following examples of appropriate incentives.[27]

A businessman thinking of stepping out of semi-legality into the light of day might consider his choice as a kind of "deal." The service he receives is the rule of law, and the price he pays is tax. One major factor in the growth of the private sector is the impressive speed at which the legal system has developed. A range of new laws have been passed, including company, bankruptcy, banking, and accounting acts. A succession of others are being drafted, but it would be desirable to speed up the process. Let us hope that this legislative process will be accompanied by reinforcement of the courts and acceleration of their work. Private entrepreneurs will be attracted toward legality if that is the only way they can gain legal protection for their property. They will also be able to count on the just treatment of their complaints at court if they come into conflict with the bureaucracy.

Legalization of business transactions helps in enforcing private contracts. This benefits both the entrepreneur and the other party to the contract, which provides grounds for hoping that the state can find allies among the public. Here, however, all parties to a contract encounter a dilemma. Let me give two illustrations.

The rate of value-added tax is very high at present. If no receipt is provided by the seller or requested by the buyer, both sides can gain at the state's expense. However, a buyer who wants to complain later, for instance, because the quality is poor, has no legal redress. The more active the legal protection of buyers becomes in the future, the more common it will become for buyers to demand a receipt, even if that means paying a higher price, covering the value-added tax.

For the second example, consider that nowhere else in the world do the employer and the employee together have to pay a higher sum for social security, pension contributions, and unemployment insurance than they do in Hungary. It amounts to 55% of gross wages, and there are plans to raise it further to cover the increasing expenditures on

27. The economic development in Italy and Spain is enlightening in this respect. The legalization process there continued for some years and has probably not ended yet (see C. Sabel, 1982; L. A. Benton, 1990). The problems of legalizing the Hungarian informal private sector are analyzed by I. Ékes (1991) and A. Seleny (1991).

unemployment benefits.[28] If employers fail to register employees or if wages are underreported, then employers and employees can divide the saving in wage-related mandatory contributions between them. In many cases, employees do not lose much by it, since they can still qualify for many social benefits.[29] However, if a higher proportion of social benefits depended on the employer's and employee's own contributions, employees could become the treasury's allies in legalizing employment.

All these issues tie in with the question of the citizens' relations with the law and the state. The suspicion, indifference, and even antagonistic feelings toward the state which are very prevalent among citizens are a legacy from the old order. A sizable part of the population does not consider tax evasion to be immoral.[30] For a long time it was a form of civil courage to defy the state, and that attitude cannot be altered by ceremonial pronouncements alone. Experience has to prove that the state will be a good steward of the taxpayers' money; it must win the public's trust by its actions.[31]

The private sector will be drawn toward legality if it can expect far greater *economic* advantages than it does at present. Here let me mention just one example: access to the legal credit and capital market. The large commercial banks, for instance, treat small private firms quite ungenerously because they are used to links with the large state-owned firms, with which they are closely bound up, and because they consider it riskier to lend to the private sector. If the behavior of the financial sector changes, and banks show more readiness to extend credit to legal private businesses, including small and medium-sized

28. In comparison, the social-security contributions as a proportion of wages are in the range of 30–40% in Austria, Portugal, Spain, and Sweden, and 20–30% in Greece (U.S. Department of Health, 1990, pp. 12, 98, 208, 238, and 246).

29. There are a great many opportunities for this. People may be on sick leave, paid maternity leave, or registered as unemployed, and they can receive benefits on that basis. Or, they may spend some of their working time in the state sector, which qualifies them for social-security benefits, while doing work illegally, without registering, in the private sector as well, thus saving part of the wage-related taxes.

30. A public-opinion poll of the Hungarian Gallup Institute found that 44% of respondents agreed with the following statement: "People prosper in whatever way they can, and so they should not be blamed if they hide some of their earnings from the tax authorities" (R. Manchin and L. G. Nagy, 1991*a*, pp. 8–9).

31. Hungary still has a long way to go in this. People were asked in one survey whether various institutions really served the public interest. Only 42% of respondents said this was so of the government, while the churches, the press, the Constitutional Court and the parliamentary opposition received far higher confidence ratings (R. Manchin and L. G. Nagy, 1991*b*, pp. 10–11).

undertakings and new ventures, private business people will have one more reason to become legal.[32]

To sum up point C, the transition sets yet another *fiscal trap*. The larger the private sector's share of production, the harder it becomes to collect taxes. To put it another way, the more successful the transformation of property relations, the greater is the risk of budgetary troubles. All incentives that help to increase the relative weight of the law-abiding, tax-paying segment within the private sector as a whole must be used. This may bring with it an increase in tax revenues. Regrettably, I cannot rule out the possibility of the process being protracted and, thus, plagued with severe fiscal problems caused by loss of budget revenue in the meantime.

D. Welfare Expenditures

One of the largest items in the consolidated budget, which also includes for statistical purposes various funds handled separately, is "welfare expenditures," under which the following can be grouped: (1) benefits in cash such as old-age pensions, disability pensions, maternity and child-care allowances, sick pay, family allowances, student scholarships, social assistance, and unemployment compensation; (2) benefits in kind, such as medical care, medicines, public education, training, nursery schools and after-school centers, nursing homes, and labor-market services provided free or at concessionary prices; and (3) price subsidies on consumer goods and services, including the prices (and rents) of housing.[33] Most of the observations in this study refer to welfare spending as a whole; there is no room to deal here with special problems posed by education, culture, and housing.

Tables 5.6 and 5.7 use international comparisons to show that welfare expenditures are very high in Hungary. Considering only the aggregate figures as a proportion of GDP, such spending in Hungary exceeds the level in the group of countries close to it in terms of economic development (Greece, Spain, and the lower-income OECD

32. E. Gém (1991) provides a thorough description and analysis of the credit-supply situation of private firms.

33. Several thorough studies of these issues have been made in Hungary. I recommend in particular the works by Zs. Ferge (1991*a*), (1991*b*) and the report by the company Fraternité Rt. (1991). The descriptions and analyses prepared under the auspices of international agencies are extremely instructive, particularly the studies of the World Bank (C. Kessides et al., 1991) and the International Monetary Fund (G. Kopits et al., 1990). My study draws many ideas from these studies.

Table 5.6
Social expenditures: International comparison

Country	Government expenditures as a percentage of GDP					
	Total social expenditures		Health		Pensions	
	1980	1986	1980	1986	1980	1986
Greece	12.6	19.5	3.6	3.7	5.8	10.6
Italy	23.7	26.4	5.6	5.2	12.0	12.2
Norway	24.2	24.8	6.5	6.6	7.9	8.8
Spain	15.6	17.0	4.3	4.3	7.3	7.6
Sweden	33.2	32.0	8.8	8.3	10.9	11.4
United States	18.0	18.2	3.9	4.5	6.9	7.2
West Germany	26.6	25.2	6.3	6.3	12.1	11.4
Hungary	**21.8**	**24.4**	**3.3**	**4.1**	**7.8**	**9.1**

Sources: C. Kessides et al. (1991, p. 7). Statistics for OECD countries are based on OECD data bank sources; Hungarian data extracted from Central Statistical Office, *Statistical Yearbooks* (Központi Statisztikai Hivatal, various years); information provided by the Social Security Administration, government officials, and estimates by World Bank staff.

Notes: In line with OECD definitions, the Hungarian data on total social expenditures do not include consumer and housing subsidies.

Table 5.7
Net social insurance tax and transfers: International comparison

Statistic	(As a percentage of GDP)		
	OECD lower-income states[a] 1986	OECD welfare states[b] 1986	Hungary 1989
Total social insurance contributions (employees + employers)	8.3	12.0	15.2
Total social expenditures	21.0	31.0	25.4[c]

Source: C. Kessides et al. (1991, p. 13). For more detailed information on the data in this table, see the sources of table 5.6.

a. Average of Greece, Ireland, Portugal, Spain, and Turkey.

b. Average of Belgium, Denmark, Finland, France, Netherlands, Norway, and Sweden.

c. In accordance with OECD definitions; see note to table 5.6.

countries as a whole). Although the ratio is lower than in the developed "welfare states" (Sweden or Denmark) it approaches those in such developed European countries as West Germany or Italy, which are not normally placed in the "welfare-state" category.

Table 5.8 presents a Hungarian time-series demonstrating that governmental expenditures on social-security programs are increasing continually. Meanwhile, one hears many complaints from the Hungarian public, and a substantial part of them are quite warranted. For example, though the number of doctors and hospital beds per capita are very high, there are serious problems with medical care, such as tragically low life expectancy and high infant mortality. While the system of old-age pensions goes a very long way in some respects, pensions are only partially indexed, so in times of rapid inflation the retired face devastating difficulties. Moreover, inequality is increasing: the postsocialist transition allows some of the population to grow rich, but others are impoverished or actually sink into penury, and the regulations and institutions in existence up to now are insufficient to halt the process of decline. This paradoxical situation presents perhaps one of the gravest dilemmas of all the problems discussed in this study.

The Hungarian welfare state was born "prematurely." There is generally a close positive correlation between a country's level of economic development and the scale of its welfare services. Development is not the only factor, but it is undoubtedly among the decisive ones. Hungary was "ahead of itself" in this respect. To a certain extent, the

Table 5.8
Major social-security programs in Hungary

	Expenditure on benefits	
Year	Billions of forints	As percentage of GDP
1985	167.0	16.2
1986	181.5	16.7
1987	200.3	16.3
1988	255.2	18.1
1989	317.1	18.6
1990	414.7	19.9

Source: Organization for Economic Co-Operation and Development (1991, p. 67).
Notes: The OECD data are compiled in accordance with a definition of social-security programs that is narrower than the definition underlying the World Bank statistics presented in Tables 5.6 and 5.7. Nevertheless, both tables 5.6 and 5.8 reveal a similar trend in increasing social expenditures.

classical, prereform socialist system rushed ahead when it made a constitutional commitment that it would satisfy a number of basic needs free or for minimal recompense. It introduced free medical services and education and introduced a pension scheme covering almost the entire population, it subsidized the prices of foodstuffs, set rents for state housing at an almost nominal level, and so on. Later on it proved incapable of keeping its promises. Chronic excess demand appeared for the free or unrealistically cheaply priced services, and the quality of them was often very poor.

Added to the unkept promises of the classical system were the new concessions introduced during the process of reform that began in 1968. It was one of the characteristics of the Hungarian reform, sometimes referred to as "goulash communism," that it tried to turn its back on the previous policy of forced industrialization and devote greater attention to the needs of the general public. A measure of liberalization was accompanied by a growth in the political influence of the forces known as the "living-standard advocates." However, the gulf between promises and their fulfillment remained and in fact widened due to the slowdown and then the stagnation in economic growth. Some new concessions were granted, while others were withdrawn.

Finally came the political turning point, and the population—understandably from a psychological point of view—expects the new system to fulfill the promises made, but not kept, by the old. People are irritated by the state interfering in their private lives and harassing individuals, but many of them still want a caring, paternalist state as well.

So what can be done? Everyone agrees that the institutions of welfare policy and social security must be reformed. There could also be a substantial improvement in utilization of resources and allocative efficiency.[34] The incentives for the providers of services could be substantially improved, and the administrative costs could be reduced. Detailed proposals have been prepared, and they extend to these details and beyond. It may be that they could all achieve some cost reductions. However, it would be wrong to convey the impression that the problem can be solved by improving administrative efficiency.

34. For example, there are too few nursing homes for the aged in Hungary, and the majority of them are ill equipped. On the other hand, the hospitals are used to a great extent to care for old people who in fact do not need hospital care. This is far less beneficial for the old people concerned, and at the same time it is much more costly.

Some radical proposals have also been put forward for rapidly and greatly reducing the state's role in this sphere, at least to the scale found, for instance, in the present-day United States. It is argued that a fast rate of decentralization and privatization should take place in both medical care and the pension system, apart from a narrow band financed by the state.

I do not feel it is my task in this study to comment on the American situation. There is a debate going on, for example, about whether there should be a national health service or whether the health care of the majority of the population should continue to be based on private insurance. All I would like to emphasize here, in the spirit of the first chapters of the study, is this: it is extremely important to remember where one is moving from and to. It is one thing to decide whether a state should give its citizens a right they have not enjoyed before and another to decide to withdraw from them a right they have gained and become accustomed to. A curious *institutional ratchet effect* can be seen here. The cogwheel of historical development turns one way, but it cannot turn back in the opposite direction. If Britain had not had a national health service already, the government of Margaret Thatcher would certainly not have proposed introducing one; but as it existed before Mrs. Thatcher's time, her government did not suggest closing it down.

The citizens of postsocialist society are suffering many uncertainties they did not know before. I have already mentioned the depressing experience of unemployment. Many people's sense of security would be shaken if in addition the medical care, pension system, and other welfare services ensured by the state were to collapse around them.

There is great resistance to the idea of a swift drastic cut in the welfare services provided by the state, along with decentralization and privatization of welfare assignments. In fact, the economic problems of the transition add new expenditures to the list as well. Mention has already been made of unemployment benefits. In addition it must be said that the great transformation of society is accompanied by a redistribution of incomes, and there are many sections in society whose material living conditions are rapidly deteriorating. They expect the social-security net at least to save them from crashing to the ground. Unfortunately, the net has big holes, and to weave a denser one would generate additional demands on the state budget at a time when drastic cuts in budget spending are desperately needed.

No easy escape from this dilemma exists, and it will take patience and tact to get closer to a more acceptable situation. The most important guide should be the principle of *voluntariness and free choice.*[35] Let me give a few illustrations of how these principles can be applied in this field.

The evolution of a decentralized network of for-profit and nonprofit insurance companies and pension funds which employers and employees can join voluntarily must be affirmatively promoted, not just permitted. It would be worth introducing a law that specifies that these new institutions should receive valuable, truly income-generating portfolios of securities during the privatization of the state-owned firms, as a free contribution to their initial capitalization.

More leeway must be given to private medical practice and private providers of other social services ranging from child care, through nursing of the sick, to care for the aged. They should receive a market rate of remuneration for their activities.[36]

In other words, it would be worthwhile to ensure that the private sector grows rapidly in this sphere as well, under appropriate governmental supervision. I agree with the view that the desirable *final state* after the transformation would be a combination of three basic forms: a minimal level of certain services must be guaranteed as a civil right; other services must be provided in accordance with contributions paid by the beneficiaries and their employers; and finally, some services can be available to individuals through private insurance or through a direct act of purchase on the market. Let individuals be given as much scope as possible to choose between schemes providing welfare benefits. However, in view of the initial conditions, this final state can only be approached gradually. Those who have no means of making a real choice cannot be presented with a *fait accompli.*[37]

35. In an earlier work of mine (J. Kornai, 1988), I tried to shed light on how the reforms taking place in the socialist countries have a bearing on the growth of *individual freedom* through the expansion of economic choice.

36. It is another matter to decide who should pay this remuneration. In some cases, it could be the clients availing themselves of the services or their insurers; in others, it could be the state or the social welfare fund; and in still others, remuneration could be provided by a combination of the two.

37. A young man today, for instance, can make a choice between alternative pension schemes, but someone near retirement age cannot be forced to transfer to a private pension fund. The state made a "contract" with him or her under the pension laws in force when they were working, and it cannot be broken arbitrarily and unilaterally.

Something perhaps more important still than providing a choice between various mechanisms for social services is to give citizens the chance to express their will through the *political process*. A far greater role in monitoring the institutions providing social services should be given to various voluntary associations for safeguarding interests. Apart from that, the legislature must have the final word on welfare expenditure and in matters of social insurance and the levies connected with it. The political parties cannot avoid this complex of problems. A far clearer connection must be made between what citizens receive from the state and quasi-state organizations and how much tax they pay for them. Not the least of the economists' obligations in this respect is to protest against cheap prevarication and to expose politicians who promise a cut in taxes alongside an unchanged welfare program. The proportion of the state's welfare spending should decrease to the extent that well-informed voters *consent to* and desire it, in order to lessen the burden of taxation. Conversely, the welfare expenditures can only be maintained in the proportion that the citizens are prepared to finance with their taxes.

To sum up point D, there is yet another fiscal trap ahead, and this may be the most painful one to writhe in. A drastic cut in state welfare spending will bring insecurity and a grave deterioration in the quality of life of many people. However, to maintain current levels of welfare spending, and still more to increase them, would be accompanied by levels of taxation that would discourage investors and therefore hold back economic growth. It is a self-evident truism to say that more production is needed to cover the welfare services provided: a bigger pie is easier to divide.

It is difficult to make a forecast about expected welfare expenditures in the years to come. I believe the likeliest outcome will be that welfare services will be partially decentralized and marketized, but with agonizing slowness.

IV General Conclusions

I have examined four problems through an analysis of experiences in Hungary. Nowadays there are countries (such as the republic-states being formed in the territory of the former Soviet Union) battling with problems even more staggering and elemental in force than these, such as deciding what to do to ensure that the population has food, that money has real purchasing power, and that the dive in production is halted. There is hope, however, that sooner or later all postsocialist countries will progress beyond the baneful state of chaos and crisis, and then they will all find the questions I have discussed in my study on their agendas.[38]

Bitter conclusions can be drawn from this discourse. Even where the elemental tasks of macrostabilization have been more or less accomplished, grave problems are constantly reproduced. Even where there has been some success in approaching budgetary stability, serious pressure on public finances persists. On the one hand, an increase in various kinds of spending is still being urged by a variety of political and social forces, and on the other, the difficulties of collecting taxes are increasing. The danger of budgetary deficit is here to stay. Covering the deficit with loans from the central bank can constitute a perilous contribution to the inflationary pressure. Any success in monetary macrostabilization can easily slip through our fingers. Covering the deficit by issuing state bonds can crowd out productive investments, which will impede growth.

Any kind of quick-fix solution can only be proposed by economic dilettantes or political tricksters. I have repeatedly mentioned potential traps in order to emphasize that there is no easy way out of any of the problems discussed in the study. What present themselves are painful trade-offs and choices between bad and worse.

Strong and persistent efforts must be made to repress the former hyperactivity of the state and concurrently to reduce state spending, while combatting the bureaucratic, centralizing tendencies that constantly revive. The change is likely to occur slowly; it will be a good while before today's big government has been reduced to government on a desirable scale, far smaller than the present one.

Although I cannot make optimistic short-term forecasts, the outlook in the longer term is more favorable. The political change has released the spirits of autonomy, freedom, and entrepreneurship, and these are the primary driving forces of economic progress. It seems justified to expect the low point to be followed by a rise in production, one effect of which will be to make it easier to solve the fiscal problems dis-

38. Among the factors compelling a reduction in state spending and taxation is Hungary's desire, shared with several other Eastern European countries, to join the European Community. One requirement for membership is that these rates should not exceed the far lower European norms.

cussed in this study. This will broaden the tax base, which is a precondition for a reduction in the tax rates. The latter stimulates investment, which in turn creates new jobs. A decrease of unemployment ultimately reduces the social-security burdens of the state.

A wise and efficient government can accelerate this development, and governmental errors and omissions can impede it, but the final outcome of the transition is not in the government's hands. Under the new postsocialist system, the state can at most influence the economy. It cannot run the economy, which is propelled by the interests of those participating in it. This is one of the main advantages a market economy has over centrally managed socialism.

References

Aberbach, Joel D., Putnam, Robert D., and Rockman, Bert A. 1981. *Bureaucrats and Politicians in Western Democracies*. Cambridge, Mass.: Harvard University Press.

Bator, Francis M. 1958. "The Anatomy of Market Failure." *Quarterly Journal of Economics* 72 (3): 351–379.

Baumol, William J. 1965. *Welfare Economics and the Theory of the State*. Cambridge, Mass.: Harvard University Press.

Benton, Lauren A. 1990. *Invisible Factories: The Informal Economy and Industrial Development in Spain*. Albany: State University of New York Press.

Buchanan, James, and Tullock, Gordon. 1962. *The Calculus of Consent: Logical Foundations of Constitutional Democracy*. Ann Arbor: University of Michigan Press.

Ékes, Ildikó. 1991. "A második gazdaság az átmenet időszakában és a piac fejlődése" (The Second Economy in the Period of Transition and the Development of the Market). Mimeo. Budapest: Központi Statisztikai Hivatal.

Esti, Nóra. 1991. "A magyarországi kisvállalkozások helyzetének és lehetőségeinek alakulása 1991-ben" (The Trend in the Situation and Outlook for Small Business in Hungary in 1991). Mimeo. Budapest: Gazdaságkutató Intézet.

Ferge, Zsuzsa. 1991*a*. "The Social Safety Net in Hungary: A Brief Survey." In *Social Safety Nets in East/Central Europe*. Mimeo. Cambridge, Mass.: Harvard University, Kennedy School of Government.

Ferge, Zsuzsa. 1991*b*. "Marginalization, Poverty, and Social Institutions." *Labor and Society* 16 (3): 417–438.

FRATERNITÉ Rt. 1991. *Jelentés a társadalombiztosítás reformjáról* (Report on the Reform of the Social Security System). Budapest.

Gém, Erzsébet. 1991. "Hitelt—de honnan? A vállalkozásfinanszírozás rendszere Magyarországon" (Credit—But Where From? The System of Financing Entrepreneurship in Hungary). Mimeo. Budapest: KOPINT-DATORG.

Hall, Peter A. 1986. *Governing the Economy: The Politics of State Intervention in Britain and France*. New York: Oxford University Press.

Helpman, Elhanan. 1990. *Monopolistic Competition in Trade Theory*. Princeton: Princeton University Press.

International Monetary Fund. 1990. *Government Finance Statistical Yearbook*. Washington, D.C.

International Monetary Fund. 1991. *Government Finance Statistical Yearbook*. Washington, D.C.

Jantscher, Milka Casanegra de, Silvani, Carlos, and Vehorn, Charles L. 1991. *Modernizing Tax Administration in Eastern Europe*. Washington, D.C.: International Monetary Fund.

Kessides, Christine, Davey, Kenneth, Holzman, Robert, Micklewright, John, Smith, Andrew, and Hinayon, Carlos. 1991. *Hungary: Reform of the Social Policy and Distribution System*. Washington, D.C.: World Bank.

Kopits, George. 1991. *Fiscal Reform in European Economies in Transition*. Washington, D.C.: International Monetary Fund.

Kopits, George, Holzman, R., Schieber, G. and Sidgwick, E. 1990. *Social Security Reform in Hungary*. Washington, D.C.: International Monetary Fund.

Köllő, János. 1990. "Munkaerőpiac: Mitől legyünk pesszimisták" (Labor Market: Why One Should Be a Pessimist). In *Társadalmi riport 1990*, edited by Rudolf Andorka, Tamás Kolosi, and György Vukovich. Budapest: TÁRKI.

Köllő, János. 1991. "A foglalkoztatáspolitika igazi dilemmája" (The Real Dilemma of Employment Policy), *Figyelő* 35 (August 22): 3.

Kornai, János. 1988. "Individual Freedom and Reform of the Socialist Economy." *European Economic Review* 32 (2-3): 233–267.

Kornai, János. [1989] 1990. *The Road to a Free Economy. Shifting from a Socialist System: The Example of Hungary*. New York: W. W. Norton.

Kornai, János. 1992. *The Socialist System. The Political Economy of Communism*. Princeton: Princeton University Press, and Oxford: Oxford University Press.

Kovács, Ilona. 1993. "Tényleg túl sokat fogyasztunk?" (Do We Really Consume Too Much?). *Közgazdasági Szemle* 40 (78): 663–679.

Lányi, Kamilla, ed. 1991. *A gyors változások területei a magyar gazdaságban* (The Areas of Rapid Changes in the Hungarian Economy). Budapest: KOPINT-DATORG.

Lányi, Kamilla, and Oblath, Gábor, eds. 1991. *A világgazdaság és a magyar gazdaság helyzete és kilátásai 1991 végén* (The Conditions and Prospects for the World Economy and the Hungarian Economy at the End of 1991). Budapest: KOPINT-DATORG.

László, Csaba. 1993. "Mekkora valójában az államháztartás szerepe az újraelosztásban" (How Bid a Role Does the State Budget in Fact Play in the Redistribution?). *Közgazdasági Szemle* 40 (1): 63–79.

Lindbeck, Assar. 1988. "Consequences of the Advanced Welfare State." *World Economy*, 11 (March): 19–37.

Manchin, Róbert, and Nagy, Lajos Géza. 1991*a*. *Ismeretek és vélemények az adóról* (Information and Opinions on Taxes). Budapest: Magyar Gallup Intézet.

Manchin, Róbert, and Nagy, Lajos Géza. 1991*b*. *Vélemények gazdaságról, életszínvonalról, politikai intézményekröl* (Opinions on the Economy, Living Standard, and Political Institutions). Budapest: Magyar Gallup Intézet.

Móra, Mária. 1990. "Az állami vállalatok (ál)privatizációja" (The (Pseudo-)privatization of State-Owned Firms). Mimeo. Budapest: Gazdaságkutató Intézet.

Móra, Mária. 1991. "The (Pseudo)-Privatization of State-Owned Enterprise." *Acta Oeconomica* 43: 37–58.

Murrell, Peter. 1990. "An Evolutionary Perspective on Reform of the Eastern European Economies." Mimeo. College Park: University of Maryland.

National Bank of Hungary. 1991. *Quarterly Review*, No. 4, Budapest.

Niskanen, William A. 1971. *Bureaucracy and Representative Government*. Chicago: Aldine.

Offe, Claus. 1984. *Contradictions of the Welfare State*. Cambridge, Mass.: MIT Press.

Organization for Economic Co-operation and Development. 1991. *OECD Economic Surveys: Hungary 1991*. Paris.

Pénzügyminisztérium. 1991. "Az 1991. VII–VIII. havi és várható éves gazdasági folyamatokról" (On Actual and Expected Economic Development in the July–August Period and for the Whole Year). *Pénzügyi Szemle* 35 (11): 847–852.

Sabel, Charles. 1982. *Work and Politics*. Cambridge: Cambridge University Press.

Schumpeter, Joseph A. [1911] 1968. *The Theory of Economic Development. An Inquiry into Profits, Capital, Credit, Interest and the Business Cycle*. Cambridge, Mass.: Harvard University Press.

Schumpeter, Joseph A. [1942] 1976. *Capitalism, Socialism and Democracy*. New York: Harper and Row.

Seleny, Anna. 1991. "The Political Economy of Property Rights and the Transformation of Hungarian Politics: 1949–1989." Mimeo. Cambridge, Mass.: MIT.

Skocpol, Theda. 1985. "Bringing the State Back In: Strategies of Analysis in Current Research." In *Bringing the State Back In*, edited by P. B. Evans, D. Rueschemeyer, and T. Skocpol. Cambridge: Cambridge University Press, 3–37.

Stiglitz, Joseph E., et al. 1989. *The Economic Role of the State*. Oxford: Blackwell.

U. S. Department of Health. 1990. *Human Services Research Report* 62 (May).

6 The Evolution of Financial Discipline under the Postsocialist System[1]

Financial discipline, as I see it, means the enforcement of four simple rules:

1. Buyers: Pay for the goods you buy.
2. Debtors: Abide by your loan contract; pay back your debt.
3. Taxpayers: Pay your taxes.
4. Enterprises: Cover your costs out of your revenues.

Self-evident though these rules may seem in a market economy, they were far from obvious in a socialist command economy. That was based on a quite different kind of discipline, which consisted chiefly of enforcing planning commands, above all the fulfillment of output targets and compliance with input quotas. How postsocialist society should learn to observe the new kind of discipline is the subject of this study.

The analysis rests on Hungary's experiences; other countries are only referred to in a few places. But in my view, the *problems* raised in the discussion are general ones that inevitably arise in other postsocialist countries as well. So I attempt at the end of the study to draw some general conclusions.

---

1. The study was prepared as part of a research project entitled "Hungary's Transition into Market Economy," with support from Hungary's National Scientific Research Foundation and the European Bank for Reconstruction and Development. I must express thanks for the help I have received from Annamária Balogh, Béla Bártfai, Imre Fertő, Erzsébet Gém, Marianna Holló, Mária Kovács, László Muraközy, Sándor Piskolti, Jane Prokop, and György Rózsahegyi in gathering the material for the lecture. I am grateful to Brian McLean and Julianna Parti for their excellent translation of the Hungarian text.

I A New Contract Between the State and the Enterprise

Analysis of the problem requires a conceptual framework. Let us look upon the relationship between the state and the enterprise as if there were a *long-term contract* between them. (This study does not deal with the other areas in which financial discipline is manifest, for instance, discipline within the bureaucracy or within the firm.) The relationship, in fact, might be interpreted as a specific kind of *insurance contract.*

Under the old contract that ran under pre-reform socialism, the insurance company (i.e., the state) covered the losses in full. If an enterprise found itself in financial trouble, the state bailed it out unconditionally. A variety of techniques were used for the purpose: extending financial subsidies, granting tax concessions or postponing tax commitments, rescheduling loan repayments, or providing new soft loans. The state also guaranteed the survival of chronic loss-making enterprises. All these techniques involved constantly breaking rules 2, 3, and 4 of financial discipline (loan discipline, fiscal discipline and market cost-coverage discipline). This is the group of phenomena that I termed *softness of the budget constraint* in my earlier works. Also apparent was a side-effect well known in insurance theory: the so-called moral hazard. If policy-holders know that the insurer will pay for all damage, it is not worth them making efforts to avoid damage, which in this context means that enterprises are insufficiently motivated to avoid losses by raising efficiency.

A mature market economy is marked by a different kind of insurance contract between the state and the enterprise. This policy only partly covers the damage, with the insured party paying the dominant share. There can be no question of losses being covered automatically and unconditionally. Only in certain privileged sectors (like banking) will the state assume a sizeable part of the losses that may occur. Irrespective of whether the state's role as an "insurer" extends only to these privileged sectors or to others as well, the cover will apply only under exceptional, rigorously determined conditions. So the survival of an enterprise is not guaranteed; sooner or later, a chronic loss-maker will have to make an exit from the economic scene. Rules 2, 3, and 4 are rigorously enforced. To use the terminology introduced earlier, *the budget constraint is hard.*

There are several signs that Hungary has moved towards the long-term insurance contract characteristic of a market economy. This seems to be confirmed by table 6.1, which shows a substantial reduction in subsidies—from 12% to under 3% of GDP. Moreover, tables 6.2 and 6.3 betray a jump in the number of bankruptcy and liquidation proceedings, which means the number of state rescue operations has fallen. Let me recall that an average of 26 enterprises a year ceased activities between 1976 and 1982,[2] and even with this tiny number of exits, there were not financial reasons, but other factors behind them in many cases. To make another comparison, more liquidation proceedings were commenced in a single month of 1992 than in a whole year in the period 1986–1988.

In actual fact, of course, there is no written contract between the state and the enterprise. But the promising branch of theoretical economics known as "contract theory" has identified countless cases in which an *unwritten* contract applies; custom and habitual behavior induce the parties to observe the terms of the contract.[3] Each party, counting on the other continuing to behave in the habitual way, itself

Table 6.1
Flows between the government budget and the enterprise sector

Years	From the enterprise sector to the budget	From the budget to the enterprise sector	Net flow to the budget
		(as a percentage of GDP)	
1987	29.6	12.3	17.3
1988	20.4	9.9	10.5
1989	15.4	6.7	8.7
1990	16.2	4.7	11.5
1991	12.4	2.8	9.6
1992	9.8	2.7	7.1
1993	10.0	2.6	7.4

Source: L. Muraközy (1993, pp. 25 and 39).
Notes: [This table was revised in the course of editing this volume. Referred to as *Revised table* hereafter.] Figures for 1993 are government projections. The first column includes the net profits surrendered by state-owned enterprises to the government budget, and profit taxes paid both by state-owned and private enterprises. The second column excludes consumer subsidies.

2. See J. Kornai and Á. Matits (1987, p. 100).
3. G. S. Becker (1992, p. 338) in his study of habitual behavior and traditions states the following: "... habits, addictions, traditions, and other preferences that are directly contingent on past choices partly control, and hence commit, future behavior in predictable ways. Indeed, habits and the like may be very good substitutes for long-term contracts and other explicit commitment mechanisms."

Table 6.2
Number of bankruptcy proceedings in 1992 and 1993

Months and years	Number of filings	Number of official announcements by the court
January to March	786	285
April	2,259	205
May	201	465
June	145	482
July	154	300
August	113	69
September	151	104
October	150	190
November	118	225
December	154	175
Total in 1992	**4,231**	**2,500**
Total in 1993	**987**	**887**

Sources: 1992: Pénzügyminisztérium (Ministry of Finance), (1992, pp. 4 and 7) and T. Szalai (1993, p. 79); 1993: Pénzügyminisztérium (Ministry of Finance), (1994, Table II/3.3).
Notes: *[Revised table.]* The figures in the first column record the initiations of bankruptcy proceedings. The figures in the second column refer to public announcements regarding the start of bankruptcy proceedings. It is the responsibility of the court to publish the announcement in the official gazette.

abides by the unwritten terms of the contract. So this social relationship rests on firm long-term expectations.[4]

Under the old contract, characteristic to the pre-reform, classical socialism, the enterprise could be sure about what help it would receive from the state in overcoming a financial crisis. But what happens if there is an insufficient basis for long-term expectations because the behavior of one party (in this case the government) has suddenly changed? Neither economics nor social psychology provides adequate reliable information about a dramatic *change* in preferences, habits and expectations. This alone makes it very difficult to find an answer to the questions explored in this study.

4. To analyze a long-term implicit contract, in other words, a constantly renewing social relationship based on "the rules of the game," the mathematical models most commonly used are those of "repeated games." For a theoretical description, see for instance, the book by D. Fudenberg and J. Tirole (1991, pp. 147–206). The interpretation of the theoretical models from the social sciences' point of view is presented in a more popular form in T. C. Schelling (1978, pp. 115–133) and K. Binmore (1992, pp. 345–381).

Table 6.3
Number of liquidation proceedings

Months and years		Number of filings	Number of official announcements by the court
1986 to 1988		n.a.	159
1989		n.a.	141
1990		n.a.	233
1991		n.a.	526
1992			
	January to March	2,617	120
	April	1,281	161
	May	837	202
	June	927	166
	July	699	219
	August	701	210
	September	797	482
	October	782	211
	November	751	233
	December	692	223
Total in 1992		**10,084**	**2,227**
Total in 1993		**7,242**	**2,593**

Sources: Figures for the period 1986–1991 from M. Móra (1992, pp. 18–23); 1992: Pénzügyminisztérium (Ministry of Finance), (1992, pp. 5 and 9) and T. Szalai (1993, p. 79). 1993: Pénzügyminisztérium (Ministry of Finance), (1994, Table II/3.3).
Notes: *[Revised table.]* The period covered by the first figure started on September 1, 1986 and ended on December 31, 1988. The figures in the first column record the initiation (filing) of liquidation proceedings. The figures in the second column refer to public announcements regarding the start of liquidation proceedings. As in the case of the bankruptcy proceedings, it is the responsibility of the court to publish the announcement in the official gazette.

The conceptual framework just described provides an appropriate structure in which to discuss the problem. Let us look first at government, and then at enterprise conduct.

II The Conduct of the Government

Conflicting Objectives

The prime requirement before a government can change the long-term contract previously in force is the *political will* to do so. This is a function of the political goals. When a government sets its political objectives concerning financial discipline, it has to weigh the benefits and costs to be expected from it. Let us look first of all at the *benefits* of enforcing financial discipline.

• A smoothly operating credit system is essential to a modern market economy, but it cannot appear without an assurance that credit contracts will be observed.

• Very grave problems arise during the postsocialist transition with balancing the budget. One requirement for overcoming them is to improve the collection of taxes.

• Relative prices have been distorted by the system of differentiated, non-uniform taxes and subsidies. Discontinuing these helps more reliable price signals to develop.

• Tougher financial discipline will send the chronic loss-making producers out of production. This becomes particularly opportune once the system of relative prices is giving a sufficiently true reflection of the costs and relative scarcities. Apart from that, the discipline encourages the surviving old enterprises and the emerging new ones to reduce costs and adjust better to demand.

To sum up, tightening financial discipline provides a strong incentive to increase *efficiency*. Hungarian experience also shows that some of the benefits appear immediately, but others only after a delay.

The most spectacular result was the rapid adjustment made by Hungarian production to the collapse of Comecon. The threat hanging over Hungarian enterprises was expressed by two World Bank staff

Table 6.4
Destination of exports

Year	European Community	Countries in transition and non-market economies	Other
	Share of total exports (%)		
1987	20.1	56.5	23.3
1988	22.6	51.2	26.2
1989	24.8	47.3	27.9
1990	32.2	37.7	30.1
1991	45.7	23.6	30.7
1992	49.8	23.3	26.9

Source: Központi Statisztikai Hivatal (Central Statistical Office, 1993, p. 106).
Note: [Revised table.]

members, K. Dervis and T. Condon, in their 1994 study as "export or perish." A picture of the export performance is provided by table 6.4. The share of exports directed to the European Community doubled in a very short time.

Less conspicuous, but extremely important is the effect that imposition of tougher financial discipline has on the reorganization of production, the process known as restructuring and reorganization. Judicial bankruptcy proceedings do not necessarily signify the beginning of the end, since they initially provide legally regulated forms for deferring the settlement of debts. During this period, the enterprise's affairs must be set to rights, if that is possible. The process is often accompanied by a full or partial change in the top management and the appointment of new, better managers. Nor, of course, do the liquidation proceedings bring about an irresponsible destruction of the material and intellectual capital. They promote the sale of as much of them as possible, if only in order to satisfy the creditors to a greater extent. During liquidation, a previously vast enterprise is often split up into smaller units, and its various assets are sold. Both bankruptcy proceedings and liquidation can create improved conditions for privatizing the original enterprises or the successor firms.

Finally, there is the least conspicuous, longest delayed, but most important effect of tough imposition of financial discipline, which appears in the shaping of people's thinking. This I will return to later.

Let us turn now to the other side of the balance, the *costs*.

The tightening of financial discipline, including the wave of bankruptcy and liquidation proceedings, contributes to the fall in production. This is not the sole reason why a recession appears in all postsocialist economies without exception, but it is undoubtedly one of the factors behind the contraction of the economy.

The closure of whole factories clearly causes a loss of jobs. Moreover the surviving enterprises also try to reduce their costs, and lay-offs are among the results. Table 6.5 presents the changes which have taken place on the labor market. The number of vacancies still exceeded the number of jobseekers before May 1990. The scales since then have tipped to the side of unemployment, which continues to grow month after month. This produces a particularly grave trauma in a country where the labor force has become accustomed over decades to full employment, in fact to a labor shortage. The appearance and growth of unemployment are a great affliction that is only alleviated in part by unemployment benefits. In any case, there is not only the financial loss

Table 6.5
Job vacancies and unemployment

Months	Number of registered vacancies	Number of registered unemployed	Unemployment rate (%)
03/1990	34,048	33,682	0.7
06	37,859	43,506	0.9
09	26,969	56,113	1.2
12	16,815	79,521	1.7
03/1991	13,583	144,840	3.0
06	14,860	185,554	3.9
09	15,351	292,756	6.1
12	11,529	406,124	8.5
03/1992	15,124	477,987	8.9
06	25,346	546,676	10.1
09	25,634	616,782	11.4
12	24,097	663,027	12.3
03/1993	35,760	697,585	13.4
06	30,771	657,331	12.6
09	35,784	669,761	12.9
12	28,089	632,050	12.1
03/1994	33,341	610,994	12.2

Source: Reports of Országos Munkaügyi Központ (National Labor Center, Hungary), 1991–1994.
Note: [Revised table.] The statistical definition of the unemployment rate has been adjusted beginning in January 1992 to the definition used in Western labor statistics. The data for 1990 and 1991 are calculated according to the old definition, since no recalculation was made. The unemployment rate would be somewhat lower in this period on the basis of the new definition.

caused by unemployment to be considered, but the psychological effect produced by the loss of job security.

Moreover the enterprise under the socialist system, particularly in its pre-reform stage, was not simply an employer. It provided numerous welfare services: apartments or hostel accommodation, canteen meals, holidays, medical treatment, kindergartens and child-minding centers. As the enterprise turns into a profit-motivated employer, it steadily brushes aside these tasks. So social security provided at firm level is eroded at the same time as job security is lost.

Confrontation of the benefits and costs leads to a difficult choice between conflicting objectives. Much attention is devoted in the economics of macrostabilization to the trade-off between inflation and unemployment. The curbing of inflation, which requires a rigorously observed regime of restrictive monetary policy, is regularly accompanied by an increase in unemployment, and conversely, measures to reduce unemployment increase the danger of inflation speeding up. This trade-off applies also to the postsocialist economy, and places a heavy burden upon it. Hungary's annual rate of inflation has fallen somewhat, but in 1992 and 1993 it was still around 22–23%, while the unemployment rate has already risen above 12%. But underlying this there is another trade-off that is still more serious because it has a deeper effect: that of *efficiency versus security*. Improvement of efficiency, in the short, medium and long term, goes hand in hand with abandonment of full employment and job security, and erosion of the social security originating from the welfare services provided by the enterprise.

International comparison shows that in terms of facing this serious dilemma, Hungary has gone furthest in imposing financial discipline and hardening the budget constraint, and consequently in promoting an improvement in efficiency. Poland, the Czech Republic, Slovakia, and Slovenia have taken steps in the same direction, but so far they have hesitated, for example, about introducing a modern bankruptcy law and applying it consistently. To give the ultimate counter-example, Russia's central bank in the second half of 1992 was extending almost incalculable sums in credits to sustain state-owned enterprises on the brink of bankruptcy, or at least to make sure they could keep on their workers and pay their wages.

Credibility and Commitment

Let us return to a more general level of discussion. Let us assume there comes a point when the government decides that from now on it will rigorously impose financial discipline and harden the enterprise's budget constraint. The question is, will it have the perseverance to continue this policy consistently? And even if it promises to do so, will the enterprises believe this promise? One condition for applying the new contract mentioned at the beginning of the study is that the government should have *credibility*, in general terms, and in the specific context of our discussion, credibility for its "no bail-out" commitment. The theory of conflicts and contracts draws attention emphatically to credibility, above all to the central importance of the credibility of threats. Here the picture Hungary presents is far from clear; a curious ambivalence can be found instead.

Let me recall at this point the story of Ulysses and the Sirens.[5] The bewitching voices of the Sirens would entice sailors towards them into shipwreck and destruction. When Ulysses's ship approached the Sirens' island, he blocked his men's ears with wax and told them to tie him to the mast, so that he could not yield to the temptation. The more he begged them to release him, the tighter they were to tie his bonds.

Turning from the metaphor of temptation and commitment to Hungary's real situation, let us first examine the *temptations*. There are a great many influences on the government tempting it to loosen the financial discipline and soften the budget constraint. The political forces behind the government can use financial bail-outs to win clients by playing the part of a patron. They can make concessions to political pressure and the requests of industrial or regional lobbies. They will clearly have in mind the next parliamentary and local-government elections, so that bail-outs can serve to gain them a cheap popularity.

This constitutes a very real political temptation whose effects can actually be observed. Since the period of tougher financial discipline began, exceptional procedures have been followed in several cases, in many of which the bargaining led to agreement. The remnants of the soft budget constraint are plainly visible. There is a danger that the frequency of the exceptions will undermine the credibility of the government's pledges concerning the tough financial discipline.

The function of Ulysses's *bonds* is performed mainly by *constraints and pre-commitments* that bind the government's hands. An absolute, doctrinaire application of the "no bail-out" principle cannot be expected, because of the macroeconomic requirements and the efforts to defuse political tensions, but the government must ensure that the financial bail-outs are infrequent, i.e., they occur only on very rare occasions. The criteria and procedures for bailing out enterprises must be laid down by law, not left to *ad hoc* administrative bargaining processes. Only temporary financial assistance is permissible, and whatever form the assistance may take (postponement of tax arrears, debt rescheduling, budgetary subsidy, etc.), it must follow a clear timetable that extends the assistance over a strictly determined and not too distant deadline. Instead of confidential agreements reached behind closed doors, there should be full publicity for each bail-out, so that it

5. J. Elster's book *Ulysses and the Sirens* (1979) makes manifold use of this metaphor in its philosophical analysis of temptation and commitment.

takes place under the public scrutiny of a parliamentary committee and the press.

Regrettably, politicians usually behave in a different way from the Ulysses of Homer. There is no question of them telling their sailors to bind them hand and foot. On the contrary, they do all they can to keep a free hand, feeling they need room to maneuver and improvise. "Unpredictability is power," as Albert Hirschman put it.[6] Obscurity suits politicians much better than clarity.

The outcome depends greatly on whether the public, particularly the economists' profession, can extract binding pledges from the government and make sure it keeps them. Whatever happens, the test of the credibility of the government's promises about financial discipline will be the practice it pursues in the years to come.

The Mechanism for Imposing Discipline

Let us now assume the existence of the political will to apply financial discipline continually and consistently. That still leaves open the question of whether the *means* are available to perform the task.

Discipline under the socialist economic system was imposed by the bureaucracy itself, often by arbitrary and brutal means. Postsocialist society must become a *constitutional state,* and that applies in connection with financial discipline as well.

Let us begin with *legislation*. Hungary has made significant progress: modern accounting, banking and bankruptcy laws that meet the requirements of a market economy are already in place. The legislative process is itself an instructive one of experimentation. A particular law may be full of mistakes, and sooner or later need amending, which makes it harder for the effect of it to be incorporated into the awareness of the actors in the economy.[7]

---

6. See A. O. Hirschman (1977, p. 50).

7. Of the regulations on bankruptcies and liquidations, one particularly worth noting was the measure known ironically as the "harakiri clause." The responsible manager of an enterprise was obliged to file for bankruptcy once it was clear that the firm would be unable to fulfill its payment commitments. If the manager failed to do so and this could be proved to cause loss, he or she could be sued personally for damages in the civil courts. This provided a very strong inducement to file for bankruptcy if the enterprise got into financial straits.

The "harakiri clause" exacerbated the wave of bankruptcies to such an extent that it was withdrawn recently at the same time that other, lesser amendments were made. Experience will show whether this amendment has substantially weakened the Bankruptcy Act or not.

But although the necessary legislative steps have been taken, there is a problem with *enforcing* the law. The work load of the courts dealing with business cases has grown by leaps and bounds. The number of competent professionals is too small. There is a shortage not only of judges, but of receivers, chartered accountants, lawyers, economic analysts and business administrators with the qualifications and experience to conduct bankruptcies, liquidations, auctions, mergers, demergers, and reorganizations.[8]

Let us take another example, in which an enterprise has broken rule 1 of financial discipline: it has not paid for what it has bought. The seller requests the court to issue a warrant of payment. This is a warning which is followed, if the payment has still not taken place, by an official auction. Table 6.6 shows that the number of such cases has multiplied by six in four years. It can be three to four months before the court issues the warrant of payment and the official bailiff begins auctioning the debtor's sizable assets.

It is hardly surprising that some entrepreneurs feel they must take the law into their own hands. There have been reports in the press on the existence of one or two obscure firms that specialize in debt collection by curious means: a few strong young men with a resemblance to boxers are sent to a debtor's home to remind him, at least in menacing words, of his obligation to pay.[9] There have also been cases where the message was underlined by beating up the debtor or warning him that

Table 6.6
Warrant for payment cases at the Budapest Court in 1992

Years	Number of cases	Total value of claims (HUF bn.)
1988	11,000	6
1989	31,000	19
1990	64,000	45
1991	61,645	43
1992	31,470	38

Source: Communication by S. Piskolti, the former head of the Economic Bench of the Budapest Court.

8. G. S. Becker and G. J. Stigler (1974) in a study on enforcing the laws show that the mechanism for the purpose is not an invariable. If the interests of society's members are served by so doing (as they clearly are in this case), the scale, methods, and organizational forms of the apparatus can be adjusted to the greater demands; the quality of its activity can be improved, for instance, with requisite incentives.
9. See, for instance, the news report in the daily paper *Népszabadság* on October 19, 1992.

his property would be damaged or his dependants attacked. So there we have the mafia method of imposing financial discipline. . . .

This is alarming and intolerable. But, unfortunately, such methods must be expected to appear as well, because it will be some time before the legal infrastructure for enforcing financial discipline has developed.

Although legal enforcement of financial discipline is essential, it is by no means sufficient in itself. It must be augmented by a change in the moral attitude of the public towards financial transactions.[10] This leads to the second part of the study, which concerns the conduct of enterprises.

III The Conduct of Enterprises

An Example: Forced Credit Between Enterprises

The new contract between the state and the enterprises, determined in the spirit of a market economy, requires a change not only in government conduct, but in the behavior of enterprises. To see how this second change has failed to occur sufficiently in Hungarian business, let us look at the phenomenon of forced credit between enterprises. Enterprise *B* has delivered goods for production to enterprise *A*. The buyer has received them, but it has not then paid the bill. One could put it like this: enterprise *A* forces enterprise *B* to extend credit without prior agreement, and then does not pay its debt. By doing so, enterprise *A* commits a grave breach of rules 1 and 2 of financial discipline. In a similar way, enterprise *C* is not paid for its goods by *B*, one of whose troubles is that it has not been paid by *A*. The neglect of payments and debt settlements spills over onto other enterprises, to form

10. Economic history shows that private contracts based on the honesty and mutual respect of the parties to them were widely made *before* the legislative regulation and legal enforcement of them. When the first commercial laws were then passed, they dealt unceremoniously with those who failed to pay their debts. England's Lex Mercatoria (Law Merchant), passed in the thirteenth century, stipulated that if a debtor did not pay his debts, the creditor first had to seize his moveable property: "And if the debtor have no moveables whereupon his debt may be levied, then shall his body be taken where it may be found and kept in prison until he have made agreement, or his friends for him." The quotation is from W. D. Mitchell (1969). For more on the history of commercial law, see L. E. Trakman's book (1983).

So from the Middle Ages onwards, there were strict laws to induce respect for private contracts and financial discipline among the actors in the commercial world. Only centuries later, when the need for discipline had been historically fixed in their minds, did the legal sanctions become "tamer."

long, interlocking chains of forced credits.[11] It was continuously growing until April 1992, as shown in table 6.7.

In the second half of 1992 the amount of forced credits decreased substantially. It seems to indicate that the wave of bankruptcies have already had a favorable effect on the strengthening of financial discipline. In addition, various attempts are made to resolve the problem with the cooperation of the banking sector. It would be possible, for

Table 6.7
Forced credit

Years	Number of involuntary creditor enterprises	Total forced credit (HUF bn.)
1979	52	7.9
1980	25	3.8
1981	27	4.7
1982	85	15.2
1983	167	33.8
1984	159	38.4
1985	127	28.3
1986	82	14.0
1987	82	14.0
1988	208	45.5
1989	314	72.8
1990	432	90.5
1991	1,017	159.8
Apr. 1992	1,143	197.0
Dec. 1992	642	104.0
Dec. 1993	638	99.0

Source: Period 1979–1991: É. Várhegyi and L. Sándor (1992, p. 25); 1992 and 1994: Communication by É. Várhegyi. The figures are based on the data of the Hungarian National Bank.

Note: [Revised table.] 1991 figures refer to data for November 30, 1991. All other figures refer to the volume of involuntary credit on December 31 of the year stated. The figures for the volume of involuntary credit only cover credits larger than HUF 25 mn. The total volume, including smaller-scale involuntary credit, would presumably be much larger. For the sake of comparison, consider the volume of total outstanding bank credit to all enterprises, in billion Hungarian forints: 144.3 in 1990, and 121.4 in 1991. The ratio of forced credit to bank credit was 63% in 1990 and 132% in 1991.

11. This means that the creditors wait in line in front of the debtor firm to have their debts settled. So the expression *queuing* has become widespread in Hungary for this phenomenon.

instance, to settle some of the reciprocal debts, even in several different chains, through a clearing system. Some of the interfirm trade credit could be converted into bank credit. Though the amount of forced credits decreased considerably, the reoccurrence of an increase of forced credits is not excluded as long as fundamental and lasting changes do not occur in the observance of financial discipline. To ensure that forced credit is at most sporadic, instead of ubiquitous, enterprises must accept the following two prohibitions:

"*Buyer:* Never leave goods unpaid for without the seller's prior agreement. If a debt should remain, you may well be in legal trouble: the seller may take you to court and have your assets seized. Apart from the legal complications, there will be a blot on the business reputation and goodwill of your firm, and your creditworthiness rating will fall."

"*Seller:* Refrain from delivering your goods until you are convinced that the buyer will pay for them and is really creditworthy."

The second warning is particularly worth emphasizing. The extenders of forced credit are often presented as "innocent victims" who demand justice. They think they have a right to expect the state to rush to their aid, as if they were the victims of a natural disaster. I think this argument is faulty. It must be accepted that the market is not "just." Entrepreneurs, as their name suggests, take a risk. If the deal goes well, they can make a lot of money, but if it comes out badly, they suffer a loss. If the buyer happens not to pay, they must try to collect their debt by legal means. If they do not succeed, that is their problem alone. If they have not lost heart, they will be more cautious next time about who they deliver their goods to.

In this respect as well, we must get used to the change. In a socialist economy, what counted was how much a firm managed to *produce.* Once the production had taken place, it could be reported to the statistical office, and the quantity of products was chalked up as a contribution to the fulfillment of the plan. What actually happened to the goods was quite immaterial from the enterprise's point of view. In a market economy, however, the sole thing that counts is what the firm manages to *sell,* how much money it can get for its products.

Having considered this instructive example, it is time to analyze the conduct of enterprises on a more general plane. Here it is worth examining separately the two segments of the economy: the new private enterprises, and the old state-owned enterprises.

The New Private Sector: "Imprinting"

To shed light on the behavior of the new private firms that arise during the reform-socialist period and the postsocialist transition, I would like to borrow a concept from evolutionary biology: the expression "imprinting."[12] (The dictionary definition is to impress or stamp, and the figurative meaning to impress indelibly on the memory.) Observations of animals provide firm evidence that habits acquired in the *initial, particularly sensitive stage* of life have an extremely strong influence. They become impressed deeply and almost irreversibly in the memory, and prompt the animal concerned to repeat the experience.[13]

It is most important for the new private firms to learn from the outset that they must observe the rules of financial discipline strictly. Resistance appears to this requirement. Private entrepreneurs may argue that if state bail-outs are still being instituted for state-owned enterprises, why is the same not done for them? I think it would be a big mistake to yield to this pressure. Disregarding some rare, truly justified exceptions (mentioned already), private enterprises must not be rescued financially with the help of the state. Let them struggle to survive. There is no cause for alarm if even 10–15% of new businesses, especially small and medium-sized firms, cease trading each year. The healthy, natural process of evolution and selection requires a large number of entries and exits.

The Old State Sector: Education by Trauma

The same argument makes people skeptical about what can be expected of state-owned enterprises if they remain in state hands. The knowledge that loose financial discipline was tolerated and the budget constraint was soft has been deeply "imprinted" in the minds of those running state-owned enterprises and many of those employed by them. Is it possible to alter this imprint at all?

It may be possible to change it, at least to some extent, if (and only if) the other contracting party, the state as "insurance company," is

12. See E. H. Hess (1973) and W. Sluckin (1973).

13. Goslings follow the mother goose on their walks in single file. One of the discoverers of "imprinting," Konrad Lorenz, observed that if goslings hatched in an incubator became acquainted with him, a man, in the first hours of their lives, they would follow him in single file when he went for a walk, instead of their real mother, even though the goose was nearby. This habit of theirs remained, despite the presence of their mother.

strict and steadfast about abiding by the new market economic contract.

State-owned enterprises have become dependent on the paternalist helping hand of the state and the constant availability of a bail-out, just as many weaker-willed individuals become addicted to the relief of smoking, alcohol or drugs. This is worth pondering upon as an analogy. How do those who actually manage to stop smoking, drinking or taking a narcotic go about giving up their addictive habit? The most important step is to recognize it is *harmful and dangerous*. In most cases the recognition comes through the influence of explanatory writings or lectures, while in many the final push comes from a shattering experience, for instance when the toxic habit causes a tragedy in the immediate environment of the hesitant subject, or serious illness in the addict himself or herself.[14]

Tables 6.2 and 6.3 showed that chronic loss-making and grave insolvency have become mortal dangers to the survival of enterprises in Hungary. If this pressure becomes permanent, managers will come to believe sooner or later that observing financial discipline is a matter of life and death.

This is what *may* happen, but it is not certain that the situation will really develop in this way. Observation of addictive habits, in fact, shows how easily any temptation can cause an old habit to recur. Every recurrence of the state's old conduct—toleration of infringements of financial discipline, softening of the budget constraint—may be taken by the managers of state-owned enterprises to mean that they need not take the matter so seriously after all. Then they too will revert to the old conduct.

So there is a chance of new expectations, accompanied by new habitual behavior, developing in state-owned enterprises, but it cannot be fully relied on. This can serve as an extra argument, alongside the other well-known ones, for privatizing state property, as the new kind of conduct can really be expected only from enterprises based on private ownership and accustomed to financial discipline right from the start.

---

14. A study by I. Swenson and J. A. Dalton (1983) of the factors inducing the cessation of smoking contains the following figures: 67.9% of the sample of former smokers cited the fact that they had been deterred by learning of the statistics on the mortal dangers of smoking; in 57.6% of the cases they mentioned damage to the respondent's own respiratory system, and in 29.2% of the cases the smoking-related death of a family member or friend. Similar findings are reported by S. Curry, E. H. Wagner, and L. C. Grothaus (1990).

IV General Conclusions

A number of general conclusions emerge from an analysis of the situation in Hungary.

A long preparatory phase was needed before the government and judiciary really set about imposing financial discipline with a firm hand. A range of prior conditions were required for this to happen. There was a need for the private sector to attain a critical mass, so that it could become, both as a supplier and an employer, capable of at least partly replacing the state-owned enterprises, if they disappeared in large numbers. There was also a need for the market institutions and legal infrastructure to attain a critical mass, for an apparatus to handle unemployment, and above all for organizations to distribute unemployment benefits and to act as a labor exchange.

Later, when financial discipline is being applied more forcefully, another quite long period must pass before the actors in the economy start believing that the state's conduct in this respect has changed for good and all. The expectations of managers are shaped above all by their own experience, not just by the pledges the government makes. Once they can see *in retrospect*, over a period of years, that a new, tough and consistent regime of financial discipline has really come into being, the new enterprise conduct will consolidate as well.

The two lessons drawn so far point to a common conclusion: consolidation of financial discipline is a lengthy process of evolution that extends over several years.

This is a painful process that cannot take place smoothly or without grave social costs. This is chiefly because it has painful side-effects like falling production and lay-offs, but also because the upheaval and trauma are themselves part of the education process.

The imposition of stronger financial discipline inevitably becomes a *political issue*. It can only be done if there is broad enough public support behind it. It assumes the presence of a consensus on a certain scale, at least in an implicit and passive sense. The requirement for its development, in other words, is that no significant force in the political arena attack the policy of reinforcing discipline from the rear.

The final lesson is that forceful steps taken towards financial discipline entail a *risk*. Tension is caused by the negative side effects, the falling production, the unemployment, and the weakening of social security. A marked rise in this tension can exercise a destabilizing effect and undermine the still fragile democratic institutions. More than one alarming warning has already been heard in Eastern Europe about the danger of "Weimarization," where populist demagogy, extremist nationalism and racial hatred find a response in the discontent caused by the economic ills.

I would like at this point, at the end of the study, to make my own position clear on this issue. While the conflict remains one between various economic and welfare goals, I for my part would lay very great emphasis on raising efficiency and imposing financial discipline to that end. But if a sober, objective political analysis revealed that democracy was threatened by the drastic economic measures being taken, I would accept a more cautious advance towards reinforcing financial discipline in order to avert that danger. If it comes to a conflict between efficiency and the cause of democracy, I am sure that defense of the institutions of democracy is the supreme task.

References

Becker, Gary S. 1992. "Habits, Addictions, and Traditions." *Kyklos* 45 (3): 327–346.

Becker, Gary S., and Stigler, George J. 1974. "Law Enforcement, Malfeasance, and Compensation of Enforcers." *The Journal of Legal Studies* 3: 1–18.

Binmore, Ken. 1992. *Fun and Games. A Text on Game Theory*. Lexington: D. C. Heath and Company.

Curry, Susan, Wagner, Edward H., and Grothaus, Louis H. 1990. "Intrinsic and Extrinsic Motivation for Smoking Cessation." *Journal of Consulting and Clinical Psychology* 58 (3): 310–316.

Dervis, Kemal, and Condon, Timothy. 1994. "Hungary—Partial Successes and Remaining Challenges: The Emergence of a 'Gradualist' Success Story?" In *The Transition in Eastern Europe*, edited by O. J. Blanchard, K. A. Froot, and J. D. Sachs. Chicago: University of Chicago Press, pp. 123–152.

Elster, Jon. 1979. *Ulysses and the Sirens. Studies in Rationality and Irrationality*. Cambridge: Cambridge University Press.

Fudenberg, Drew, and Tirole, Jean. 1991. *Game Theory*. Cambridge, Mass.: MIT Press.

Hess, Eckhard H. 1973. *Imprinting. Early Experience and the Developmental Psychobiology of Attachment*. New York: D. Van Nostrand Company.

Hirschman, Albert O. 1977. *The Passions and the Interests. Political Arguments for Capitalism before Its Triumph*. Princeton: Princeton University Press.

Kornai, János, and Matits, Ágnes. 1987. *A vállalatok nyereségének bürokratikus újraelosztása* (The Bureaucratic Redistribution of Firms' Profit). Budapest: Közgazdasági és Jogi Könyvkiadó.

Központi Statisztikai Hivatal (Central Statistical Office). 1993. *Magyar satisztikai évkönyv 1992* (Hungarian Statistical Yearbook, 1992). Budapest.

Mitchell, William D. 1969. *Essay on the Early History of the Law Merchant*. New York: Burt Franklin.

Móra, Mária. 1992. "Változások a csődkezelésben—nyolcvanas évektől napjainkig" (Changes in the Way of Handling Bankruptcies—From the 1980s to Our Days). *Vezetéstudomány* (4): 18–23.

Muraközy, László. 1993. "Az átmenet költségvetése Magyarországon, 1986–1992" (The State Budget in the Transitional Period in Hungary, 1986–1992). Mimeo. Debrecen: Kossuth Lajos Tudományegyetem.

Pénzügyminisztérium (Ministry of Finance). 1992. *Előterjesztés a Kormány részére a csődeljárásról, a felszámolási eljárásról szóló törvény makrogazdasági hatásairól* (Report to the Government on the Macroeconomic Effects of the Bankruptcy and Liquidation Act). Budapest, October.

Pénzügyminisztérium (Ministry of Finance). 1994. *Tájékoztató az 1994. Évi gazdasági folyamatokról* (Report on the Economic Development in 1994). No. 11–12. Budapest.

Schelling, Thomas C. 1978. *Micromotives and Macrobehavior*. New York: W. W. Norton and Company.

Sluckin, W. 1973. *Imprinting and Early Learning*. Chicago: Aldine Publishing Company.

Szalai, Tamás. 1993. "Konstruktív bizalom" (Constructive Confidence). *Heti Világgazdaság* 15 (February 20): 78–80.

Swenson, Ingrid, and Dalton, Jo Ann. 1983. "Reasons for Smoking Cessation among a Random Sample of North Carolina Nurses." *Women and Health* 8 (Winter).

Trakman, Leon E. 1983. *The Law Merchant: The Evolution of Commercial Law*. Littleton, Colorado: Fred B. Rothman and Company.

Várhegyi, Éva, and Sándor, László. 1992. *A sorban állások kialakulásának okai és visszaszorításuk lehetséges módjai* (The Causes Behind Queuing and the Possible Means to Eliminate It.) Mimeo. Budapest: Pénzügykutató Rt.

7 Transformational Recession: A General Phenomenon Examined through the Example of Hungary's Development[1]

All the postsocialist countries without exception are suffering from a grave economic recession. This is made clear by figure 7.1. The course of the recession is conspicuously similar in every case, even though these are countries whose starting points and specific circumstances differ substantially. The history of the production decline in Poland, the prime example of "shock therapy," is similar to the one in Hungary, where the transition has been gradual. Production has fallen sharply in countries which started with high international debts, and done the same in Romania and Czechoslovakia (or the Czech Republic and Slovakia), which were untroubled by this problem at the beginning of the transition. Production has fallen where there was no reform before the political turning point, and also where there was a process of reform taking place over many years. This strong similarity has prompted me to concentrate in this study on the factors that are common to the histories of this group of countries. Although the discussion throughout this study is about Hungary, I hope that the analytical approaches in it will prove useful when examining other postsocialist countries as well.

Since the phenomenon differs substantially from the cases discussed hitherto in the theories of economic fluctuation, there is justification for giving it a separate name. To distinguish it from them, I have called it *transformational recession*.

1. I am most grateful to Mária Kovács for her wide-ranging assistance with the research, to Álmos Kovács and György Surányi for their valuable comments, to Brian McLean and Julianna Parti for their excellent translation of the Hungarian text, and to Hungary's National Scientific Research Foundation (OTKA), the European Bank for Reconstruction and Development, and the AustriaLotto for their financial assistance to the program.

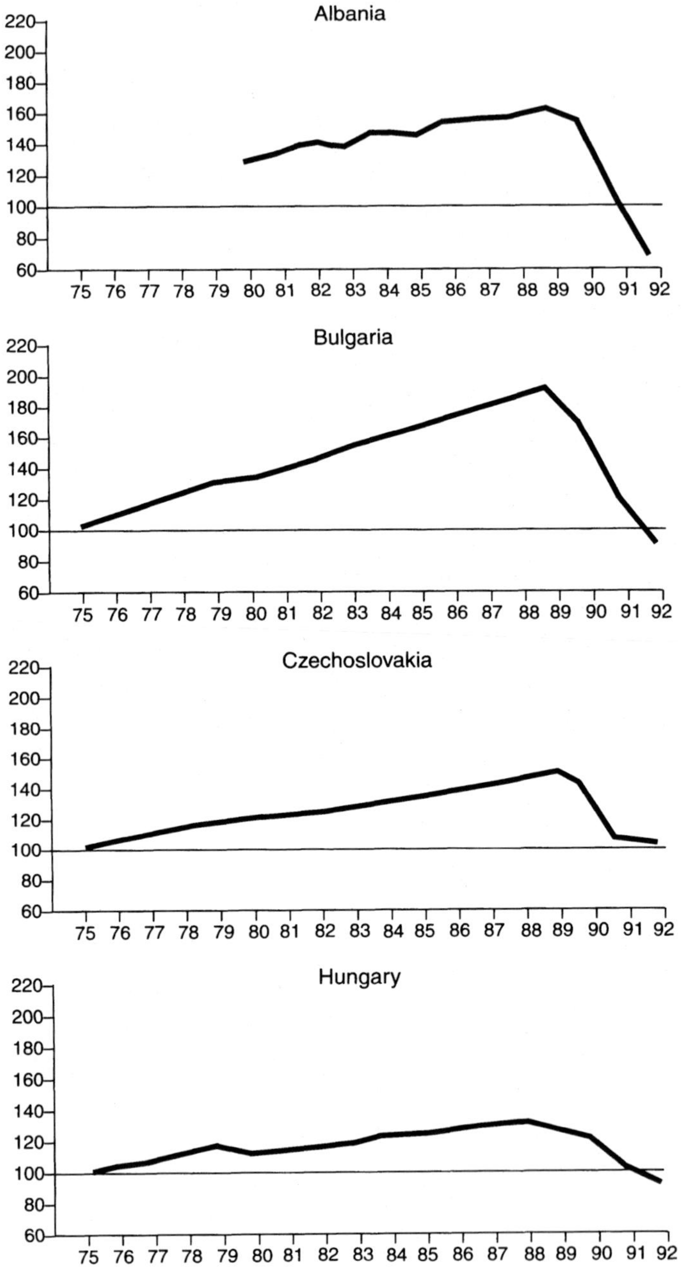

Figure 7.1
Gross industrial output (indices, 1975=100).
Source: Economic Bulletin for Europe, 1992, vol. 44, p. 29, on the basis of national statistics and ECE secretariat Common Data Base. *Note:* Industrial output changes for 1992 estimated by the ECE secretariat.

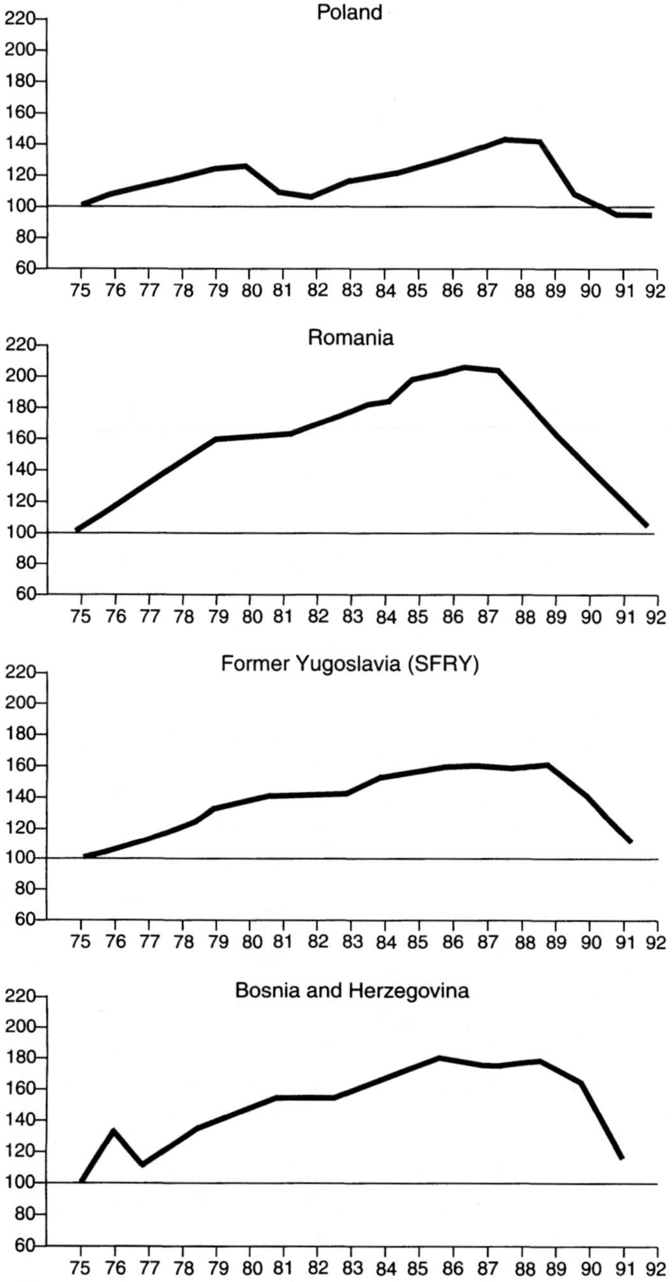

Figure 7.1 (continued)

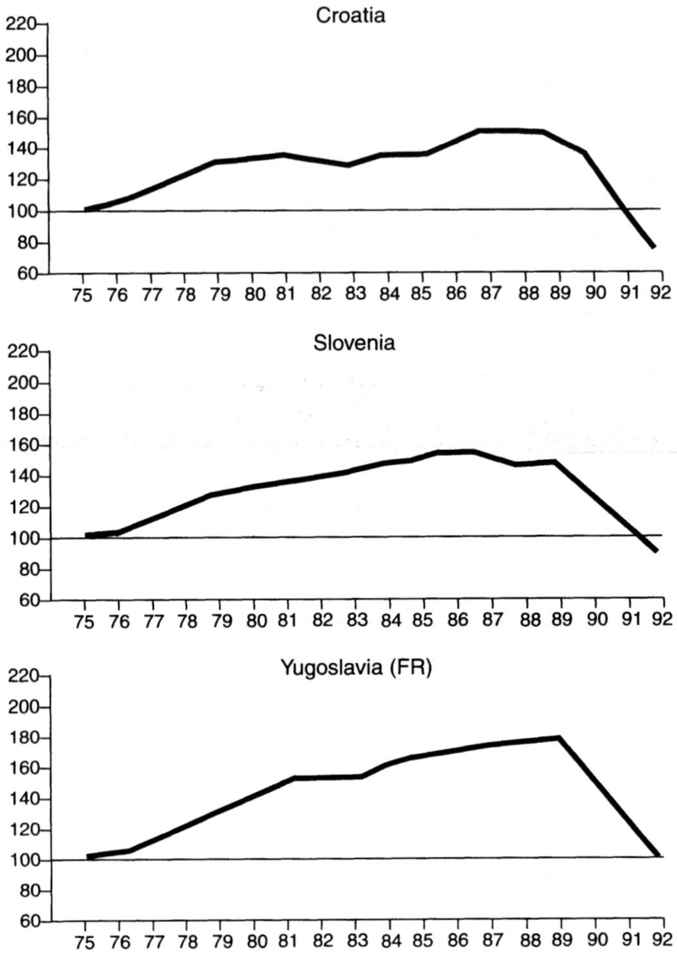

Figure 7.1 (continued)

The figures for Hungary are shown in tables 7.1 and 7.2 (see also table 6.5 on p. 148). These make it clear that the fall in production, which followed a long period of stagnation, is deeper than the one that took place in the Great Depression of the early 1930s. Total production has fallen by 19% instead of 7% as then, and industrial production by 39% instead of 12%. Yet the recession in Hungary so far has been relatively milder than in most other countries in the region.[2]

It was generally expected that the transition would be accompanied by a range of difficulties, but to my knowledge, very few economists predicted this large-scale decline in production.[3] A growing number of

Table 7.1
Indices of GDP and industrial production in Hungary, 1980–1992

Year	GDP	Industrial production
	(1989 = 100)	
1980	86.3	89.8
1981	88.0	94.3
1982	91.3	98.7
1983	91.9	100.5
1984	94.4	103.2
1985	94.1	100.9
1986	95.5	100.4
1987	99.4	103.6
1988	99.3	102.1
1989	100.0	100.0
1990	96.5	92.3
1991	85.0	75.7
1992	81.2	71.1

Source: Központi Statisztikai Hivatal (Central Statistical Office), (1993*b*, p. 71.).
Note: [Revised table.]

2. It can be assumed that the share of the informal sector (the "shadow economy") in total production grew in the same period. If this was really so, the fall in the total GDP including both the formal and informal sectors was smaller than the official statistics show.

3. The public in the postsocialist region was not prepared for this eventuality by the new parties and leading politicians, or by the new democratic governments. Nor can any forecast of the serious recession be found in the early theoretical writings to outline the program for the transition. So it is absent, for instance, from my own book, *The Road to a Free Economy* [1989] (1990), and from the oft-cited study written by O. Blanchard and other famous Western macroeconomists (1991). Among the very few exceptional early warnings was the writing of K. Laski (1990).

Table 7.2
Output, investment, and employment indices in Hungary under the Great Depression

Year	Net national product	Industrial production	Capital formation	Industrial employment
1929	100.0	100.0	100.0	100.0
1930	103.3	94.6	75.6	91.3
1931	101.0	87.4	59.1	82.9
1932	96.2	81.9	54.5	73.0
1933	93.6	88.2	43.5	73.6
1934	102.0	99.2	34.9	79.9
1935	102.7	106.8	34.5	85.9
1936	107.8	118.4	41.8	94.7
1937	115.1	129.5	54.3	104.0
1938	112.5	125.3	60.7	112.3

Source: Net national product and capital formation: B. R. Mitchell (1976, p. 786); industrial production and employment: League of Nations (1939, pp. 67, 181).

economists have been dealing with the question since then, but the profession has failed to arrive at a consensus about how to explain the phenomenon. Some ascribe it to a single cause (or at least a single main cause) like the collapse of Comecon trade, including the Soviet market. Such simple theories do not seem convincing to me. In my opinion, this is a complex, compound phenomenon that requires a *multi-causal explanation*,[4] and my research is aimed at contributing to a synthesis of various explanations.

The first chapter of the study points out a few *general* factors inducing the recession. The second chapter examines the *special* factors that cause the contraction of the main elements of macrodemand (investment, consumption, government spending, and exports). Both chapters discuss causal factors that can be traced back to a common ultimate cause: the postsocialist transformation itself. I am not arguing that no part of any kind is played by factors other than the group of factors associated with the process of transformation. A contribution to the decline in the postsocialist region has certainly been made, for instance, by the fact that the outside world, including the developed capitalist countries, is going through a recession as well. Apart from the direct economic drawbacks of this (tougher export conditions, a

4. Efforts to provide one are apparent in the articles by T. Erdős (1992), S. Commander and F. Coricelli (1992), S. Gomulka (1991*a*), (1991*b*), and G. W. Kolodko (1992). I have taken over several important ideas from these in this study.

smaller influx of capital), it has an unfavorable social-psychological effect. It is unfortunate that the former socialist world should have begun to move towards capitalism just at a time when this system was not in its best form. This factor, however, is not covered in my study, which deals solely with *internal* effects rooted in the transformation itself.

The third and final chapter draws conclusions from the causal examination described in the previous two chapters. The emphasis in all three chapters is on positive description and analysis, but normative proposals also appear in them, in most cases simply as illustrative examples.

It is worth saying what the study does *not* set out to do. It does not provide a numerical forecast, and it does not put forward a detailed program of government action. Instead of contributing to the debate on the current situation of the Hungarian economy, I would like to analyze a few major tendencies in the last and next few years, and comment on some strategic problems that arose.

I The General Factors Inducing the Recession

Not even in the recessions of a mature capitalist economy does the production of each and every firm and product decline. Even near the trough, successful, expanding enterprises are found at least sporadically. In a transformational recession, this is not exceptional at all; this duality is one of its characteristic features. Contraction and expansion, failure and success, mass exit and mass entry can be observed side by side. To use the phrase of Schumpeter's so often quoted these days, "creative destruction" takes place at tempestuous speed. But it is still possible to refer to a recession in the macro sense because the balance of the two processes is negative; for the time being, the pace of the contraction process is greater than the pace of the parallel process of expansion.

This recognition dictates that the examination should not be confined exclusively to the factors that explain the *absolute* decline. The final balance between the expansion and contraction processes with their opposite signs is affected by everything that promotes or impedes either growth or decline.

Each and every trade cycle under capitalism has specific features. Even so, I will attempt a measure of abstraction, by comparing the individual features of the transformational recession with an "ideal type," the typical recession that occurs in a mature capitalist economy.

From a Sellers' Market Toward a Buyers' Market

In the normal state of capitalist economy taken here as a basis for comparison, macro-level monetary equilibrium applies as the long-term trend: macrosupply and macrodemand are in balance at the prevailing level of prices. The usual attendant phenomena are unemployment corresponding to the natural rate, excess capacities accompanying imperfect competition that governs the bulk of the market, and a constant process of entries and exits. The balance of power between the producer-cum-seller and the buyer in this kind of economy is tipped in the buyer's favor. There is a buyers' market, in which the sellers compete for the buyers' money, and precisely this is one of capitalism's greatest advantages, because it encourages adaptation to the demand, respect for consumer sovereignty, improvement in quality, and the introduction of new products.[5]

Compare this with the normal state of classical socialism, a chronic shortage economy, in which macrosupply and macrodemand are not in equilibrium at the prevailing level of prices. The attendant phenomena are a shortage of labor, unsatisfied demand for many products and services, widespread queuing, and forced substitution. The expansion of production regularly runs up against bottlenecks and constraints on physical resources.[6] The balance of power between the producer-cum-seller and the buyer in this kind of economy is tipped towards the seller. This is a sellers' market, in which the buyers compete for the products for sale.

Not even at the peak of the trade cycle in mature capitalism does the state of the market switch over to a general, intensive and chronic shortage economy. The ball remains in the same half-court, i.e. the buyers' market basically continues to prevail, and at most the balance of power shifts slightly in the direction favorable to the seller. At the trough, there is an increase of unemployment and underutilization of resources, which intensifies the competition even more.

---

5. On the advantages of a buyers' market, see the articles by T. Scitovsky [1951] (1971), (1985) and E. Domar (1989). A detailed comparative discussion of the buyers' and sellers' markets appears in chapters 11 and 12 of my book (1992*a*).

6. In an open socialist economy the desire to increase production often runs up against constraints on the availability of hard foreign currencies.

Transformational recession, on the other hand, is combined with a profound and *unique* change. The game moves to the other half-court, so that the economy changes from a sellers' into a buyers' market—from a supply-constrained economy into a demand-constrained economy. This is a process that is to some extent consciously controlled by economic policy (monetary and fiscal policy, as well as pricing policy), out of a desire to bring the shortage economy to an end. But its course is influenced by several uncontrolled, spontaneous circumstances as well. There is a complex mutual influence between recession and the switch of "market regime" (the change from a sellers' to a buyers' market), so that neither process can be plainly said to have *caused* the other.

In the countries that were moving away from the classical form of socialism before the political turning point—Hungary in the first place—the transition to a buyers' market began earlier. Table 7.3 is instructive in this respect, because it shows how the supply constraints (shortages of labor, materials, semi-finished products and components, for instance) eased steadily over a period of seven years. Already it is rare for physical resource constraints to constitute a direct obstacle to production growth. The kind of low frequency with which production in Hungary runs up against input constraints can be found in any mature market economy as well. It can be established from this table (and from numerous other facts) that the shortage economy in Hungary has ceased; there is no longer a general, intensive and chronic shortage. Parallel with this very substantial change, the role of the demand constraint increases. The table shows clearly how this is now the obstacle that the desire to raise production encounters most often. (A very important role is additionally played by the financing constraints, which are discussed later.)

To simplify somewhat, this long period of transition in Hungary can be divided into two stages (table 7.4). In the first, repressed inflation that constituted one feature of the shortage economy turned into a moderate rate of open inflation. The gradual, increasingly widespread freeing of prices worked in this direction; a price level developed at which macrosupply and macrodemand could reach equilibrium. This was also helped by supply factors: the emergence of the private sector, the easing of the conditions for entry into production, and the partial liberalization of imports. The rate of inflation speeded up, reaching a peak in June 1991, when prices were for 38.6% higher than a year before. These processes presumably soaked up the unspent purchasing

Table 7.3
Impediments to production: Hungarian survey data (in percent)

Quarter	Insufficient demand	Shortage of labor	Insufficient supply of raw materials and spare parts			Financing problems
			Domestic origin	Imported from ruble area	Imported from dollar	
1987/1	26.0	22.2	41.2	42.6		31.2
2	27.4	23.7	42.3	46.7		24.3
3	21.3	24.1	46.6	50.4		22.1
4	24.1	15.8	39.4	41.8		20.4
1988/1	28.0	15.7	50.0	16.6	32.8	32.7
2	28.3	24.7	44.1	17.2	35.3	36.4
3	27.3	23.0	45.3	18.2	64.0	35.0
4	30.7	19.3	38.5	14.9	22.4	40.1
1989/1	38.0	21.5	37.6	14.4	17.9	49.6
2	40.1	22.0	28.7	11.0	11.8	46.1
3	40.4	21.9	27.5	10.3	8.9	46.8
4	51.2	13.4	21.4	8.0	6.3	49.4
1990/1	51.3	12.1	13.8	5.8	3.9	57.8
2	56.1	13.9	13.0	3.4	2.2	45.2
3	51.0	10.3	15.3	4.6	2.6	51.9
4	54.5	4.3	11.3	3.2	3.7	48.7
1991/1	60.6	4.3	9.4	2.3	2.6	53.2
2	70.1	4.0	7.1	1.5	2.4	54.1
3	66.8	3.3	6.2	1.2	2.0	52.7
4	65.9	3.0	7.2	0.5	1.0	47.3
1992/1	65.1	3.3	5.8	0.3	1.0	51.0
2	62.2	7.4	5.9	0.7	1.5	45.9
3	56.1	4.4	10.6	1.7	3.1	47.8
4	54.5	4.8	8.7	0.7	2.3	42.9
1993/1	57.7	2.2	6.1	1.3		45.5
2	68.8	3.0	6.0	3.2		47.3
3	67.9	3.7	7.5	3.1		48.6
4	62.5	4.3	9.4	2.4		47.3

Source: KOPINT-DATORG (1994).
Note: *[Revised table.]* The survey applies the methodology elaborated by the German research institute IFO and used in several other countries as well. Respondents are asked to mention "impediments of production." Each respondent can mention as many impediments as he or she likes. The figures refer to relative frequencies in percentage. (E.g., in 1987, 1 out of 100 respondents 26 mentioned insufficient demand, beside mentioning other factors as well.) There are other impediments mentioned by the respondents but not included in this table. "Ruble area" refers to the former member countries of Comecon. The survey did not separate the "ruble area" and the "dollar area" in 1987 and in 1993; the data refer to the lack of imported raw materials and spare parts.

Table 7.4
Consumer price indices in Hungary, 1980–1993

Year	Average annual rate of change (in percent)
1980	9.1
1981	4.6
1982	6.9
1983	7.3
1984	8.3
1985	7.0
1986	5.3
1987	8.6
1988	15.5
1989	17.0
1990	28.9
1991	35.0
1992	23.0
1993	22.5

Source: Period 1980–1990: Központi Statisztikai Hivatal (Central Statistical Office), (1991, p. 218); 1991–1992: Központi Statisztikai Hivatal (Central Statistical Office), (1993*a*, p. 34); 1993: The data were given by the Central Statistical Office of Hungary.
Note: [Revised table.]

power or "monetary overhang." In other words, there was an end to the macroeconomic situation that some economists characterize as a general excess demand.

The *disinflationary* efforts of the financial administration commenced in 1991 and became more perceptible in 1992. The rate of inflation reached its lowest level so far in July 1992, when the price level was 20.1% higher than twelve months before. Since then it has fluctuated within the range of 20–26% annually. To some extent demand had actually been held in check even earlier by monetary policy. Though no orthodox monetarist economist would call the financial policy of the late 1980s and early 1990s "restrictive," as scope constantly remained for a very sizeable inflationary growth in the money supply, demand clearly did not "run away."[7] In fact, it fell appreciably in volume terms, and the gap between demand and the earlier maximum

7. A part was played in curbing demand by the institutional reforms and the changes that took place in the behavior of the economic actors as well. To some extent the budget constraint became harder, and that was accompanied by a lessening of the investment hunger; firms, and even the state budget, became less prodigal in their spending.

supply, i.e., the potential GDP, steadily widened. Ultimately, the economy on the macro level tipped from the state of excess demand to insufficient demand.

The "market regime" can be graphically demonstrated by using a synthetic index that shows the composition of stocks. In a shortage economy, firms mainly accumulate stocks of inputs, while outputs are soon taken up by the buyers. When the shortage economy ends, the proportions change; there is no more need to hoard inputs, but output stocks build up due to sales difficulties. This change is shown in table 7.5. The index in Hungary stood earlier at around 6—input stocks were six times as big as output stocks. This compares with a value of around 1 in the mature and developed market economies. The present value of the index shows a dramatic fall to below 3, but it has yet to reach the figure typical of a mature market economy.

From all this can be drawn a range of conclusions important to our subject, recession.

The recession cannot be explained solely in terms of insufficient demand. Even now, only half the firms consider the insufficiency of demand as the obstacle to production.[8] We currently face a "half-

Table 7.5
Ratio of input and output stocks

Countries Periods	Input stocks/ output stocks
Capitalist countries, 1981–1985	
Austria	1.06
Canada	0.92
Finland	1.92
Japan	1.09
Portugal	1.66
United States	1.02
West Germany	0.71
Hungary	
1981–1985	6.10
1988	5.16
1989	4.65
1990	3.50
1991	2.67

Source: The table was compiled by A. Chikán.

8. Nor does inadequate demand become the sole obstacle to production in a mature,

Keynesian" situation, for whose treatment a doctrinaire Keynesian therapy is not suitable *in itself*. But the other half of the comment must be added immediately: precisely because the situation is already half-Keynesian, demand plays a very marked role in determining output. So the second chapter of the study analyzes this in detail. In a postsocialist transformational recession, the "brake" has not been applied by central controls on supply, as was the case when investment and production were curbed in the socialist economy. Although we are not faced with a recession produced *exclusively* on the demand side, the demand side has assumed the primary role.

When I first asked myself, twenty three years ago, how a supply-constrained sellers' market would turn into a demand-constrained buyers' market, I hoped this could be accomplished without a fall in production.[9] I thought the supply would continue to grow, while the growth in demand would decelerate (but still remain positive) to an extent that finally tipped the situation from excess demand to excess supply. The idea, or rather hope, that I had at that time is shown in figure 7.2a, taken

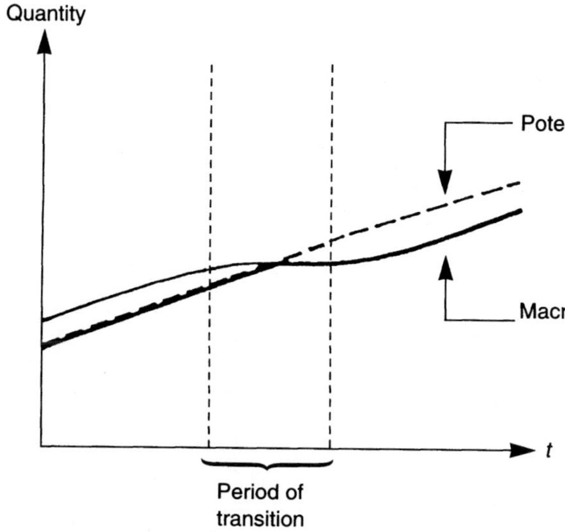

Figure 7.2a
The concept put forward in 1971.

developed capitalist economy, even during the downward phase of the trade cycle. The frequency there is at most 70–80%. See J-J. Laffont (1985, p. 354).

9. See *Anti-Equilibrium* (1971, p. 325). At that time I used other terminology ("suction" and "pressure"), but in later works, and in this study, I adopted the more widespread expressions.

from my 1971 book. Unfortunately the transition takes place differently in practice, for a number of reasons. Well before the change of system in Hungary, the growth of production had decelerated and been followed by a long period of stagnation. To transfer from excess supply to excess demand under such circumstances, the curbing of the growth of demand and (in volume terms) its absolute reduction inevitably drags down the supply as well, and these interact with each other in a vicious circle to deepen the recession. When the postsocialist economy transfers from one secular market regime, a sellers' market, to the other secular market regime, a buyers' market, it *tips over too far*, instead of arriving at an ideal state of equilibrium. The actual trend of supply and demand appears in a stylized form in figure 7.2b. The actual volume of production falls back steeply from its previous peak; the state of the economy resembles in this respect the trough in the customary fluctuation of the capitalist trade cycle.[10]

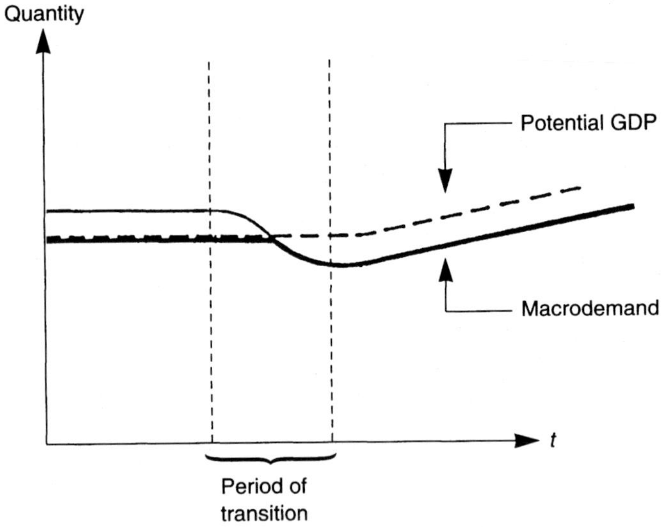

Figure 7.2b
The reality of the 1990s. *Note:* The bold line represents the actual GDP. The actual GDP is the smaller of the potential GDP and macrodemand. The curves in figure 7.2a coincide with those of figure 22.2 in *Anti Equilibrium* (1971); I modified only the denominations of the variables as to follow the generally used terminology.

10. The 1992 annual report of the United Nations Economic Commission for Europe considers it a mistake not to recognize the alteration in the macroeconomic conditions in Eastern Europe. "Emerging unemployment, the elimination of shortages and restoration

In fact, I have a bad conscience about using the expressions *general* excess demand and excess supply, because they simplify the description of the situation. I have been campaigning for a long time against rash use of aggregate macro categories in this subject-area. Unsold goods also existed under the conditions of the shortage economy. Occurrences of excess demand and excess supply can coexist at the micro level. Some producers run up against supply constraints while others meet with demand constraints. This caution is now more apposite than ever before, but it leads on to the next factor, the transformation of the real structure of the economy.

The Transformation of the Real Structure of the Economy

When we were looking at the restoration of macro monetary equilibrium just now, one question was left open: why does the change of market regime, the development of the sellers' market into a buyers' market, have recessionary effects?

Prices are gradually (or in some other countries suddenly) freed, which brings about a new system of relative prices. The greater the extent to which this is accompanied by liberalization of foreign trade (which in Hungary took place in parallel to a substantial extent), the more strongly and immediately the effects of foreign relative prices are felt. It suddenly emerges that there is insufficient demand for a range of products and services at the earlier high prices or at slightly lower ones; but if the prices plummet, the firms producing them make a loss. If the firms are deprived (either gradually or suddenly) of their financial subsidies at the same time, they are forced to cut or completely cease their production. Meanwhile the prices of other products rise due to the appearance of hitherto suppressed demand, therefore it becomes profitable to produce or import them. So the new relative prices and the concurrent new product composition of demand generate an adjustment in the supply, *i.e.*, a transformation of the real structure of production. But the adjustment of the quantities to the new prices always takes time, and for several reasons it is particularly sluggish during the period of the postsocialist transition. (Some of these reasons will be returned to later.)

---

of the basic monetary equilibrium are all symptoms of transforming the Kornai-type, supply-constrained economies into Keynesian-type, demand-constrained ones" (p. 51).

The strategy of forced growth under socialism gave rise to a production structure unadjusted to user requirements, including domestic consumption, but utilization of these products was imposed on buyers by central allocation and shortages. In the reform period a gradual change in the product composition of output took place. This transformation has accelerated in the last few years. At branch level, this primarily consists of a fall in the share and absolute volume of industrial production and a rise in the share and absolute volume of services (table 7.6). Within this process, thousands of alterations, great and small, take place on the micro level in the specific product composition of output.

In this respect the transformational recession has characteristics that are far more Schumpeterian than Keynesian. It is not simply that aggregate demand is insufficient. The demand for the output of some sec-

Table 7.6
Composition of GDP in Hungary

	Sources of GDP by economic branches (in percent)			
Branches	1986	1988	1990	1991
Industry	36.7	34.1	31.8	30.7
Construction	6.6	7.7	6.6	6.3
Agriculture and forestry	20.7	16.6	16.2	14.8
Transportation, post, and telecommunication	8.9	8.0	8.2	8.8
Commerce	9.4	10.1	11.5	11.1
Water management	1.4	1.4	1.3	1.3
Other material activities	1.2	1.1	1.3	1.4
Material activities	**84.9**	**79.0**	**76.9**	**74.4**
Personal and economic services	4.6	5.0	5.6	-
Services by financial institutions	-	1.5	2.0	-
Health, social, and cultural services	6.2	8.7	9.4	-
Community, public administration, and other services	4.3	5.8	6.1	-
Non-material activities	**15.1**	**21.0**	**23.1**	**25.6**

Sources: 1986: Központi Statisztikai Hivatal (Central Statistical Office), (1989, p. 57); 1988 and 1990: Központi Statisztikai Hivatal (Central Statistical Office), (1992*a*, p. 95); 1991: Központi Statisztikai Hivatal (Central Statistical Office), (1992*b*, p. 61).

tors of the economy fell dramatically, while the demand for that of other sectors did not fall at all, but may actually have grown. Let me give just two examples. Long-postponed demand led to an almost explosive development of businesses concerned with personal computers, electronics, modern information systems and telecommunications, so that for a long time this broad sector experienced a positive boom in the midst of the recession. The new relative prices and the new structure of demand caused the catering industry and services connected with tourism to flourish.

The change in the product composition and branch structure is connected with two other processes of change:

Property relations alter. There is a fall in the proportion of the sector in purely state ownership and a rise in those of the purely privately owned sector and the mixed-ownership sector that covers various combinations of state and private ownership. This occurs in such a way that the production of the purely state-owned sector decreases in absolute terms, while that of the private and mixed-ownership sectors increases.

A change takes place in the size distribution of firms. The small and medium-sized enterprises were almost totally eliminated under the classical socialist system. Small and medium-sized firms began to return during the period of reform socialism between 1968 and 1989, but they have only begun to multiply rapidly since the change of political system. The proportion and absolute production volume of the large-firm segment are falling, while those of the segment of small and medium-sized firms are rising.

These three kinds of restructuring do not overlap completely, but they coincide to a significant degree. It is not far wrong to say that the two most characteristic actors in a postsocialist economy are the large, contracting, state-owned industrial firm and the small, expanding, privately owned service firm. A more general and accurate way of putting it is to refer to contracting and expanding segments of the economy, without specifying their ownership, scale, and product classifications. The desirable state would be if the expansion were faster than the contraction, so that the balance between them yielded a positive increment. The opposite is unfortunately the case: the contraction of the first segment is faster than the expansion of the second, not because anyone intended it should be, but because there are a number of factors retarding the expansion of the growing sector. More will be said about these retarding factors later.

A painful process of "natural selection" takes place, but the trauma has a healthy, cleansing effect. In fact, a similar process occurs during the normal capitalist trade cycle; the idea features large in the cycle theories of A. Spiethoff and J. Schumpeter.[11] In the transformational recession, this process is far more intense and comprehensive. At the end of a capitalist trade cycle, the real structure of the economy has changed comparatively little since the beginning of the cycle, whereas it can be assumed (or rather hoped) that the situation after the transformational recession will be drastically altered.

Disruptions in Coordination

Many people had the naive idea that the elimination of central planning and bureaucratic coordination would be followed immediately and automatically by the appearance and operation of market coordination. In fact there is a curious "no-man's land," where bureaucratic coordination *no longer* applies and market coordination does *not yet* apply, and economic activity is impeded by disintegration, lack of coordination, and anarchy.[12]

The lack of coordination assumes various forms, of which I will pick out a few:

- The old behavioral norms of the economic actors have ceased, but they have not yet learned the new behavior to suit the new situation.
- Certain earlier institutions of bureaucratic coordination (organizations and legal regulations) have ended, but the erection of the new market institutions has either not begun yet, or is progressing very slowly. The network of market connections is still very loose, and it will take time before a dense network has been woven.
- The information structure of bureaucratic coordination has gone, but the new system of signals has not yet developed, or the economic actors are not yet sufficiently capable of assessing and processing the new kind of information.

11. See A. Spiethoff's (1902) and J. A. Schumpeter's (1934), (1939) works. An excellent account of these two cycle theories can be found in A. Hansen's well-known summarizing work (1964).

12. G. A. Calvo and F. Coricelli refer in their study (1992) to a trade "implosion." The trade relations are destroyed by the absence of market institutions.

The phenomenon they describe is an important constituent of the wider group of phenomena referred to above as the yawning gap and lack of coordination between the two kinds of coordination mechanism.

• Bureaucratic coordination, especially in its more consolidated periods before the final disintegration, supplied a kind of order and predictability. The market by its nature involves its participants in a lot of uncertainty and risk. This, however, is multiplied in the present unsettled situation. Most of the actors are at a loss, anxious, and hesitant about their decisions.

This phenomenon takes its ultimate form in many of the republics that have replaced the Soviet Union, but it also plays a major part in other countries like Albania and Bulgaria. This in my view is one of the main causes (possibly *the* main cause) behind the recession in these countries.

In Hungary the supplanting of bureaucratic coordination began much earlier, in 1968, after which gradual progress was made, with successive relapses. So the phenomenon just described appears in less dramatic forms than in countries which jumped almost directly from classical socialism to postsocialism. But it is worth recalling that there were areas of "no-man's land" even throughout the period of partial reforms implemented under the socialist system, a state described at the time by Tamás Bauer as one that was "neither plan nor market."[13]

The process of transformation has not been completed in Hungary either. The confusions of coordination and the phenomena of "no-man's land" still appear from time to time, at least in certain branches, and they contribute greatly to the recession. Let us look at two examples of this.

One is agriculture, where production has taken a real nosedive. Cooperative production based on collective ownership complemented by private farming on dwarf household plots holdings was not efficient in many respects, but nonetheless it worked and scored some successes. All the elements of coordination were adjusted to these property forms at the time: the central administration, the allocation of investments, the credit and tax system, the setting of prices, the commercial relations between producers and users, etc. The old property forms have been shaken, but mature new property forms have not arisen in their place. Everything is in a fluid state. The old institutions and organizations of coordination cease to function under these conditions. But the requisite new system of coordinative institutions—an up-to-date new wholesale and retail network to link the smallholders with the consumers, a new credit system for smallholders, and a

13. See T. Bauer (1983).

stability-enhancing price and subsidy system in line with European practice—have still not developed. All these factors gravely impede production. They are compounded by a succession of big government mistakes, above all over the compensation of formerly expropriated land-owners and the reorganization of the cooperatives.

The other example is the building industry, and in connection with it, housing construction and urban planning. Although this sphere was relegated and neglected under the socialist system, it still had an established organization and system of institutions. There were periods when the performance was relatively good, at least in terms of the number of housing completions, even though the quality of the housing completed was poor. Now the sphere is in a state of collapse as well, even though there is a great demand for housing. The market institutions have not yet developed, a credit system to suit the specific features of the housing market still hardly operates, the network of real-estate agencies is rudimentary, developers able to undertake the development of whole neighborhoods have not yet appeared, and there is confusion in the system of rents and social subsidies. There is an undoubted need for state supervision over the market processes in this field, and in certain respects for state regulation as well (for instance in applying urban-planning and social-policy criteria). Instead of a harmonious combination of bureaucratic and market coordination, one encounters repeated confused conflicts between them. As a result of all this, housing construction has fallen back seriously, whereas it might have been one of the leading sectors in the postsocialist transition.

The development of market coordination takes time, which is one reason why the recession is protracted in many fields. But the period of development can be shortened by appropriate legal regulations and state initiatives. The government has committed many sins of omission in this respect: it dawdled over drafting and implementing the legislation to support market coordination, over organizing supervisory agencies in conformity with the market economy, and over supplying a system of state guarantees in certain areas requiring it.

Financial Discipline and Enforcement of Efficiency

A hardening of the firms' budget constraint can be observed in the Hungarian economy.[14] The most tangible manifestation of this is the

14. This process is analyzed in greater detail in the sixth study.

forceful implementation of the bankruptcy legislation, even if some mitigation of this originally very strict piece of law has come onto the agenda since. A large number of insolvent firms are undergoing reorganization through bankruptcy proceedings, and many of them are being liquidated.

A private firm is under a hard budget constraint from the outset. Although there are attempts to soften it here as well, the growth of the private sector entails the spread of a hard budget constraint.

What effect do these changes have on recession, the phenomenon discussed in this study? Some of the firms go bankrupt and exit, which means lay-offs and an end to the firm's demand for inputs. The survivors, which from now on are truly profit-maximizing firms that use market instruments to fight for their survival, economize in their expenditure better than they did, which means that their demand for inputs is decreasing. They try to use up their swollen stocks from the past. This too has a demand-reducing effect. They dismiss workers who have become superfluous. The unemployed usually generate less consumer demand than the employed.

Even if the managers of state-owned firms bring themselves to dismiss workers, they remain somewhat disinclined to undertake a radical reduction of their excess labor. Table 7.7 shows that employment in industry falls slower than production, so that the productivity of labor is deteriorating. Presumably there is still a great deal of "unemployment on the job." Once state-owned property is privatized, the situation changes. Experience in many cases confirms what would be expected in theory: the first thing the new owners do is to dismiss the workers they judge to be superfluous.

Privatization is widely considered to be the main means of overcoming the recession and inducing growth, but this is a simplified misconception of the real relationship. *In the long term,* efficiency really will be increased by the spread of private ownership, the privatization of assets previously owned by the state, and the enforcement of financial discipline, a hard budget constraint, in all sectors of the economy, and that will make the growth trend steeper. *In the short term,* however, privatization has a different effect, because as we have described already, it raises unemployment, reduces demand and so contributes to the recession. Choosing between a short-term, anti-recessionary goal and a long-term growth goal is one of the gravest dilemmas to be faced during the postsocialist transition.

Table 7.7
Gross production, employment and labor productivity in Hungarian industry, 1980–1992

Year	Output	Average number of employed	Gross production per employee
		(1989 = 100)	
1980	89.0	116.1	76.6
1981	91.2	113.7	80.2
1982	93.2	111.4	83.8
1983	93.9	109.2	86.0
1984	96.3	108.6	88.7
1985	97.2	107.9	90.2
1986	98.9	107.1	92.4
1987	102.7	104.4	98.4
1988	102.1	101.7	100.5
1989	100.0	100.0	100.0
1990	89.8	94.5	95.0
1991	74.9	84.1	89.1
1992	67.5	73.1	92.5

Source: Központi Statisztikai Hivatal (Central Statistical Office) (1993*b*, p. 95).
Notes: The output data are based on the gross production of economic organizations belonging to the category of industry. The table does not cover the construction sector.

The Backwardness of the Financial Sector

The problem to be discussed now is in fact part of the previous two, but it deserves separate treatment because of its special importance. Only now, when the financial sector's backwardness has become one of the obstacles to growth, can the full significance of the difference between a wholly monetized capitalist economy and a semi-monetized socialist economy be appreciated.

Let me return to the column in table 7.3 showing the proportion of firms that consider insufficient financing to be one of the obstacles to growth. It is worth noting that while this factor was mentioned by 20–30% of the respondents in 1987, the frequency is 45–50% nowadays.

The banking system under classical socialism did not operate as a real bank. Its actual function was to provide a nationwide bookkeeping and cashier service, coupled with some aspects of the supervision of producer firms. Its guiding principle was that if a real action was declared necessary by the plan or the state bureaucracy, it would provide the money for carrying it out. Where a start was made to reforming the economy before the change of political system, as it was in Hungary, transformation of the banking system also began, so that it came somewhat to resemble its counterpart in a true market economy, although the development can certainly not be taken as complete.

This study does not set out to make a comprehensive analysis of the financial sector, and so only a few problems directly related to the subject of recession and growth will be dealt with here.

One problem is the rash and irresponsible way in which credit risks are assumed when they are motivated by non-commercial considerations. This problem that ties in with the question discussed in the previous section, i.e., financial discipline, still appears very sharply in the successor states of the Soviet Union. There thousands of loss-making firms are being kept alive with bank credits, this way fueling inflation and impeding the enforcement of financial discipline. This phenomenon does not occur on a mass scale in Hungary, since we are past that stage. But not even in Hungary has the special relation of the state-owned commercial banks and the large state-owned firms ceased altogether. The owner of both is the state, and in a sense a "personal union" applies. The banks are at times more indulgent with their old customers than they are with their new customers, the private entrepreneurs, when it comes to pressing their claims. Sometimes a similar partiality can be seen in the extension of new credit as well.[15] Settlement of the situation with unrecoverable loans was a very long time coming. This "soft" behavior by the banks towards the state-owned firms' sector hinders the process of natural selection described earlier. The situation is further exacerbated by the fact that from time to time a high-ranking figure in the government and political life will intervene, usually in an informal way, in the activity of the commercial banks in state ownership, exerting pressure on their credit-extension decisions.

In some credit relationships there is a disregard for risks, and in others there is excessive caution and real cowardice about extending credits, particularly when the applicant is a small or medium-sized private firm or a household. It must be admitted that there is a real dilemma here. The banks are just beginning to get used to the idea that

15. The bias is not shown exclusively to state-owned firms. The banks have also rashly extended vast credits to a good many large private firms, and find it hard to bring themselves to take harsher measures to force repayment.

they must pursue *commercial* activity, which taken as a whole will yield a profit. They should learn that a bank is not an institution for distributing money on orders from above or friendly recommendations from politicians. That may be so, but they now apply the lesson they have learnt with eager zeal and are inordinately averse to risks. They have yet to master the second part of the lesson: a bank, as a commercial undertaking, must live and prosper by extending credit. No venture in a market economy can make lasting profits by "holding goods back."

So a paradoxical situation has developed. A huge stock of liquidity has accumulated in the banking system, but it is stuck there. On the one hand the commercial banks are shy of lending it on a broad scale, but on the other, entrepreneurs are shy of drawing credit, because they think it is too risky as well.

For a long time the nominal rate of interest was very high, and it only began to fall quite recently. The real interest rate was less alarming because of the steep rate of inflation, but still high enough to deter many entrepreneurs from borrowing. There is a debate taking place about the role played in decisions on borrowing under current Hungarian conditions by the magnitude of the interest rate. For want of a strong enough argument to support a decided opinion on this, I can only give my impression. It seems that at the real rate of interest prevalent at the time of writing even a moderately successful business could service a loan on such terms. I tend to agree with those who say the *main* cause of the reluctance to borrow is the uncertainty.[16] There are too many unpredictable aspects of the future legal situation, property relations, taxation and other public levies, the future trend in relative prices and inflation, and not least the forecasts about the general state of the economy. On the creditors' side, the interest rate has probably come down enough to make the banks even less inclined to lend, precisely because of the uncertainty about the economic conditions.

To follow up the line of argument begun in the previous section, I can point to the continued absence of a whole range of institutions and organizations very necessary in general for the operation of a market economy, and especially important for stimulating Hungary's transitional economy. Let me give just a few examples. There has not yet emerged a system of collaterals and guarantees that does not just copy

16. See, for instance, the article by Á. Valentinyi (1992).

the rules and conventions in the mature market economies, but allows for the immaturity typical of the Hungarian economy and the initial problems of the entrepreneurial stratum. There has not yet developed fully one of the elementary tools of all modern financial systems: a system of current (checking) accounts. Transfers and payments of claims through the banking system are still very slow and expensive. Credit cards are not widespread. The network of various kinds of investment funds, venture-capital companies, pension funds, and other financial intermediaries has still not consolidated. The development of the capital market is at its early stage.[17]

Mention must again be made of the two branches referred to earlier: agriculture and housing construction. Throughout the world, both of these employ special credit and investment schemes. In Hungary, the development of these proceeds very sluggishly, which has greatly contributed to the grave recession in these two branches.

Development of the financial sector inevitably takes a long time, of course, but a great many omissions by the government can be blamed for the fact that progress has not been faster. This applies to all the phenomena used to demonstrate the backwardness. Yet another typical example of government neglect was the delay and procrastination before conditions for the so-called "E-credits" available to entrepreneurs were eased, thus widening access to them. (This is a specific credit scheme, which grants loans to private entrepreneurs for investment at favorable terms with the help of governmental assistance.) Hesitation and a lack of imagination have been shown in a field where there is a real need for constructive governmental initiative.

Calvo and Coricelli, in the study mentioned earlier,[18] take the disturbances in the credit system and the scarcity of credit to be one of the main causes of the recession. This statement seems to be correct, but at least in Hungary's case it needs some refinement. I do not think the main problem is the tightness of the total credit supply permitted by central monetary policy. There is even some redundancy here. In my

17. It is particularly worth noting that the country is facing problems of immaturity not only in the banking sector in a narrow sense, but in the broader financial sector. It would be a mistake for credit to play an excessive role in financing the firms, and so relegate their own capital into the background. Difficulties appear in assembling initial capital and obtaining investments needed for capital injections. A very high degree of uncertainty about the chances of value-preserving, profitable investments, as well as the underdevelopment of the organizations managing investments, is deterring many possessors of money from bringing their savings to the capital market.

18. G. A. Calvo and F. Coricelli (1992).

view the problem lies in the excessive friction and low efficiency with which the financial system operates as an intermediary between the possessor of money—the depositor-saver—and the borrower of loans.

To sum up the first chapter of the study, it can be stated that the postsocialist transformation necessarily gives rise to processes that tend towards a reduction in aggregate production. This painful consequence of the transformation has been examined in five "dimensions." These five processes, intertwined with and reinforcing each other, hinder growth and retard production. Their negative effects are compounded by mistakes on the government's part.

II On the Four Components of Macrodemand

Attention was drawn in the first section of the previous chapter to the conspicuous and constantly expanding role played by the demand side in determining output during the period of the postsocialist transition. So let us consider the principal components of demand one by one, employing the categories customarily used in macroeconomics. (A summary of the changes in these is provided by Table 7.8.)[19] But I would like to stress in advance that I do not confine myself exclusively to examining the demand (utilization) side; mention will also be made of some aspects of the supply (production) side. Although in each case I take a macro approach as the point of departure for examining the phenomenon, I will also refer several times to the microeconomic and institutional aspects.

Investment

Let us begin with the most important category from the point of view of medium and long-term growth: investment. The volume of investment has seriously declined (table 7.9), in fact to 27% below its peak. The proportion of investment in the utilization of the steadily declining GDP has fallen (table 7.10).

19. The text of this study uses the customary categories of macroeconomics: investment, private consumption, government consumption, and export surplus or net exports. The classification of the official statistics for the utilization of GDP differs somewhat from this, which can be seen in table 7.8, for instance. The macroeconomic categories can each be made to correspond more or less with a statistical category. Since I am not at this point making a quantitative analysis, it can be hoped that the deviations between the two kinds of classification will not cause confusion.

Table 7.8
Gross domestic product or expenditure

GDP on comparable (1988) prices, HUF mn.					Volume indexes, %				
Components	1988	1989	1990	1991	1989/1988	1990/1989	1991/1990	1992/1991	1992/1989
Private consumption	873,814	893,586	861,112	811,591	102.3	96.4	94.2	97.8	88.8
Collective consumption	175,000	164,000	168,300	163,755	93.7	102.6	97.3	98.9	98.7
Final consumption	*1,048,814*	*1,057,586*	*1,029,412*	*975,346*	*100.8*	*97.3*	*94.7*	*98.0*	*90.3*
Gross fixed capital formation	310,801	332,529	308,800	272,925	107.0	92.9	88.4	93.6	76.9
Changes in stocks	49,941	32,685	40,947	-1,136	-	-	-	-	-
Gross capital formation	*360,742*	*365,214*	*349,747*	*271,789*	*101.2*	*95.8*	*77.7*	78.6	58.5
Total domestic use	*1,409,556*	*1,422,800*	*1,379,159*	*1,247,135*	*100.9*	*96.9*	*90.4*	*93.8*	*82.2*
Exports	530,395	536,815	508,132	430,345	101.2	94.7	84.7	-	-
Imports	491,738	500,737	479,425	437,038	101.8	95.7	91.2	-	-
Net exports	38,657	36,078	28,707	-6,693	-	-	-	-	-
Total GDP	**1,448,213**	**1,458,878**	**1,407,866**	**1,240,442**	**100.7**	**96.5**	**88.1**	**95.5**	**81.2**

Source: Központi Statisztikai Hivatal (Central Statistical Office) (1993*c*, table 1.3.2), Központi Statisztikai Hivatal (Central Statistical Office) (1993*a*, p. 105), and National Bank of Hungary (1992, p. 129).
Note: [Revised table.]

Table 7.9
Fixed capital formation in Hungary, 1980–1992

Year	Investment 1980 = 100 (on the basis of comparable prices)
1981	95.6
1982	94.2
1983	90.9
1984	87.7
1985	85.1
1986	90.6
1987	99.4
1988	90.3
1989	95.0
1990	86.8
1991	76.8
1992	72.8

Source: The data were given by the Central Statistical Office of Hungary.
Note: *[Revised table.]*

Table 7.10
Fixed capital formation in Hungary, 1980–1991

Year	Fixed capital formation as a percentage of GDP (at current prices)
1980	28.8
1981	26.5
1982	25.2
1983	24.5
1984	23.0
1985	22.5
1986	24.0
1987	24.7
1988	20.6
1989	20.3
1990	17.8
1991	19.1

Sources: Period 1980–1987: Magyar Nemzeti Bank (National Bank of Hungary), (1990, p. 97); period 1988–1990: National Bank of Hungary (1991, p. 129); 1991: J. Vígh (1993, p. 22).

There was a constant insatiable investment hunger apparent under the classical socialist system. The investment stimulus of what Keynes called "animal spirits" never flagged. The decision-makers at every level from the works manager to the prime minister were driven by expansion drive. The fact that the bill for the investment was always paid in the end out of public funds, so that the financial failure of the investment was overcome, guaranteed permanent optimism about growth.

This attitude, already dulled by the quasi-reforms, was completely eradicated by the political turn and the institutional changes that followed it. The investment hunger came to an end, to be replaced by caution, and even cowardly fear in many people.[20] Let us take the various spheres of investment decisions in turn.

1. In the government sector, in which I am not including state-owned firms here, investment activity has declined. This is connected, of course, with the troubled fiscal situation. Similar tension under the socialist system would not have deterred the top leadership from undertaking great investment expenses, as the decision could be taken behind closed doors. However great the investment expenditure was, it could be covered by taxes levied indirectly on the public. There can be no question of this now, because Parliament decides how the taxpayers' money will be spent, in the full glare of publicity.

In order to overcome the recession, it would be desirable for the investment proportion of government spending to increase. The state needs to play a bigger part, especially in infrastructural investment.

2. The state-owned firms in the category likely to remain in long-term or permanent state ownership need investment to secure their survival and to modernize. The trouble is that also many of these firms are up against serious financial difficulties and are not sufficiently creditworthy. If an investment project shows a loss, they cannot count on automatic assistance. So their old self-confidence has been lost; their managers are hesitant and do not dare to invest. This must change. The decision-makers, of course, owe a responsibility for these investment decisions, which they cover out of public money after all. But this should not stop such decisions being made at all; public

20. Looking at the behavioral motives, this phenomenon relates to the one described earlier in connection with credit. A strong aversion to risk is apparent in both spheres.

The two spheres are not identical, although they overlap. Some investment is not financed from credits, and some credits are not extended for investment purposes.

opinion of the business community should also encourage the state sector to invest.

3. The situation is even worse with firms that are still in state ownership but known to be destined for privatization in the future. Here almost all investment activity has been paralyzed; no one dares to initiate anything while waiting for the new owners. In fact there is quiet disinvestment—depletion of the assets invested earlier. Several practical conclusions can be drawn from these observations:

- An acceleration of the change of ownership is also urgent from the investment point of view. The immediate proceeds of the sale should not be the main criterion. Consideration should be given, alongside the general objectives of social transformation, to the likely results of the investment and job-creation program promised by the new owners.
- Before the privatization takes place, it must be ensured at least that the assets will reach the new private owners in the best possible condition. A fundamental element of this is the conservation and careful maintenance of assets. Many firms need reorganizing, which usually entails larger or smaller amounts of investment as well.
- The firms' managers must be given a far bigger incentive to carry out the tasks just described, so that the assets privatized are as valuable as possible, not in a run-down condition.

4. In the private firms, in fact, the "animal spirits" referred to by Keynes are alive, as the large number of entries and firms being founded shows. They are alive, or rather would be if the propensity to invest were not cooled by several unfavorable circumstances. Two have already been mentioned when the financial sector was discussed: the uncertainty, which in fact is much greater than is usual in a market economy, and the financial sector's backwardness and reluctance to lend to private firms. Coupled with these are the weakness of the capital market and the fact that the tax system is not friendly enough towards investment. Many would also include among the factors curbing the propensity to invest the high level of interest rates. (This question has been mentioned already.)

Overcoming these unfavorable circumstances is the key factor in recovering from the recession.

5. A major figure in the investment sphere is the household, which can finance the construction of an owner-occupied apartment or house

from its own savings and from credit. For the sake of completeness, let me repeat that housing construction in general, including housing construction financed by households, has seriously declined. Stimulation of this activity with more easily accessible credits and with tax concessions, for instance, could play an important part in overcoming the recession.

Consumption

As table 7.8 showed, the volume of private, personal consumption has fallen, but to a smaller extent than GDP and total real income.

Under the mechanism of central planning, the predominant part of household incomes was regulated by the state, and the savings proportion was fairly stable, so that the central management of the economy could accurately forecast the consumer demand from the general public. There is no question of this now. Let us take the determinants of the demand in turn:

1. A smaller part of incomes derives from the budget, while the greater part depends on agreement between employers and employees. Although this is influenced by collective bargaining and interest reconciliation taking place at the highest level, on which the government has a great, though not exclusive influence, the actual wage agreements are decentralized. The central agreement is at most taken into consideration as a suggestion.

2. Once households possess a cash income and some stock of previously accumulated savings, the decision on how much to spend and how much to save is in their own hands. This may be influenced by government action (for instance a monetary and fiscal policy that tries to affect the interest rate), but the strength of this influence is doubtful.

Although the future spending intentions, i.e., aggregate demand of households will have a great effect on the recession, they remain hard to predict. Households themselves are just getting acquainted with the new situation and learning to make savings decisions of a new kind. No economist can yet know the result of that learning process or yet recognize what the regularity in it is, and what represents a one-off departure from some future regularity.[21] Let me pick out a few hypothe-

21. Household savings can be described by a variety of stock and flow indices. Let us take here just one stock indicator, used in Hungarian financial statistics: the "net financial position" of the general public, i.e., the household sector. The indicator is calculated by subtracting total debt from accumulated gross savings (whose main components are

ses that seem not merely to apply to the present situation in Hungary, but to have a more general validity: [22]

- Citizens who can rely less and less on the assistance of the state build up a safety reserve against illness or unemployment, and for their old age.
- Also appearing as "household savings" is the accumulation of the operating business capital for new private ventures (including unregistered, gray, or black businesses).
- The savings-to-earnings ratio of the higher-income strata is generally higher than that of the lower-income strata. So it can be assumed that the income differentiation that took place in recent years tended to raise the average savings rate. All these tendencies can be expected to continue.

What can be concluded from this in terms of an economic policy aimed at overcoming the recession? It would be a mistake to work for a growth in consumer demand through unbridled wage rises. Though perhaps popular initially, it is a dangerous weapon that can easily overshoot the target. There could also be an unexpected change in the spending-saving ratio, so that a still greater volume of intended spending spills onto the market from the excessive surplus of income. This would not only boost production, but price rises as well, leading to a big inflationary push. There is still a great need in the future for moderation and sobriety on the part of employees and organizations representing them. But if excessive wage pressure should appear after all, let us hope the employers (including the biggest, the state) will put up resistance.

Rash handling of wages would affect employment unfavorably as well. There is a generally recognized macroeconomic connection here. Very many firms would be obliged to dismiss workers if they were burdened by too high a wage bill under the present cost and labor productivity conditions.

---

cash, savings deposits, and securities). This index suddenly grew in 1991 and in the first part of 1992; a contribution was certainly made by the strong incentive given to pay back housing loans immediately.

Even after the easing of the sharp rise, the net position of the general public in real terms shows a great increase since three years ago: it was 71% higher at the end of 1992 than at the end of 1989. (Source: communication with the National Bank of Hungary and Magyar Nemzeti Bank, 1993, p. 122.)

22. Some hypotheses that seem convincing are advanced in this respect in an article by J. Király (1992), and I also make use of these in what follows.

Although there is still a need for caution and discipline over wages, there are some well-aimed measures that could help households as well to contribute by their economic decisions to overcoming the recession. The government and the financial sector, which is still mainly in state hands, have not shown enough initiative in this respect either. Let me give just a few examples.

• More should be done to ensure that the banking system is not the exclusive route by which private savings can turn into investment. Households should be involved to a greater extent in the capital market, primarily through the mediation of investment funds, insurance companies, and decentralized pension funds. This would tie down and so stabilize a high proportion of savings.

• Here let me repeat something mentioned before: it is desirable for a sizeable part of the savings by households to be used for financing housing construction.

• As a legacy from the socialist economy, too little scope is left in all the postsocialist countries, including Hungary, for consumer credit, which is far more limited than it is in the mature market economies. The spread of consumer credit can provide an easily controllable increase in demand, with favorable effects on production.

Government Consumption[23]

The state budget, from which government consumption is financed, has become a constant topic in day-to-day politics. This study is not a contribution to these debates. I remain within the bounds of my subject by dealing exclusively with the relationship between the budget and the recession. Looking beyond the immediate situation, I examine a few more general problems concerned with this relationship.

Hungary is in a vicious circle. Declining production is necessarily joined by declining state revenue, while most state expenditure is not

23. The "government consumption" category (i.e., total government spending, minus governmental investment expenditures) does not coincide exactly with the statistical category "collective consumption" (see table 7.8), although there is quite a large overlap between them. There is a third category, "total budgetary expenditure," which differs from both, for one reason because it includes the investment financed from the budget as well.

It is not the task of this study to compare these categories in detail or to work out the numerical deviations between them. What I have to say is confined to presenting qualitative tendencies. These appear most of all in the part *common* to all three expenditure aggregates, i.e., the collective consumption financed out of the budget.

related directly to the quantity of production. So a recession may produce a budget deficit in all economies. But once the deficit is there, it becomes hard for a government to bring itself to inject into the economy a fiscal stimulus, which is the most obvious method of overcoming the recession quickly.

It has been a truism since Keynes's day to suggest that it is advisable in times of recession to take fiscal measures to raise macrodemand, even at the cost of a budget deficit. The policy of governments that raised taxes and cut spending during the contraction phase of the trade cycle were described subsequently in the works of economic history written in a Keynesian spirit as gravely mistaken, because these measures reduced total demand.

This line of thinking suggests the following statement. If the deficit had been lower in past periods (if spending had been less and revenue more) and all other circumstances had been equal, the fall in production would have been greater than it actually was. The budget deficit acted as an anti-cyclical stabilizer.

The same line of thinking gives rise in the short term to the following conclusion: it would be dangerous now to reduce the deficit quickly and to a large extent (assuming the administration were capable of doing so at all.) A rapid and drastic cut (for instance by a sharp increase in taxes) would suddenly reduce the macrodemand and abruptly push the already very deep recession even deeper. In saying all this, I do not want to ignore all the well-founded arguments about the seriously damaging nature of the budget deficit. It entails an inflationary risk; moreover, the financing of it squeezes out the investment so necessary for recovery and growth. I merely want to draw emphatic attention to the existence of a direct connection between these two grave diseases in the Hungarian economy: the recession and the budget deficit. Treating one problem without sufficient circumspection will have harmful side-effects and may hinder recovery from the other disease.

It is far from my intention to encourage a deficit increase. On the contrary, the goal must be to take concerted measures to whittle down the main totals in the budget, i.e., to reduce expenditure, revenue, and the deficit concurrently. But an eye must be kept on the following: the reduction must happen in such a way that the demand lost from government consumption is replaced, if possible in full, by investment demand. The hope is that this desirable reallocation of resources will be ensured from a future reduction in the credit demand for financing the budget, in other words, the mitigation of the crowding-out effect.

This must be combined with a rise in the proportion of investment spending within total budgetary spending at any time. In this case there will be a favorable rearrangement of the composition of aggregate demand. Total investment demand of all sectors (governmental, business, and household) will have more beneficial multiplicator effects than the demand from government consumption.

Exports and Imports

The logic of the discussion has left foreign trade until last, although there is no doubt that of all the events inducing the recession, the serious decline in trade with the former Comecon countries, including the breakdown of the former Soviet market, has caused the greatest upheaval.[24]

Some of the authors dealing with the question have described this occurrence as an "external shock." In my view this is not an apt name for it. It is certainly true that the shock from foreign trade is external to each country concerned in a geographical sense, but all the characteristics of Comecon trade can be traced back to the fundamental features of the socialist economic order; its effect is deeply imbedded in the regularities of the system. The sellers' market was able to work because there was a Comecon buyer even for the articles least desired at home; if all else failed, the sale could be forced by a tie-in. The expression "external shock" is normally applied to an event that suddenly appears and then vanishes again, so that the economy, after some adjustment, gets over it and continues from where it left off before the shock. The collapse of Comecon trade, however, has lasting, definitive effects. The structure of these economies must be altered once and for all before they can prosper without it.

Table 7.8 shows that in the period of 1989–1991 exports fell back dramatically. The Hungarian economy successfully took the first steps of adjustment, proving capable of redirecting a very high share of its export potential to the OECD markets (see table 6.4 on p. 146). This made sure that the Hungarian economy stayed on its feet, that the fall in production did not assume catastrophic proportions, and the country's international payments position consolidated.

Unfortunately this cavalry attack cannot be sustained; the growth rate of exports has already slowed down, and the first warning signs of a decline can be discerned. We are unlucky, because a recession (far

24. An attempt to quantify this effect numerically was made in a study by D. Rodrik (1992).

milder than ours) appeared in the Western world just at the time when we had the greatest need to expand onto their markets.

Another problem is that the first great advance was made according to the old formula: "export at any costs." Many firms, particularly in the state sector, shouldered great losses in forint terms just to be able to export and not have to shut down production. But this cannot continue in the future, as the budget constraint hardens. Instead the struggle now must be for all possible additional exports that are really profitable without a state subsidy. On the other hand, the restriction of domestic demand has eased somewhat, so that firms sense to a lesser extent that they have to export or perish.

On top of all this are the serious problems with agricultural exports, which have been caused by several factors, not merely the unfavorable weather, but the growing tendency to protectionism shown by importing countries and the crisis in agricultural production discussed earlier in the study.

I agree with those who say that exports constitute one of the growth-inducing branches for small open countries in the long term. But it is another matter to decide to what extent exports can contribute under the present circumstances to the urgent short-term task of overcoming the recession as soon as possible. Some of the means mentioned earlier in connection with the stimulation of investment can self-evidently be applied to exports as well. Particular attention should be paid to the private investments aimed at producing for export as well.

Detailed analyses do not support the proposition that imports always squeeze the domestic producers out of the domestic market. There are examples of this, but it is far from general. A whole range of firms without an import rival have sunk into deep crisis, and on the other hand, many firms manage to carry on producing and selling successfully in spite of competition from imports. None of this is an argument against giving temporary protection to some domestic product or group of products on a considered basis of economic rationality, but not under pressure from lobbies. This can contribute to curbing the recession. But the protection must only be temporary, until the necessary adjustment has been made, and in line with the prescriptions of GATT, the international tariff agreement, so that it does not lead to protectionist retaliation by foreign trading partners.

The concerns about both imports and exports make it necessary once again to rethink the exchange-rate policy. If the present policy of allowing real appreciation of the Hungarian currency is continued, the chances for exports and domestic production facing import competition may deteriorate further, which will tend to deepen the recession. The campaign against recession must include a revision of the exchange-rate policy.[25]

Devaluation is known to give a boost to inflation.[26] Whichever way Hungary goes, either one problem (recession) or the other (inflation) will get worse. This dilemma arises in connection with most of the measures to be considered, and so it must be faced also in its more general form, which the final chapter of the study will do.

To sum up the second chapter, it can be established that the contraction observable in all four components of macrodemand is largely the result of the transformation process itself. But a role in the development of macrodemand is also played by the economic policy of the state; the severity of the recession is partly attributable to errors and mistakes on the part of the government.

III Conclusions

Priorities

In my view there are now grounds for reorganizing the priorities. Two or three years ago, there were very strong political and economic arguments in favor of the following priorities:

1. The increase in indebtedness had to be halted; the country's international liquidity position had to be improved.
2. Inflation had to be slowed down as much as possible.
3. Unemployment had to be "handled" from the point of view of welfare policy.

Neither the political statements and government programs nor the writings of economists included among the urgent priorities the need to guard against recession, or later the need to halt or combat the recession.

I now propose the following new priorities:

---

25. This idea is argued in detail in a study by G. Oblath (1994); I agree with its conclusions.

26. The inflationary effect is particularly serious if nominal wages are allowed to rise to compensate for the devaluation. So a condition for the success of the exchange-rate policy is that it should be based on a social consensus.

1. We must forestall any further recession. Recovery from the recession must be promoted. The economy must be diverted onto a growth path. As a likely by-product of this, perhaps after some delay, unemployment will cease to increase, after which employment will start to grow.

2. We must prevent a renewed acceleration of inflation. The inflation rate must be gradually brought down to the 12–18% band known as the range of "moderate inflation."[27] The attainment of single-figure inflation must be taken off the agenda for the time being. Preparation for this will become opportune once the economy is on a growth path again.

3. We need not work for a further sharp reduction in the total stock of foreign debt or rise in the foreign-exchange reserves.[28] A slight deficit on the current account is tolerable temporarily, although any marked deterioration on the balance of payments must be prevented, and we must not enter a new spiral of debt accumulation.

I have tried to phrase these new priorities as accurately as possible. On the basis of bad experience in the past, I would like to protest in advance against the eventuality of any opponent of mine in debate twisting one or other of these a little and leaving out some qualification, and then take issue with my proposals presented in a distorted form.[29]

There is no justification for relaxing attention to inflation and the balance of payments. In fact the danger of inflation and accumulation of debt will be greater than ever before, precisely because measures are being taken against recession. Countries that only have to cope with one of these three painful problems—only with inflation, for

27. Experience in many countries shows that an economy can remain within this band for several years without reaching single-figure inflation, but still avoid the danger of a renewed acceleration of inflation. See the study by R. Dornbusch and S. Fisher (1993) on this.

28. This last proposal should be understood as follows. The yardstick is not the absolute size of the exchange reserves, but the ratio between them and the volume of imports. Point 3 embraces the suggestion that it is not worth increasing this ratio further.

29. Inaccurate interpretations have not been confined to my opponents in debate. When I presented this line of argument in public in Budapest, one daily paper in a short report interpreted the priorities I put forward as a *temporal sequence*. According to the report, I was proposing that growth should be achieved first, then after that had happened, we should defend ourselves against inflation, and when that had been done, we should tackle the balance of payments. In fact, these are simultaneous tasks.

example, or only with recession and the accompanying unemployment—are in an enviable situation. The Hungarian economy is suffering from several grave problems at once, which makes it extremely difficult to decide what to do, because whichever way we take, the desired beneficial effect will be accompanied by undesired side-effects. It is impossible to find a solution satisfactory in every respect. The only choice before us is to decide which disease to devote most attention to treating in the immediate future, which disease we consider most acute.

I would like to say a separate word about the problem of inflation, where some disquieting phenomena are appearing. There is a danger of inflationary pressure entailed in the rapid rise in the money supply (notably the high-powered money, i.e., "monetary base") and the accompanying "surplus" of money building up in the banking system. The rate of inflation is easing more slowly than expected and promised by the government. So the emphasis throughout this study is on "growth-friendly" measures that might give a boost to production *without* causing a general rise in aggregate demand, i.e., ones less prone to have side-effects that speed up inflation.

My proposal is a *half-turn* towards growth, not a U-turn in which our backs are turned to the earlier priority tasks of tackling inflation and the growth of indebtedness. This cannot be confined to adopting "half-turn" as a slogan. To make it will require a convincing, detailed, practical program whose implementation must begin at once.

What justification is there for rearranging the priorities? It would be a shame to commit the big mistake of rigid thinking. These economic-policy tasks, whether expressed in the earlier or the present set of priorities, are not among the *ultimate* goals and primary values of economic activity that must be stuck to at all times. They are *intermediate* goals and instrumental values that need choosing in a way appropriate to a specific situation and rearranging if the situation alters. No universally, eternally valid order of priority can be established between production growth, reduction of unemployment, curbing of inflation, or improvement of the international payments position. So the question at the beginning of the paragraph could be put more specifically like this: what alterations in the *situation* justify reappraising the priorities? Let me pick out a few circumstances.

First, as I pointed out in the introductory paragraphs, the recession has proved much deeper than anyone expected two or three years ago, and protraction of it cannot be ruled out. This is causing very serious damage. The country is suffering from a variety of problems: technical backwardness, widespread poverty, with the threat of further worsening of the financial position of the poor, neglect of the health service, education and infrastructure, and so on. None of these problems can be solved satisfactorily by redistribution, by transferring from elsewhere resources to carry out tasks that have been put off or neglected. Only a growing economy can slowly but surely resolve these and other problems not mentioned here.

Secondly, while the private sector is the force for overcoming the recession on which we can most rely, insufficient demand is already holding back private-sector development as well. It is increasingly hard for many private firms coping with the difficulties of start-up to keep their heads above water.[30] If the total volume of the private sector's production should start to decline, the prospects for recovery would become almost hopeless.

The third (and possibly weightiest) factor is that the reduction in the real income of a sizeable proportion of the population and the previously unknown phenomenon of mass unemployment have produced broad economic discontent. If the strength and extent of this discontent reaches a critical threshold, it will pose serious dangers for the young Hungarian democracy. Politicians have several times warned that there could be a "Weimarization" of the postsocialist region, including Hungary.[31] It should be remembered that they were mass unemployment and waves of inflation in Weimar Germany that led to mass disillusionment and rejection of the institutions of democracy and the parliamentary system. This economically induced disillusionment provides a fertile breeding ground for demagogy, cheap promises, and desires for iron-handed leadership.

We must guard against Weimarization in the political and ideological sphere. Not as a substitute for political action, but as a parallel effort conclusions need to be drawn in terms of economic policy. This is what the half-turn proposed in this study sets out to do.

30. This concern was voiced by the heads of the biggest private companies in Hungary, who referred to "the private sphere contracting because of the recession" and drew attention to the fact that the economic decline was making it impossible to attain the turnover required to finance the debt stock of the large firms which had rapidly expanded. (See Sz. Hámor, 1993.)

31. In my reading, I first encountered this expression in an article by G. M. Tamás (1990).

Confidence and Credibility

There are political and social-psychological requirements for an economic recovery. This is not an assumption suggested only by politicians or experts outside the economists' profession, like psychologists or sociologists. The truth in this realization has penetrated fully into modern economics as well. It is worth drawing attention to the following connections:

- Study of expectations has come to the fore in modern macroeconomics. In the first wave of studies concerning the Phillips Curve, it was thought that all disinflation was plainly accompanied by a specific rise in unemployment. Since then, however, a modification of the theory has been devised. There is already general acceptance for the view that the Phillips Curve can shift depending on the inflationary expectations.[32] The more the actors in the economy expect the inflation to continue, the greater the unemployment sacrifice required to overcome that expectation. The more they believe that inflation will decelerate, the smaller the sacrifice required. Applying this line of thinking to our case, the following can be established: parallel progress in both growth and the macroequilibrium can only be made if the government program to achieve this has credibility in the eyes of the actors in the economy.[33] But if people expect that the recession and the inflation will continue whatever the government may promise, the expectation will be self-fulfilling.
- Keynes and other economists underlined that optimism—confidence that the economy will pick up—is required to reinforce the propensity to invest. In this connection it can be said that either optimism or pessimism will be self-fulfilling.
- A feeling of stability, a knowledge that the existing laws and institutions are lastingly stable, not fickle or arbitrarily changeable is needed to strengthen the propensity to invest, and, beyond that, for business activity on a private-ownership basis.

---

32. This theory was first expounded in articles by M. Friedman (1968) and E. Phelps (1968). New impetus to the examination of the connection between inflation and unemployment has been given since then, primarily by the theory of rational expectations.

33. The statement that the credibility of a stabilization program plays a decisive part in its success has been proved not only theoretically, but historically. This was proved with a force that swept all counterarguments aside in a famous study by T. Sargent (1982) entitled "The Ends of Four Big Inflations."

Unfortunately there are great troubles with these socio-psychological phenomena. For the sake of illustration, I mention only one study. From table 7.11, showing some results of an international opinion poll organized by Western researchers, the Hungarians emerge as the most pessimistic group of respondents.

Can this public attitude be reversed? Could a convincing government program backed by a broad political consensus emerge? This study was written in June 1993, nine months before the next parliamentary elections are due. It would be self-deceptive to count on this consensus in the months ahead, when political divisions and rivalries are likely to become sharper than before. It would be much more sound to expect (and even this is far from certain) that the situation will at least not deteriorate further, and that the political configuration after the elections will provide conditions more favorable to implementing a credible, confidence-inspiring program.

Table 7.11
Sense of personal optimism/pessimism in Western and Eastern European nations in 1991[a]

	Personal optimism or pessimism					
Countries	Progress[b] %	Neither %	Decline %	Optimism[c] %	Neither %	Pessimism %
United Kingdom	43	28	29	51	37	12
France	36	34	30	42	39	19
Italy	41	34	25	51	32	17
Spain	34	43	23	39	48	13
West Germany	45	38	17	42	46	12
Bulgaria	16	24	60	56	20	24
Czechoslovakia	29	22	49	41	33	26
East Germany	34	33	33	62	29	9
Hungary	18	25	57	26	40	34
Poland	27	21	52	36	40	24
European Russia	21	22	57	40	36	24

Sources: M. Kaase (1992, p. 23), on the basis of Times-Mirror (1991, 21–23, tabular appendix). Missing data for the past and present averaged one to two percent. The future was not assessed by an average of 20 percent. Cases with missing data were excluded from this calculation.

Notes: a. Row percentages, Cantril-type, 0–10 ladder scale. b. Progress/Decline is based on a comparison of five years ago/today. c. Optimism/Pessimism is based on a comparison of today/five years from now.

The Role of the State[34]

In theory there are two ways out of the recession: forward or back. *Back* means to restore the old structure of the economy with subsidies, to support inefficient exports, to sustain state-owned firms in financial crisis artificially and many jobs along with them, to defend all domestic producers from import competition by protectionist means, and to maintain unemployment on the job in the surviving firms and the low productivity that goes with it. This constitutes overcoming the recession by abandoning further transformation and partially restoring the old economic system. If we now ignore the political conditions, this is certainly a program that in an economic sense can be realized by a combination of "hyper-Keynesian" demand-inflating monetary and fiscal policy with bureaucratic interventionism. Ideas of this kind appear in several places, tinged with the various colors of the Hungarian political spectrum.

The way *forward* out of the recession is to try and get over the gravest difficulties, in other words, to eliminate the loss-making jobs and concentrate our energies on ensuring that the private sector expands, new and efficient jobs are created, the necessary structural adjustment takes place, and profitable exports develop.

But even among those who agree with the progressive line that requires a consistent transformation, two views can be found on the strategy to be followed. In one, the confidence in the spontaneous force of the market and private initiative is very strong. It is a matter of waiting before the internal forces of the economy lift the economy out of the trough. These forces are so strong that they can prevail even against an incompetent government that makes repeated mistakes. I must admit that I myself inclined to this view for a good while, all the more because I share the attitude of those whose past experience leaves them with little confidence in governmental wisdom.

But I am now obliged to adjust this perhaps too doctrinaire position somewhat. I am induced to do so by awareness of the political danger

---

34. Here and elsewhere in the study, I mean by the "state" the ensemble of all the branches of state power (the legislature, the government, and the judiciary). I emphasize this because many readers will follow ingrained habits and immediately identify the "state" with the government of the day, not taking into account the roles of Parliament, the head of state and the courts, including the Constitutional Court, as "checks and balances" on the government. These have great powers, and share responsibility for the development of the country with the government.

of "Weimarization," mentioned in the previous section. Another argument for adjusting it is a recognition that simply to await a spontaneous, self-engendered movement in the present political and economic situation in Hungary could set what is known in economics as a "low-level equilibrium trap." This state in Hungary's case would exhibit the following characteristics:

There would be a prolonged slackness in the propensity to invest. Mass unemployment would stabilize at a high level and the utilization of the other resources would also be low. The growth of the private sector would stick at its present level for lack of entrepreneurial spirit. Foreign capital would lose interest in investing in Hungary. The fiscal crisis would be perpetuated; there would be insufficient money for infrastructural development, education, medical care, and welfare services. The budget deficit could not be overcome without production growth, but production would be unable to grow because of the high taxes and the crowding-out effect of the budget deficit. There would be repeated surges of inflation, followed by repeated painful measures to slow it down. Although the slump in the economy would halt, it would be unable to climb out of the trough.

This is no mere nightmare. There are countries in the Third World where this slow stagnation has been typical for a long time. Whatever happens we must climb out of the trough, and economic activity by the state is essential for doing so.

I am no advocate of superabundant state intervention and bureaucratic micro regulation. This would lead to the very endeavor from which I strongly dissociated myself just now: combatting the recession by partially restoring the old system.

It is worth referring, in my view, to two grades of justified and desirable state engagement. The first grade, in fact, is no more than what the state should do in a modern market economy even according to a libertarian concept: introduce laws and ensure they are enforced, pursue a fiscal and monetary policy, and exert supervision where this is essential (for instance, over the financial sector or the natural monopolies). It must do all these things in such a way that they serve the priorities of the present day.

The second grade expects more than this from the state during the postsocialist transition. It must *initiate and actively assist* the development of the new institutions required by a market economy, the establishment of certain new organizations and abolition of others, and the transformation of property relations. The study has put forward plenty of examples of these as well.

So I do not support those who propose that the state should do nothing. That would relieve of responsibility both the legislative and executive branches of power. Within a well-defined field, the state should certainly do its job. If the recession accompanying the transformation proves too protracted and involves too great a loss, the government is also responsible for this.

The Responsibility of the Economists' Profession

In a time of sharpening political struggles, there is a danger that politicians in government may opt for measures which are harmful in the long term but popular in the short term. There is similarly a danger that opposition politicians may try to turn public opinion against the government by making extravagant promises. At times like this, an even greater responsibility devolves on research economists, who have a professional duty to speak out against both these threats.

During the public debates taking place on the recession and the country's economic situation in general, many politicians and political journalists, along with some researchers as well, have "dug themselves into ideological trenches," as Tibor Erdős so graphically put it.[35] An atmosphere of mutual suspicion prevails. Those who talk about "stimulation" are suspected of supporting the government, while those who mention "restriction" are classed as liberal oppositionists. Erdős emphasizes that researchers should not climb into any ideological trenches, but should retain their objectiveness and express views in accordance with their convictions. A similar opinion is expressed by Rudolf Andorka as well, who points out that "there is no single redeeming economic-policy recipe. Pragmatism is required; ideologies and dogmas cannot be allowed to determine economic policy."[36]

I fully agree with this position. Many of us feel fed up to the back teeth with the "labelling" that has become prevalent in economic debates. The dogmatic application of half-digested economic theories and, in addition, the habit of classifying various theoretical schools around the present party structure in Hungary (this party is Keynesian, that party is Friedmanite), has a toxic effect on objective research.

35. See T. Erdős (1992, p. 1000).
36. See R. Andorka (1993, p. 17).

The problems that have to be solved are extremely difficult and unprecedented. We can all make mistakes. That means there is all the more need for composure and rational argument.

References

Andorka, Rudolf. 1993. "Gazdaság és társadalom dogmák nélkül." (Dogma-free Economy and Society). *Népszabadság*, May 15, 51 (112): 17, 19.

Bauer, Tamás. 1983. "The Hungarian Alternative to Soviet-Type Planning." *Journal of Comparative Economics* 7 (3): 304–316.

Blanchard, Oliver, Dornbusch, R., Krugman, P., Layard, R., and Summers, L. 1991. *Reform in Eastern Europe*. Cambridge: MIT Press.

Calvo, Guillermo A., and Coricelli, Fabrizio. 1992. "Output Collapse in Eastern Europe: The Role of Credit." Paper presented at the conference "The Macroeconomic Situation in Eastern Europe" organized by the World Bank and IMF, June 4–5.

Commander, Simon, and Coricelli, Fabrizio. 1992. "Output Decline in Hungary and Poland in 1990/1991: Structural Change and Aggregate Shocks." Paper presented at the conference "The Macroeconomic Situation in Eastern Europe" organized by the World Bank and IMF, June 4–5.

Domar, Evsey. 1989. "The Blind Men and the Elephant: An Essay on Isms." In *Capitalism, Socialism, and Serfdom*, edited by E. Domar. Cambridge: Cambridge University Press, 29–46.

Dornbusch, Rudiger, and Fischer, Stanley. 1993. "Moderate Inflation." *The World Bank Economic Review* 7 (1): 1–44.

Erdős, Tibor. 1992. "A gazdaság stabilizálásáról" (On the Question of Stabilizing the Economy). *Közgazdasági Szemle* 39 (11): 985–1000.

Friedman, Milton. 1968. "The Role of Monetary Policy." *American Economic Review* 58 (1): 1–17.

Gomulka, Stanislaw. 1991*a*. "The Puzzles of Fairly Fast Growth and Rapid Collapse Under Socialism," Socialist Economies Reform Unit, Country Economics Department, World Bank, *Research Paper Series*, no. 18.

Gomulka, Stanislaw. 1991*b*. "The Causes of Recession Following Stabilization." *Comparative Economic Studies* 33 (2).

Hámor, Szilvia. 1993. "Tőke nélkül ma már nincs előrelépés" (Today There Cannot Be Any Progress without Capital). *Népszabadság* May 19, 51 (115): 17.

Hansen, Alvin H. 1964. *Business Cycles and National Income*. Expanded edition. New York: W. W. Norton and Company.

Király, Júlia. 1992. "Tartós tendencia vagy pillanatnyi robbanás?" (Is It a Lasting Tendency or a Temporal Explosion?). *Napi Gazdaság*, October 17, 2 (240): 4.

Kolodko, Grzegorz W. 1992. "Stabilization, Recession and Growth in Postsocialist Economy." *Working Papers*, Institute of Finance, Warsaw, no. 29.

Kornai, János. 1971. *Anti-Equilibrium*. Amsterdam: North-Holland.

Kornai, János. [1989] 1990. *The Road to a Free Economy. Shifting from a Socialist System: The Example of Hungary*. New York: W. W. Norton.

Kornai, János. 1992*a*. *The Socialist System. The Political Economy of Communism*. Princeton: Princeton University Press, and Oxford: Oxford University Press.

Kornai, János. 1992*b*. "Visszaesés, veszteglés vagy fellendülés" (Recession, Stagnation or Recovery). *Magyar Hírlap*, December 24, 25 (302): 12–13.

Laski, Kazimierz. 1990. "O niebezpieczenstwach zwiazanych z planem stabilizacji gospodarki narodowej," *Gospodarka Narodowa* 1 (2-3): 5–9. Also published in German in *Wirtscahftspolitische Blätter*, no. 5.

Laffont, Jean-Jacques. 1985. "Fix-Price Models. A Survey of Recent Empirical Work." In *Frontiers of Economics*, edited by Kenneth J. Arrow and Seppo Honkapohja. Oxford and New York: Basil Blackwell, pp. 328–367.

Oblath, Gábor. 1994. "Economic Transition: Exchange Rate Policy, Real Exchange Rate Changes in Central Eastern Europe." In *International Trade and Restructuring in Eastern Europe*, edited by J. Gács and G. Wincler. Wien: IISA.

Phelps, Edmund. 1968. "Money-Wage Dynamics and Labor-Market Equilibrium." *Journal of Political Economy*, Part 2, July-August, 678–711.

Rodrik, Dani. 1992. "Making Sense of the Soviet Trade Shock in Eastern Europe: A Framework and Some Estimates." Paper presented at the conference "The Macroeconomic Situation in Eastern Europe" organized by the World Bank and IMF, June 4–5, 1992.

Sargent, Thomas. 1982. "The Ends of Four Big Inflations." In *Inflation: Causes and Effects*, edited by Robert Hall. Chicago: National Bureau of Economic Research, University of Chicago Press.

Schumpeter, Joseph A. 1934. *The Theory of Economic Development*. Cambridge: Harvard University Press.

Schumpeter, Joseph A. 1939. *Business Cycles*. New York: McGraw-Hill.

Scitovsky, Tibor. [1951] 1971. *Welfare and Competition*. Homewood, Ill.: Irwin.

Scitovsky, Tibor. 1985. "Pricetakers' Plenty: A Neglected Benefit of Capitalism." *Kyklos* 38 (4): 517–536.

Spiethoff, Arthur. 1902. "Vorbemerkungen zu einer Theorie der Überproduktion." *Jahrbuch für Gesetzgebung, Verwaltung und Volkswirtschaft*.

Tamás, Gáspár Miklós. 1990. "Weimar." *Beszélő*, February 12, 1(5): 5.

United Nations, Economic Commission for Europe. 1992. *Economic Survey of Europe in 1991–1992*. New York.

Valentinyi, Ákos. 1992. "Stabilizáció és növekedés Magyarországon: néhány elméleti megfontolás" (Stabilization and Growth in Hungary: Some Theoretical Considerations). *Közgazdasági Szemle* 39 (10): 908–923.

Sources of Statistical Tables and Data

Kaaxe, Max. 1992. "Political Culture and Political Consolidation in Central and Eastern Europe." Mimeo. Paper presented at the conference on "Democratic Governments and the Transition from Plan to Market," Twente University.

KOPINT-DATORG. 1994. *Ipari konjunktúrateszt eredmények* (Results of the Survey on Industrial Trade Cycle). 1993, 4th quarter.

Központi Statisztikai Hivatal (Central Statistical Office). 1989. *Statisztikai évkönyv 1988* (Statistical Yearbook 1988). Budapest.

Központi Statisztikai Hivatal (Central Statistical Office). 1991. *Magyar statisztikai évkönyv 1990* (Hungarian Statistical Yearbook 1990). Budapest.

Központi Statisztikai Hivatal (Central Statistical Office). 1992*a*. *Magyar statisztikai zsebkönyv 1991* (Hungarian Statistical Pocketbook 1991). Budapest.

Központi Statisztikai Hivatal (Central Statistical Office). 1992*b*. *Magyar statisztikai évkönyv 1991* (Hungarian Statistical Yearbook 1991). Budapest.

Központi Statisztikai Hivatal (Central Statistical Office). 1993*a*. *Magyar statisztikai zsebkönyv 1992* (Hungarian Statistical Pocketbook 1992). Budapest.

Központi Statisztikai Hivatal (Central Statistical Office). 1993*b*. *Magyar statisztikai évkönyv 1992* (Hungarian Statistical Yearbook 1992). Budapest.

Központi Statisztikai Hivatal (Central Statistical Office). 1993*c*. *Magyarország nemzeti számlái 1988–1991* (Hungary's National Accounts, 1988–1991). Budapest.

League of Nations. 1939. *Statistical Yearbook of the League of Nations, 1938/1939*. Geneva.

Magyar Nemzeti Bank (National Bank of Hungary). 1990. *Éves jelentés 1990* (Annual Report, 1990). Budapest.

Mitchell, Brian R. 1976. *European Historical Statistics 1750-1970*. Aylesbury, England: Hazell Watson and Voney.

National Bank of Hungary. 1991. *Annual Report 1991*. Budapest.

National Bank of Hungary. 1992. *Annual Report 1992*. Budapest.

Times-Mirror. 1991. *The Pulse of Europe: A Survey of Political and Social Values and Attributes*. Washington: Times-Mirror, Center for the People and the Press.

United Nations, Economic Commission for Europe. 1993. *Economic Bulletin for Europe* 44 (1992), New York.

Vígh, Judit. 1993. "Jelentés az 1991. Évi bruttó hazai termék alakulásáról" (Report on the Gross Domestic Product in 1991). *Gazdaság és Statisztika* 5 (2): 18–23.

8 Postsocialist Transition: An Overall Survey

The flow of information on the postsocialist transition has swollen into a flood. Apart from the reports in the daily press and the media, there are hundreds of studies and books appearing and a large number of scientific conferences devoted to assessing the changes and outlining the tasks. I cannot go into the details of particular aspects of the problems in this study. Instead, I would like to offer some help in processing and systematizing this great mass of information. I will outline a conceptual framework that I hope will be useful in analyzing the changes.

Instead of dealing with the specific situation in some country or other, I will attempt to arrive at a broad generalization, to put forward statements that apply to the postsocialist region as a whole. I will, however, refer sometimes to the Hungarian experience as an example.

I have taken into consideration the fact that this study is not addressed to people who specialize in studying the issues of the postsocialist transition, but instead a broader audience of intellectuals, of any profession, who are taking part in the transformation of Eastern Europe, or are at least interested in it.

There are various possible kinds of approach, of which three are particularly worth mentioning. One is to conduct a methodical survey of the desires, hopes, and expectations. Another approach is to summarize the suggestions put to politicians and governments, endorsing some proposals and arguing for the rejection of others.[1] Finally, there

1. I summed up my own economic-policy proposals at the beginning of the postsocialist transition; my [1989] 1990 book was the first to appear in this field. I do not return to my earlier proposals in this study, my exclusive aim being a prediction of future development. An excellent summary of the normative literature and also of the practical experience gained in the first two years can be found in the (1992) report of the UN Economic Commission for Europe.

is a third kind of approach that represents an attempt to process the experiences with the transition so far and on that basis arrive at a prediction. I will try to take this third, *positive-predictive approach.* Rather than explain what kind of future Eastern Europe I would like to see, I will examine how it is likely to be according to my conjectures, irrespective of whether I am pleased with that image of the future or not.

I do not have a crystal ball for foretelling the future. The prognosis draws on several kinds of source of experience. There are three countries that are ahead in the postsocialist transition: Hungary, Poland, and Czechoslovakia. Many elements in the processes taking place in them will certainly appear in other countries as well. Important knowledge can also be gained from the recent history of Spain, Portugal, and certain Latin American countries. I am referring here to countries that never had a socialist system, so that the economy did not alter radically, but they did undergo a profound political transformation, because dictatorship was replaced by democracy. Finally, there are some notable lessons to be drawn from the more distant past as well, from the period when the capitalist market economy was developing in the framework of the pre-capitalist society and economy.

A high degree of caution is advisable; the most that should be attempted is stochastic prediction. Several alternative outcomes are possible for each process, and great courage is needed even to make statements about the relative likelihoods of the alternatives.

This study describes seven *tendencies,* advancing the prediction that these tendencies are very likely to apply. The word "tendency" conveys that we are dealing here with the flows and directions of movements in society and the inner propensities, inclinations, and trends among those taking part in the process, not with absolute certainties that can be determined in detail beforehand.

Tendency No. 1: Marketization

Under the socialist system, the integration of economic activity was mainly supplied by the mechanism of bureaucratic coordination.[2] The most important means of coordination is the command. A superior authority gives an order to a subordinate leader to carry out a certain

2. The operation of the socialist system is examined in detail in my 1992 book.

task, and not only provides a material and moral incentive to perform it, but uses administrative compulsion if need be.

There also exists a market mechanism within the socialist system, but in the period before the reforms it is confined to a very narrow field and largely operates underground. Later, but before the great political change, a somewhat wider scope is opened up for the market by the reforms.

The marketization tendency speeds up to a radical extent after the political change and becomes irresistible. The command economy is wound up, at a stroke in some countries and by degrees in others. Sooner or later, at a faster or slower pace, the prices hitherto set by the state are freed. Bureaucratic allocation of products and resources is replaced by voluntary commercial contracts between producers and users, buyers and sellers. Competition develops, including competition between domestic production and, more or less, liberalized imports.

A variety of yardsticks can be used for measuring how far marketization has gone. One of the most expressive measures expresses the proportion of GDP traded at free prices. Once this part of goods turnover has become dominant, once it accounts for an overwhelming proportion of turnover as a whole, the economy concerned can rightly be called a true market economy, at least in this respect. Now, by this measure Hungary can already be classed as a market economy. It can be predicted that the tendency towards marketization will apply strongly in all the postsocialist countries.

But, let no one think that we are witnessing a triumphant advance toward perfect competition. (So-called "perfect competition" is not characteristic of most of the markets of the developed capitalist countries either, come to that.) Large state-owned monopolies remain for a long time, and new monopolies emerge alongside them (or out of them, where state-owned monopoly firms are privatized). Foreign investors often move in with the express intention of gaining a monopoly position. Free competition is still curbed by numerous economic and administrative factors, even where the curbs are economically undesirable.

The state in the new democracies cannot find its rightful place. It is hyperactive when there is no reason to be so and passive in areas where there is a great need for state regulation or control, or occasional or constant state intervention.

Tendency No. 2: The Evolution of the Private Sector

There cannot be a smoothly operating market without a predominance of private ownership. *By definition,* it is an indispensable feature of the market that the actors in it make voluntary contracts with each other. But that requires real autonomy, in other words, decision-makers not acting on the instructions of the authorities. This independence can only be guaranteed by private ownership.

A warning about this connection was given by Ludwig von Mises long before the socialist system was actually applied. This idea was later brought up very emphatically in the work of Friedrich von Hayek.[3] Despite the admonishing signs, there developed an influential intellectual trend bent on implementing "market socialism," whose guiding principle can be summed up like this: "Let us combine the state ownership and the market mechanism." An attempt to apply the concept was made in socialist countries that took the road of reform, for instance in Hungarian practice under János Kádár or later in the Soviet Union under Mikhail Gorbachev's leadership.

The reforms inspired by the ideas of market socialism failed to live up to their advocates' expectations. They certainly helped to loosen the old Stalinist system and prepared many participants in the economy for accepting the mentality of a true market economy, but they did not achieve their purpose, which was far more ambitious than that. There was no creation of a kind of "Third System" that would prove its economic superiority over Stalinist socialism and modern capitalism alike, and be capable of stabilizing and standing on its own feet.

The ideas of "market socialism" have not disappeared and must be expected to revive over and over again. But I can add that even if these ideas gain influence once more, they are only doomed to failure again.

A further prediction: the postsocialist countries will be marked for a long time to come by a *dual economy*. The state and the private sectors will exist side by side.

One of the most important factors deciding the pace is the *enterprise* developing in the private sector. A swift evolution has started among the *small and medium-sized firms*. The growth of the private sector is extremely fast in the services, domestic and foreign trade, building construction and the financial sphere, but the weight of the private sector also grows in manufacturing.

3. See L. von Mises [1920] (1935) and F. von Hayek, ed. (1935).

Depending on the size of the country concerned, there are tens or hundreds of thousands of "start-ups" of new private enterprises. We see the emergence of *large* domestic investors, rarely to start with and then more frequently—investors who draw on the domestic accumulation that has taken place already. A broad new middle class develops, in a society from which the socialist system had almost eliminated the middle class and halted, or reversed, the process of embourgeoisement. This new middle class includes a new "business class" of entrepreneurs, owners and managers, a broad stratum of "burghers."

This process is accompanied throughout and reinforced by the influx of foreign capital, which in many cases involves big reputed firms and banks and multinational corporations. The new "business class" becomes involved from the outset with economic life outside the national borders.

The private sector that develops in this way presents, even today, a very varied picture. Side by side and mixed up and entangled with each other, we can find small, medium-sized and large firms, backward, "Balkan-style" workshops and modern super-factories, legally, semi-legally, and quite illegally operating enterprises. The process taking place can be compared most closely to some kind of cellular proliferation or the growth, at lightning speed, of a thousand-and-one kinds of vegetation in the jungle.

Meanwhile the shrinking of the state sector continues until it reaches the modest scale customary in the developed capitalist countries. The shrinkage takes place in various forms. Some of the state sector passes into private hands, either in its original form or after reorganization. This change of ownership may take place through the sale by the state of its property or through free distribution of it to specific groups in the population (for instance, to employees in the firm concerned, to those taking part in schemes to compensate them for property previously confiscated, or to all citizens who join in a campaign of almost gratis privatization). The various privatization schemes may be used side by side or in combination.

However, the contraction of the state sector takes place in other ways besides "privatization" in the strict sense. Some state-owned firms close down; other remain, but on a permanently reduced scale, with some parts being sold or wound up. "Decapitalization" takes place in many firms as they gradually use up a substantial part of their assets. We are faced with another phenomenon as well: the theft of some of the state's wealth, particularly its "intellectual assets," human capital, and its valuable business network and goodwill, which, in most cases informally, exploits the gaps in the provisions of the law. The dwindling of the state sector takes place slowly, accompanied by much loss and human suffering, and in more than one respect in a quite shameful way. Meanwhile, the surviving section of the state sector operates with very low efficiency. It is to be hoped, but by no means certain, that after a while the remains of the state sector will improve its efficiency under the pressure of the private economy around it.

Two kinds of calculation can be made on the basis of what has been said. One refers to the pace of privatization in the strict sense: the proportion of the initial state sector that passes annually into private hands. This process is likely to last for a long time. But there is another calculation that has a broader basis, and in my view, much greater importance. Having measured the growth of the private sector, including both the new "start-up" undertakings and the privatized ex-state-owned organizations, we then compare the growth of the private sector with the contraction of the state sector, by whatever means this contraction has taken place—privatization, liquidation, decline in production, or expropriation of assets. These two processes, with their opposite signs, can lead *together*, after a few years, to the weight of the private sector becoming greater than that of the state-owned sector. It is conceivable, for instance, that the private sector in Hungary will attain predominance in the next few years. In other countries the pace will be different, but the length of the period of history required for development of the private-enterprise economy will primarily depend everywhere *on the dynamics of these two processes in relation to each other.*

Governments can do much to speed up these processes or, on the other hand, to make the transformation of property relations slower and more painful through their clumsiness or incompetence. But ultimately it is most unlikely that any government policy blunder can "block" the change of ownership. The strength of capitalist development derives not least from the fact that, fundamentally, it takes place of its own accord, not by state command.[4]

---

4. There is a debate taking place among the economists and sociologists dealing with the postsocialist transition over the nature of marketization and the processes transforming property relations. For my part, I agree with those who stress that a profound transformation of society in the area of coordination mechanisms and property forms cannot be brought about at a stroke, by aggressive state measures, that they necessarily take place as an integral development by evolutionary means. Similar views can be found in the writings of P. Murrell (1992) and K. Poznanski (1992).

Tendency No. 3: Reproduction of the Macro-disequilibria

The new regime after the political turning point inherits serious macro imbalances from its predecessor. The following four kinds of disequilibrium appear most of all: chronic shortage, open or repressed inflation, budgetary deficit, and foreign debt. Of the four problems listed, two or three, or perhaps even all four may be afflicting the structure of the economy at once, reinforcing each other.[5]

The macro disturbances in certain of the postsocialist countries are so grave that there is no choice but to introduce a package of concurrent stabilization measures that causes a severe jolt in society. The government in other countries can choose between a more radical and swift or a gradual, slower stabilization strategy; the latter is usually chosen, for fear of political resistance.

Most experts would agree with the following forecast.

There are good prospects of overcoming one of the most painful symptoms of the socialist system—chronic and general *shortage*. The remedy for this is reached at by a combination of a whole range of measures: the swift growth of the private sector, free enterprise and import liberalization allow the excess demand to be satisfied quickly from the supply side. At the same time, demand is curbed by the freeing of prices, restrictive monetary policy, stronger financial discipline, and perhaps controls on wage rises. It can already be said of Hungary, for instance, that it can no longer qualify as a chronic shortage economy; at most there are partial shortages in one segment or other. Many other countries in the region have yet to reach this stage, but they are all likely to be able to overcome the shortage economy in the not-too-distant future.

There is far more reason for pessimism over *inflation* and the main factor inducing it, the *budgetary deficit*. Halting or even radically reducing inflation requires dramatic measures: a tough cut in public spending, restriction of credit, and a brake on the growth of nominal incomes. It may be possible to achieve temporary results and to cut back the rate of inflation substantially, but this is usually accompanied by a fall in production, associated with the appearance and steady increase of unemployment. As a consequence, there is constantly renewed

5. An analysis of the macro situation of the Eastern European region and a broad survey of the literature on the problem appear in the United Nations survey mentioned earlier (1992).

pressure on monetary and fiscal policy-makers to take measures to combat the recession, restart growth and relieve unemployment, but these can generate inflation again. So there remains a constant danger that the inflation which has once been slowed or halted altogether will accelerate again and again.

If the government, on the other hand, should issue bonds instead of financing the budget deficit by inflationary means, i.e., by printing money, it can squeeze private investors out of the credit market, which postpones the recovery from the recession. There is another course open—to finance the budget debt with foreign loans—but that increases the foreign debt.

The problem of *unemployment* has already been touched on several times. Whatever other grave difficulties the previous system occasioned, it did manage to sustain full employment, and in fact there was a permanent shortage of labor. One of the most painful concomitants of the change of economic system is the alteration that takes place on the labor market: excess demand turns into excess supply—labor shortage into unemployment. This is the combined consequence of various factors. As I have mentioned, a fall in production can be caused by the anti-inflationary policy. A cut or a complete halt in production at many factories is evoked by the adjustment of the structure of domestic demand, coupled with the realignment of foreign trade, induced partly by the collapse of Comecon, the organization that chained the socialist countries together. Privatization, and even the stronger profitability demands made on the state sector, oblige managers to tackle unemployment on the job by showing the door to a high proportion of their workforce. Each of these factors can lead separately to unemployment, which is then exacerbated by the spillover effects. A production fall in one place produces a simultaneous fall in demand that leads to a further fall in production at another point, and so on.

Two predictions can be made from what has been said. One is that the chronic labor shortage ceases and a measure of structural unemployment consolidates as a result of the transformation of the economic structure. The other is that an extended recession must be expected, and this is likely to result for several years in a level of unemployment higher than the future long-term average, the "normal" unemployment rate.

Economic policymakers in the advanced industrial countries are repeatedly faced with a difficult dilemma during the fluctuations in the business cycle: efforts to tackle unemployment can generate inflation, while the suppression of inflation can raise unemployment. This is still a grave problem even if the rate of inflation is relatively low when it arises. The postsocialist countries are afflicted by the same problem, but under far less favorable circumstances, because the economy, even at the point of departure—the time of the political turning point—suffers from grave open or repressed inflation. Society is caught in some very cruel traps: whichever of its grave problems it tries to resolve, it may exacerbate the others. So, the prospects for macroeconomic stability and equilibrium are not favorable. There is a danger of governments being deterred even further from the requisite tough, consistent policy that requires sacrifices from society, by the tensions within that society, which, in fact, derive precisely from its economic problems. Governments are more likely to prefer a policy of "muddling through," deferring measures to resolve the problems. That means the macro-disequilibria will continue to afflict society for a long time to come.

Tendency No. 4: Development of a Constitutional State

A market economy based on the predominance of private ownership cannot operate without a requisite legal infrastructure. The safety of private property must be guaranteed, the observance of private contracts enforced, and enterprises and citizens protected from arbitrary interference from the bureaucracy. At the same time, many segments of the economy need state supervision or regulation, particularly in fields where the application of private contracts and the activity of private enterprise have external effects that go beyond the parties directly involved in the transactions. The state has numerous tasks of this kind, ranging from supervision of banks and insurance institutions, through enforcement of anti-monopoly legislation, to protection of the environment.

There seem to be grounds for the following forecast: the legal infrastructure of a modern market economy will undoubtedly be erected in the postsocialist countries, because the transforming economy demands it. But the process will be quite protracted. In analyzing this phenomenon, a distinction can be drawn between three levels of state activity.

The first is *legislation*. This also promises to be a lengthy process. Dozens of earlier pieces of legislation must be replaced with new ones under circumstances in which lawyers versed in the regulation of a modern market economy are still only emerging, and the members of parliament themselves are inexperienced in the job of being legislators in a constitutional state. But, in spite of these difficulties, the lion's share of this task can be undertaken within a few years.

The second level is *enforcement of the law*. This promises to be even harder. Judges, prosecutors, attorneys, and company legal advisers must relearn their trades. Those dealing with commercial justice and litigation are already overstretched; the protraction of trials and civil proceedings undermines respect for the law and contracts.

The third and final level is the *alteration of the mentality of citizens*. This may prove to be the hardest and most protracted task of all. The previous illegitimate system destroyed people's honest respect for the law; instead they were influenced only by fear of erratic repression. Respect for private contracts was similarly lacking; it was considered almost natural in economic life not to keep one's word or pay debts. Those who cleverly circumvented some regulation or other were really admired, since that was one way of surviving. It will be a long time before public morality improves in this respect, before a stage is reached where a breach of the regulations, betrayal of public trust, tax evasion, business dishonesty or corruption is condemned.

Tendency No. 5: Development of Democratic Institutions

Everyone is familiar with the superficial slogans that present the connection between the market economy and democracy in simplistic terms, whereas in fact the interaction between them is quite complex.

I would like to present three observations.

First observation. One necessary condition for a transition from the socialist system to a market economy based on private ownership is the elimination of the Communist party's political monopoly. This concerns a special version of the one-party system, not totalitarian or autocratic political forms in general. It is a system in which the ruling party that enjoys a monopoly of power puts forward an *anti-capitalist* ideology and program. Its anti-capitalism is not some kind of secondary or tertiary element in the ideology and program, but an embodiment of its prime purpose. Let me quote the testimony of an authoritative source, the *Communist Manifesto*: "The theory of the Communists may be summed up in the single sentence: Abolition of private property."[6] This is the simple explanation why all the reforms before 1989–1990 were incomplete and inconsistent. The fundamental condition required for building up a market economy based on private property was provided by the abolition of the Communist party's political monopoly. Once that condition was fulfilled, removing the main obstacle in the path of the transition towards a market economy, the process of transformation began with full assurance in an inescapable way. (See the remarks under Tendencies Nos. 1 and 2 in my line of argument.)[7]

Abolition of the Communist party's political monopoly *opens the way* for the development of democratic institutions: rivalry between parties, free elections, creation of a parliament with real power, government based on a parliamentary majority, and so on. But the full development, maturity and stabilization of the democratic institutions is *not guaranteed* by the elimination of the sole rule of the Communist party. I will return to this question in a moment.

Second observation. All parliamentary democracies are market economies based on private ownership. There are no exceptions to this. No parliamentary democracy without a market economy based on private ownership exists. However, the economies of the various parliamentary democracies may still differ from each other in many respects. The public sector, for instance, may be greater in one than in the other, but in none of them does the public sector become the economy's dominant, preponderant sector. The role of state-controlled redistribution may be greater in one than the other, but in all of them the market remains the main coordinator and integrator of economic activity.

For the democratic institutions to be stable, there must be guarantees of individual freedom and autonomy. Among the most important of these are the right to own private property and the defense of private contracts. Where the state sector predominates or achieves an almost exclusive role, the individual employee loses the chances of "exit," since in the last resort there is only one employer: the state.

6. See K. Marx and F. Engels [1848] (1970, p. 47).

7. It is worth considering this connection when analyzing the prospects for the Chinese reform. The reform process there may yield results, but will sooner or later come up against the main obstacle, the sole rule of the Communist party. The private sector will need political representation. It would be logically and historically absurd to presume that the establishment of capitalism could be completed successfully under Communist-party leadership.

Comprehensive state ownership inevitably leads to a totalitarian political system.

But what is the position with the opposite statement? Is every market economy based on private ownership a democracy? That is clearly not true.

Third observation. Not all market economies based on private ownership are democracies. This economic form is compatible with many versions of dictatorship and other autocratic forms. You only have to think of Hitler's Reich, the Latin American military dictatorships, or South Korea in the early decades after the Second World War. In fact some dictatorships can be combined with very efficient and fast-growing economies.

The consequent argument is quite frequently advanced in the post-socialist region (if not in print, at least in private conversation):

It would be expressly advantageous for the transition from the socialist system to a capitalist market economy to be guided by an autocratic political regime. The transition is accompanied by anarchy, and so there is a need for "law and order," which can only be provided by a stern government. The transition brings about social tensions, but for the success of the transition it is important not to flinch from an economic policy that demands sacrifices. This is another argument in favor of a tough administration that can break any resistance on the part of the masses by force. The paragon for those advancing this view is the Chile of Pinochet.

I do not want to deny that there is an element of rationality in this argument. Particularly at a time of great revolutionary social transformation, there can exist a trade-off between the rate of growth on the one hand and the spread of democracy on the other. It is not certain that this trade-off exists under all circumstances; let us hope that as few countries in the Eastern European region as possible are confronted by this bitter choice as rarely as possible, but the dilemma cannot be ignored. Let me make a personal confession here. If I had to make such a choice, I would opt for democracy, not just its present achievements, but further development of it, even if the price to be paid were economic achievements. A situation may arise in which we all have to face up to this choice between basic values, and it is advisable to think out one's position on it in advance.

After the detour, let us return from a normative to a *predictive* approach. I have not put forward the last four tendencies without reservations or with full confidence, but at this point I must express further reservations. Although there may be an unimpeded advance by some country or other towards the fulfillment of democracy, there is no excluding the possibility that the institutions of democracy will be smothered, that some partially or totally autocratic regimes will arise and dictatorships come into being. The longer the social tensions last and the sharper they become, the greater danger there is of this happening. Believers in democracy within every postsocialist country must be vigilant in defending democracy, and so must the international community.

Tendency No. 6: The Redefinition of a National Community

The national problem is stifled under the socialist regime. The problem *existed* under the old system as well, but it was never debated frankly and openly. At most it began to break out here and there as the dictatorship loosened up, but even then people could only half-express their opinions.

The communist system collapsed in Eastern Europe in 1989–1990, and most importantly of all in this respect, the Soviet Union first weakened substantially and then broke up. The first things to underline in this connection are the *achievements*. It is a fine and elevating experience to know that the national sovereignty of the Eastern European countries and the states of the former Soviet Union has been restored. After almost half a century of occupation, first by the Germans and then by the Soviets, there are now no foreign troops stationed in a number of sovereign states. (However, it must immediately be added that there are exceptions to this.)[8]

The new situation which has emerged has several implications. Here, I will mention only the economic effects. Mutually conflicting tendencies can be observed in the advanced industrial countries and the postsocialist region. (For brevity's sake, although clearly inaccurately from the geographical point of view, let us call the OECD countries the West and the postsocialist countries the East.) In the West

---

8. There are still sizeable foreign forces stationed in the Baltic states, under the military control of the Commonwealth of Independent States, which took over some of the Soviet Union's functions.

The frontiers of newly formed states have become questionable during the warfare in the former territory of Yugoslavia. Taking the original borders as given, there are foreign occupation forces inside several new states that consider themselves sovereign.

there has been a steady strengthening of the centripetal forces. The national economies are developing in the direction of community, harmonization and integration. The movement of goods, capital, money, labor and knowledge across the old state borders is becoming freer and freer. In the East, on the other hand, there has been a sudden and extraordinary increase in the centrifugal forces. Earlier larger, supranational units have fallen apart; a movement can be seen in the direction of fragmentation and isolation. New, guarded state borders forming economic barriers exist where they never ran or had little validity before.

Assessing the latter tendency from a strictly economic point of view, there is cause for sadness. According to the criteria of a technocrat or an economist, large-scale integration is more efficient than fragmentation, disintegration, and small national economies that reduce cooperation and more or less isolate themselves from each other. Like almost every other obstacle to the free allocation of resources, the new situation that is emerging will presumably reduce the efficiency with which economic resources are utilized.

But this study is not intended to comment on the changes from this point of view. Its aim is to formulate predictions, not proposals. So the main thing is to *understand* the changes going on around us.

It seems to be inevitable that the national communities should redefine themselves first. *Only then* can come the development of supranational units, or accessions to the ones that already exist. Accession to a supranational organization (whether a monetary union, a customs union, a scheme for free movement of labor and/or capital, or a fuller scheme of integration) can only take place voluntarily, after the legitimate government of some state knows it has the support of its own people. It would be a great mistake to impose from outside centripetal forces and integration schemes of various degrees and types on any country that is only now beginning to feel it is truly sovereign.[9] Think back over the history of recent decades. On the one hand, Comecon collapsed because it was imposed on the other Eastern European countries by the Soviet Union; the Soviet Union and Yugoslavia have fallen apart because in many respects they were artificial creations thrust with merciless oppression upon smaller communities that

9. On the problems of foreign trade and economic cooperation among the postsocialist countries, see the article by I. Illés, K. Mizsei, and I. Szegvári (1991) and the study by P. B. Kenen (1991).

yearned for sovereignty. On the other hand, the European Economic Community has consolidated and managed to progress towards an even more comprehensive form of integration because it developed steadily and integrally from the very outset, with the legitimate governments of sovereign states relinquishing components of their sovereignty step by step and voluntarily.

It follows from what has been said that the tendency to separation and fragmentation will continue for a long time, and the tendency towards regional cooperation remain weak despite the rational economic arguments in its favor. But, within this general prediction, a variety of scenarios can be envisaged. The most favorable is for the mutual separations, divorces, and exclusion to take place peacefully by civilized agreement. The most forbidding prospect is of local wars to redraw the maps. Even where there is no war, interstate tensions may be perpetuated by passionate debates between neighboring countries, and protests at the inequitable treatment of national minorities in a neighboring state eliciting heated rejection of such criticism and jealous concern for sovereignty. These phenomena, very familiar from the history of the Eastern European region down the centuries, will conserve the mutual distrust and undermine the chances for regional cooperation.

It would be desirable, in my view, for "Europeanization" of the postsocialist Eastern European countries to speed up. But if I concentrate, in line with the general nature of my study, on prediction rather than aspirations, I must say that I do not expect swift progress to be made.

There are objective difficulties. The European Community has a great variety of norms, ranging from legal regulation of economic activity to quality standards, customs tariffs and tax rates. It will be a long time before the legal system and economic activity of any postsocialist country can be harmonized with the European norms in every respect.

At the same time it must be clearly seen that there is appreciable *resistance*, undiscernible in the official public rhetoric, but apparent in veiled forms, cant and the application of brakes on real changes. Eastern Europe contains influential groups that stir up feeling against anti-national "Westernization," spread doubts about "foreign" capital, and appeal to national sentiment when international organizations make strict demands on the economic performance of particular countries. The antagonism is common in Western circles as well. Who wants free movement of labor across state borders if it entails raising the barriers to new migrations of peoples? The business world looks kindly on Eastern exports if they prove to be profitable, but is not keen to open its markets to imports from the East.

This all explains why I expect the progress towards "Europeanization," organic integration into the European Community and its institutions on a basis of equal rights, to be sluggish.

Tendency No. 7: An Unequal Increase in Welfare

How do the tendencies discussed so far affect human beings? The previous system produced a low standard of living. People suffered under chronic shortages. But these aspects were combined with full employment and a modest measure of social and economic security. Society was marked by a certain degree of equality. The privileged stratum was fairly narrow. Even if the other people did not all live in the same way, their material standard of living was confined within a range of gray mediocrity.

Now that postsocialist society is being shifted out of its previous state by a great transformation, the *average* level of material welfare is likely to improve. But this does not occur right away; for a good while the economic problems discussed under Tendency No. 3 will tend to produce stagnation or an absolute fall in the average material consumption of the public. All this, however, refers only to the average, which is a statistical category that the individual does not perceive as a direct experience.

Some people are already among the financial winners at the beginning of the transition. This applies to quite a broad stratum of society, particularly those whose activity as an owner, manager, or in many cases even as a simple employee, is tied to a private business. It must be added that a smaller group within this stratum becomes conspicuously rich very rapidly. Meanwhile, the living standard of very large bodies of people declines, in some cases slowly and to a small extent, and in others sharply and to a large extent.

The market economy is a system in which individuals' lives depend far more on individual performance and luck than they do under the socialist system. At the same time, a far smaller effect on individuals' lives is exerted by the state, which undertook a paternalist role under the socialist system. All those who judge the change of system decide according to their own systems of values whether the dramatic rise of the individuals' role and fall of the state's role in deciding the fate of individuals is an advantage or a drawback, but as a tendency this alteration will certainly apply. This entails a far wider spread in the distribution of material prosperity, and is accompanied by a growth of inequality.

Every government and political party in the region underlines the need to maintain the *social safety net*, or where it has yet to develop, to create one. Some components of this system, such as a national health service and an unemployment-benefit scheme, already function in most postsocialist countries. But, it must be admitted that the net has plenty of holes in it. There is certainly no question of the socialist system bequeathing a mature welfare state. They are inconsistent, distorted, "premature" welfare states that have committed themselves in their inherited legal systems to welfare tasks they are incapable of fulfilling to an adequate standard due to their low level of economic development. The system of old-age pensions is very extensive, but the living standard provided by most of the pensions is one of penury; everyone is entitled to free medical care, but the health service is seriously backward. In the Scandinavian countries, where the most highly developed form of welfare state can be found, a start was made to organize such institutions and legally enacting the state's welfare obligations only *after* several decades of unbroken economic development.[10] Fulfillment of the welfare tasks undertaken by the state in the postsocialist region, amidst recession, inflation, and high foreign debt—in other words, macro-disequilibrium, promises to pose a grave and persistent problem.

For all these reasons, deep dissatisfaction among broad strata of people over the stagnating or falling material standard of living, and the unemployment and social insecurity suddenly falling on them, must be expected for a long time to come. It will be hard under the circumstances to ask people to make further sacrifices. That is another reason why the rectification of the macro-disequilibria will be protracted, not to mention the dangers the discontent poses from the point of view of maintaining democracy.

---

10. See A. Lindbeck (1990).

Summarizing Remarks on the Tendencies of Change

I have listed seven tendencies; these do not cover the sum total of the changes to be expected, but they single out the ones I consider most important. As I stressed in my introductory paragraphs, at the beginning of this study, I have not devised fatalistic prophecies. I have outlined alternative solutions and dilemmas of choice and then said which choice I take to be most likely (which is different from saying which I would most like to see). Nor is the pace of the changes predetermined. The most one can say with much certainty is that the transformation will take a long time, requiring a complete period of history. If for no other reason, fatalism would be unjustified because the factors on which the direction and pace of change depend can clearly be seen:

- They depend on the wisdom or stupidity, efficiency or incapacity of governments. Erasmus advised rulers and other officials to "avoid such bad counsellors as ambition, wrath, greed and flattery."[11] It remains to be seen how far they can resist these temptations.
- They depend on the opposition forces, on whether these are destructive and want to gain power through populist demagogy, or whether they are moderate and constructive.
- They depend on the social environment provided by the general public, whether they are disciplined and capable of making long-lasting sacrifices.
- They depend on help from the outside world, the scope of it and the forms it takes.

So, am I an optimist or a pessimist? As far as the immediate years ahead are concerned I am neither. There are too many uncertainties for it to be possible to say which combination of phenomena will arise out of the combined result of the seven tendencies listed in this study. In some countries the conditions will be bearable for the vast majority, and for a smaller group of people increasingly favorable, so bringing a chance there for a steady general improvement. In other countries, however, severe upheavals or even social explosions may occur.

In the long term, I am decidedly optimistic. The system that ultimately forms will not be a "good society." It will be full of shortcom-

11. The quotation is from his work *Institution Principiis Christiani* (The Education of the Christian Prince) [1516] (1968).

ings and display some repellent characteristics as well, but it will still be superior to the earlier socialist system, in its material achievements and safeguards for human rights. I am a long-term optimist because there are very strong spontaneous internal tendencies to guide the changes in this favorable direction even if the governance may not be in the best hands.

The Role of Academics

This study is not addressed to governments; I would like to add, in conclusion, a few words about the responsibility of academics.

Our Western colleagues are in a position to give *practical help* to the Eastern academic world in teaching and research. Invitations and scholarships to Eastern colleagues, acceptance of guest professorships in the postsocialist region, transfer of experience through joint research, books, periodicals and equipment donated to institutions in the East—these are a few of many possible forms of support. We have already received much assistance, but even if it were multiplied several times over, it would still fall short of the requirements.

Both Western and Eastern academics often serve as *advisers,* to governments, parties, movements, federations representing specific interests, international organizations and the business world. This activity is greatly needed, but there may be no harm in my adding a warning. We must try to put forward our recommendations with due modesty. What if the idea we favor is inapplicable? What if it is inadequately adapted to local circumstances with which we are insufficiently familiar? Let us not be aggressive, pushing our own ideas through at all costs, for that may rebound by discrediting the work of advisers as a whole. Let us draw inspiration from Erasmus; it is good to retain a little irony about ourselves.

The role sometimes assigned to us by circumstances is one of a *mediator* rather than an adviser; our task is to try and reconcile conflicting ideas or social and political forces. Again there is inspiration to be gained from the ideas in Erasmus's work: let us try to argue for rationality, sense, and moderation. Let us not shrink from the risk he took: those intruding with quiet words of sense between the rancorous shouts of antagonists may find themselves rejected and branded as heretics by both sides. Yet we must undertake to voice the conscience of society, issuing words of warning if human liberties are infringed, the young institutions of democracy attacked, and intelligence and patience overridden by passion.

References

Erasmus, Desiderius. [1516] 1968. *The Education of the Christian Prince*. New York: W. W. Norton.

Hayek, Friedrich A., ed. 1935. *Collectivist Economic Planning*. London: Routledge and Kegan Paul.

Illés, Iván, Mizsei, Kálmán, and Szegvári, Iván. 1991. "Válaszúton a Közép-európai gazdasági együttműködés" (Central-European Economic Cooperation at Crossroads). *Európa Fórum* 1 (2): 28–42.

Kenen, Peter B. 1991. "Transitional Arrangements for Trade and Payments Among the CMEA Countries." *IMF Staff Papers* 38 (2): 235–267.

Kornai, János. [1989] 1990. *The Road to a Free Economy. Shifting from a Socialist System: The Example of Hungary*. New York: W. W. Norton.

Kornai, János. 1992. *The Socialist System. The Political Economy Communism*. Princeton: Princeton University Press, and Oxford: Oxford Universitsy Press.

Lindbeck, Assar. 1990. "The Swedish Experience." Institute for International Economic Studies, Seminar Paper no. 482. Stockholm University.

Marx, Karl and Engels, Frederick. [1848], 1970. "Manifesto of the Communist Party." In *Karl Marx and Frederick Engels. Selected Works*. Moscow: Progress Publishers, pp. 35–63.

Mises, Ludwig Von. [1920] 1935. "Economic Calculations in the Socialist Commonwealth." In *Collectivist Economic Planning*, edited by Friedrich A. Hayek. London: Routledge and Kegan Paul, pp. 87–130.

Murrell, Peter. 1992. "Evolutionary and Radical Approaches to Economic Reform." *Economics of Planning* 25 (1): 79–95.

Poznanski, Kazimierz. 1992. "Market Alternative to State Activism in Restoring the Capitalist Economy." *Economics of Planning* 25 (1): 5–77.

United Nations, Economic Commission for Europe. 1992. *Economic Survey of Europe in 1991–1992*. New York.

Appendix: The Antecedents of the Studies and Their Places of First Publication

All the studies in this volume were originally presented as lectures. The frames in which each lecture was delivered and its venue and time are given below along with the bibliographical details of its first publication in English.

1. Market Socialism Revisited

Tanner Lectures on Human Values. These are delivered at the invitation of the Tanner Foundation at a few universities around the world every year, each by a philosopher, economist, sociologist, public figure or writer, on a subject chosen by the speaker. Lecturers in earlier years have included Raymond Aron, Arrow, Bellow, Brodsky, Foucault, Habermas, Havel, Hirschman, Kolakowski, Nozick, Popper, Prigogine, Rawls, Rorty, Joan Robinson, Helmut Schmidt and Stigler. The study was heard as part of the Tanner series of lectures at Stanford University on January 18 and 20, 1991.
First publication: "Market Socialism Revisited." In *The Tanner Lectures on Human Values*, edited by Grethe B. Peterson, Salt Lake City: University of Utah Press, Vol. 14, 1993, pp. 3–41.

2. The Affinity Between Ownership Forms and Coordination Mechanisms

The study was delivered as a lecture at the round-table conference entitled *Market Forces in Planned Economies*, organized by the International Economic Association and the Academy of Sciences of the Soviet Union in Moscow on March 28–30, 1989.

First publication: "The Affinity Between Ownership and coordination Mechanisms. The Common Experience of Reform in Socialist Countries." In *Market Forces in Planned Economics*, edited by Oleg T. Bogomolov. London: Macmillan, 1990, pp. 32–54.

3. The Soviet Union's Road to a Free Economy. Comments of an Outside Observer

Tanner Lectures on Human Values. The lecture was given at Leningrad University on June 12, 1991, shortly before the city changed its name. (Concerning the Tanner series of lectures, see the note on the first study.) This was the first Tanner Lecture to be held in the socialist and postsocialist region.
First publication: "The Soviet Union's Road to a Free Economy: Comments of an Outside Observer." In *The Tanner Lectures on Human Values*, edited by Grethe B. Peterson, Salt Lake City: University of Utah Press, Vol. 14, 1993, pp. 42–68.

4. The Principles of Privatization in Eastern Europe

Tinbergen Lecture. A lecture is organized annually by the Royal Netherlands Economic Association in honor of Jan Tinbergen, the Nobel laureate economist. The earlier lectures were delivered by Lawrence E. Klein, Edmund Malinvaud and James Tobin. The author delivered this in Utrecht on October 19, 1990.
First Publication: "The Principles of Privatization in Eastern Europe." *De Economist*, 1992, 140 (2): 153–176.

5. The Postsocialist Transition and the State. Reflections in the Light of Hungarian Fiscal Problems

Ely Lecture. Two plenary lectures are traditionally delivered at the annual meeting of the American Economic Association: the Presidential Address, and a lecture in honor of Richard T. Ely. The fifth study was heard at the annual meeting held in New Orleans on January 3, 1992.
First publication: "The Postsocialist Transition and the State: Reflections in the Light of Hungarian Fiscal Problems." *American Economic Review*, Papers and Proceedings, May 1992, 82 (2): 1–21.

6. The Evolution of Financial Discipline under the Postsocialist System

Myrdal Lecture. The University of Stockholm holds lectures at regular intervals in honor of the Nobel laureate economist Gunnar Myrdal. The author delivered this at the University of Stockholm on November 5, 1992.
First publication: "The Evolution of Financial Discipline under the Postsocialist System." *Kyklos,* Fall 1993, 46 (3): 315–336.

7. Transformational Recession. A General Phenomenon Examined through the Example of Hungary's Development

Perroux Lecture. A lecture is held at regular intervals in honor of François Perroux, an outstanding figure in French economics after the Second World War, by the foundation that bears his name. This was delivered by the author at the Collège de France in Paris on June 9, 1993.
First publication: "Transformational Recession: A General Phenomenon Examined through the Example of Hungary's Development," *Economie Appliquée,* Fall 1993, 46 (2): 181–227.

8. Postsocialist Transition. An Overall Survey

Erasmus Lecture. The leading body of the European Academy decided in 1991 to include in every annual general meeting a plenary lecture named after Erasmus of Rotterdam, the great figure in European thinking, science and humanism. The first Erasmus Lecture was delivered by the author at the Annual General Meeting of the European Academy held in Budapest on June 17, 1992.
First publication: "Postsocialist Transition: An Overall Survey." *European Review,* 1993, 1 (1): 53–64.

Subject Index

Author Index

Made in United States
North Haven, CT
10 November 2026

22096532R00141